Critical Political Theory and Radical Practice

Series Editor
Stephen Eric Bronner
Rutgers University
New Brunswick, New Jersey, USA

The series introduces new authors, unorthodox themes, critical interpretations of the classics and salient works by older and more established thinkers. A new generation of academics is becoming engaged with immanent critique, interdisciplinary work, actual political problems, and more broadly the link between theory and practice. Each in this series will, after his or her fashion, explore the ways in which political theory can enrich our understanding of the arts and social sciences. Criminal justice, psychology, sociology, theater and a host of other disciplines come into play for a critical political theory. The series also opens new avenues by engaging alternative traditions, animal rights, Islamic politics, mass movements, sovereignty, and the institutional problems of power. Critical Political Theory and Radical Practice thus fills an important niche. Innovatively blending tradition and experimentation, this intellectual enterprise with a political intent hopes to help reinvigorate what is fast becoming a petrified field of study and to perhaps provide a bit of inspiration for future scholars and activists.

More information about this series at
http://www.springer.com/series/14938

Dale L. Johnson

Social Inequality, Economic Decline, and Plutocracy

An American Crisis

Dale L. Johnson
Independent Scholar
Barva de Heredia, Costa Rica

Critical Political Theory and Radical Practice
ISBN 978-3-319-49042-7 (hardcover)   ISBN 978-3-319-49043-4 (eBook)
ISBN 978-3-030-04508-1 (softcover)
DOI 10.1007/978-3-319-49043-4

Library of Congress Control Number: 2017932744

Cover illustration: © Jeremy Hogan / Alamy Stock Photo

Printed on acid-free paper

This Palgrave Macmillan imprint is published by Springer Nature
The registered company is Springer International Publishing AG
The registered company address is: Gewerbestrasse 11, 6330 Cham, Switzerland

Contents

CHAPTER 1

Introduction

During its heyday, the Occupy Movement in the United States fingered 1% of Wall Street criminals and decried the situation of 99%. The statistic 99% is not just arbitrary figuration, although I would reduce it to 90% as at least 9% are very privileged and faithful lackeys of the 1%. The sad truth is that 90% of the American public is disadvantaged by the trends in the United States economy, polity, and society. Yet, we can expect that many of the 90% are not, in the short run, going to be massively mobilized on the streets by a resurgence of the movement, which is now a great diversity of militant groupings. In part, this is because there are many among the 90% who have had their minds so shrink wrapped by the ruling ideology that they rise in militant defense of *what is*. This was evident in the enthusiasm expressed by large rally crowds and voters for Donald Trump in 2015–2016. Still, in the medium and long run, with growing mobilizations, active subjects will achieve greater and greater gains.

I recently read a great book Richard Powers, *The Time of Our Singing* (Picador, 2003) in which he makes a statement pertinent to the American crisis of our day: *"We steer only by the grossest landmarks. Turn left at bewilderment. Keep going till you hit despair. Pull up at complete oblivion, turn around, and you're there."*

For the bewildered, disenchanted, and despairing, the political sphere seems pointless, if not in a state of complete oblivion, but with a revival

D.L. Johnson, *Social Inequality, Economic Decline, and Plutocracy*,
DOI 10.1007/978-3-319-49043-4_1

of some expectation given the relative success of Bernie Sanders' 2016 candidacy, only to be reversed by Donald Trump's election.

Trumpism has its antecedents. In the elections of November 2012, voters divided closely between Republicans, a party that now represents the extremes of retrograde, right-wing ideology, and Democrats, with more gentle rhetoric and weak defense of social programs but who, in the main, are servile to economic power and to the imperial ambition and hegemonic project that economic power pursues. Then, in 2014, the Republicans came on strong and gridlocked even the modest ameliorative efforts of the loyal opposition, while doing the bidding of the moneyed plutocracy. The electoral process is made farcical by big money and ossifies in political paralysis. The Democrats then floated a Lady Bush, the laydown kitten Hillary Clinton, as their choice for 2016. The Republicans fronted a lineup of exponents of the most reactionary thinking and flamboyant, dangerous demagoguery the nation has ever seen, with Donald Shrill Trumpet leading the pack of hungry wolves.

In the economic realm, "recovery" from the great debacle of 2007–2009 has only strengthened the hand of the 1%. Inequality continues—nay, deepens; the life situation of all the subordinate social classes declines. Unemployment went down gradually from 10% in 2010 to under 5% in 2016. However, the jobs are low-paid, part-time, or temporary so this reduction has not significantly changed the situation of gross inequality. Obama, subservient to the State of National Insecurity, continued to command a super rogue state pursuing imperial ambition with perpetual war and official terrorism. Impunity for Bush administration war criminals and for police gunmen shooting black youth was taken for granted. The judicial system opened avenues for the rule of money and wider repression, while there will continue to be closure to the use of the law to curtail the extension of the repressive apparatus or to punish the torturous misdeeds and criminal fraud of the powerful.

All the media conspire to obliterate consciousness of the injustice and perversity of *what is* by serving up lies, obfuscation, banality, and fear. Too many within the 90% are taken in by obliterated consciousness. This obliteration begins at an early age; public education, with sectors becoming privatized with charter schools, fosters standardized tests on students that measure how well teachers teach and youth grasps the necessity to fit themselves to the roles that the powerful define, and how far away education can move from imparting thinking, much less independent and critical thought. Institutions of higher learning are made so expensive they become exclusionary and change educational missions to business programs for students and research orientations for professors to get their hefty corporate grants.

Indignation is here, there, and everywhere, but submerged in disarray or sublimated to Trumpism. Actions expressing outrage, such as the mobilizations against police killings of unarmed black men and protests against the destruction of the natural environment, nevertheless break out. Yet, America, and Europe too, will likely muddle along for some time yet, suffering economic decline and under the sway of plutocrats and their servants in political power—President Trump, Republicans in Congress, and corporate Democrats. Popular consciousness will continue to be muddled by the media and a cultural milieu of social Darwinism, with discontent at ever higher levels, until the movement can mobilize the forces of unity among the 90% and do more than make some street noise.

The delusions that Republicans propound and from which Democrats hide find their home in the despair that prevails among the bewildered and suffering populace, too often oblivious to real solutions with reason and moral judgment subverted by the ruling ideology perpetuated in the media; by the now threatened privileges, however petty these may be, of previous class positioning; by xenophobia created in a climate of fear, hate, and endless, futile war; by the pervasiveness of racism and the resurgence of patriarchy and sexism; and, most of all, by the founding myths of capitalism that have turned American society, and most of the world with it, into a war of all against all wherein only the fittest of the rich are benefited. The heavy weight of plutocratic ideology too often spawns apathetic denial; feeds on insecurity and fear; spurs individual competition, social division, and disarray; and generates hopelessness. Frustration and despair breed hate, fear, displacement of anger to scapegoats, and Trumpism. We need some new landmarks constructed piece-by-piece by those no longer bewildered and despairing because they have vision and inspire redemption from the evils of savage capitalism in its degenerative phase.

I am an old-timer from the 1960s—in those days, a student activist and young professor of sociology but, now, an old curmudgeon, an aged and obdurate radical, yet inspired still by the better years and hope for resurgence. I frequently lapse to outrage that is radical in the sense of getting to the root of *what is*, without qualification of overstatements, while also expressing, rather stridently, a politically radical critique. In the more scholarly analysis I reason more, buttress facts with strong arguments and indisputable facts, even make some qualifications to radical pronouncements. In those inspiring days of the 1960s, I was like millions of youth "New Left." I expressed disdain for old line Stalinists and sectarian socialist groupings and did critiques of Soviet authoritarianism—but supported vibrant socialist revolutions in Cuba and Vietnam. I was not an anarchist, that tendency not then so prominent as today, but certainly in total sympathy with grassroots participatory democracy, as I remain today. I have no utopia or vanguard ideology to offer, only an expectation that equality, justice, fraternity, and peace shall one day prevail. My sociological thinking centers on the idea that social movements create by their actions radical visions of what ought to be as inspired or required by new historical circumstances. Today, that vision is expressed in Latin America's striving for a "Socialism for the 21st Century." In America, Europe, and elsewhere, that vision will ensue from a myriad of social struggles against the evils of the system and for justice, equality, and democracy.

Vision and struggle in changing circumstances transpires in the framework of contradictions that are explored throughout the book. Our upside down world is one of gross polarities of extremes begging resolution. Yet, the resolve of active subjects is obscured and thwarted by the subversion of popular consciousness. The dominant class has its well-defined, class-privilege-based hegemonic project, now a strong incipient American-style fascism. The counter-hegemony of the downtrodden and oppressed is yet in weak expression. Some of the discourse explores the graphics of one side of the contradiction, outrage to try to reach an inner conscience with the exhortation of resolution explicit.

The book generally moves from denunciation of *what is* and exhortation to remedy, passing through discourse on political economy, the formation of social classes and sociological analysis of class situations, analysis of ruling ideology, and, in the final chapters, to questions of class mobilization and movement strategy. The first chapters explore the nature of "the problem" of *what is*. The political economy of financialization of the economy and crisis and stagnation are examined. Social forces are mobilized in an economic context and the analysis of political economy in Chap. 4 focuses on how crisis and stagnation transform the social structure and restructure relations of social class. The fundamentals of ruling ideas imposed on the population, now globalized, are drawn out at considerable length in Chap. 5, along with the nature of the dominant class and the contradictions that rule by plutocracy impose on society. Chapter 6 examines the subordination of political reform forces, Obama and the Democrats, to the rule of capital. Chapter 8 poses questions of American-style fascism.

Chapter 7, "Rule by Divide and Conquer," is a sociological analysis of the class situation of people differently placed within a stratified social structure. Explored in some depth are the forces that create social division, especially racism, sexism, and the system-induced social stratifications that fracture social solidarity. Chapter 8 examines the most barbaric side of the present system: terror and war abroad, and heightened repression and violence at home. Chapter 9 reviews globalization by means of policies and institutions that extend and enforce neo-liberal policies that bring about degenerative development and its corresponding social consequences on a world scale. This chapter examines social forces in Latin America and worldwide that offer visions of a better future.

The initial chapters mainly focus on structural determinants to the direction of the American economy, society, and polity, and, to a considerable degree, employ the perspective of Marxist political economy. Structural forces determine in the first instance, but the other side to this is that people in determined, disadvantaged and changing class situations have imagination and creativity, and often the will to change adverse circumstances—they become active subjects, agents of change. The dialectic of structure/consciousness is examined theoretically in Chap. 10. Drawn from previous discourse are strategic concerns for genuine social change in the concluding chapters. What social forces can be mobilized to forge broader class alliances in the struggles? What strategies and tactics need to be evolved? And what obstacles must be overcome to do so?

Throughout the book, I refer to the State of National Insecurity. The concept is not, however, fully developed until Chap. 6. So, I will summarize the meaning here. Government in the United States is conceived as composed of three branches that divide and counterbalance the governing power of the state: executive, legislative, and judicial. In the present era, these three branches are subservient to the political power of plutocracy. Beyond the evident rule of plutocracy over government conventionally conceived is a Fourth Estate, created by plutocracy: the security apparatus. It is my thesis that the three branches of government are now subordinate to the (in)security apparatus. The State of National Insecurity consists of the Department of Defense, the CIA, Special Forces, the NSA mass surveillance that Edward Snowden exposed, Homeland Security, the Justice Department, the FBI, local police forces, the National Guard, and other forces that are state secrets. These agencies have privatized many of their operations and spawned a vast array of contracting corporations that do dirty work for the insecurity apparatus. The private shadow contractors take in trillions of dollars without oversight or accountability. The complex, the merger of government agencies and private corporations, does the bidding of the plutocracy, with its thirst for war and empire abroad, and social control in the homeland. The state becomes a regime of repressive lawlessness, a super rogue state that accords impunity to its Fortress America agents pursuing the dogma of the war on terror, globalizing its policy of neo-liberalism, espousing America first and American exceptionalism, imposing the creed of social Darwinism, and containing and repressing domestic opposition.

I don't have any illusions that social movements will achieve a total economic, social, and cultural transformation in the short or medium term. Neither do I have illusions that my denunciations and economic and sociological analysis will be extensively read or taken very seriously. Critical analysis that moves millions of active subjects in transformative efforts requires the development of a critical intellectual culture which is incipient in the United States but has yet to mature. I do think that *what is* can only be changed by people achieving better understanding, then acting on that understanding. That seems to me to be a place for New Left intellectuals.

Chapter 2 examines the immediate and more familiar sources of the ongoing crisis of degenerative, savage capitalism. Savagery is revealed in the extent of conditions of inequality. In the economic sphere, this crisis is rooted in the ascendance of banksters to the leading position within the capitalist class and the fact that economic dominance has led to plutocratic control of the greed-locked political sphere.

CHAPTER 2

Money and the World It Creates

The system of capitalism generates the grossest of contradictions. The confiscation of wealth and the exercise of power impel poverty and powerlessness. Elite supremacy necessarily involves mass anomie, alienation among the citizenry, and individual estrangement from the self. There is conspicuous consumption for the privileged few while the many suffer hunger and homelessness. War criminals and bankster fraud enjoy immunity, while the full weight of the injustice system falls on those forced by destitution to try to make a living on the street. The contradictions play out at multiple levels, bosses and workers, rich and poor, privileged and underprivileged, white and black, Anglos and Latinos, Christians and Muslims, men and women, police and citizens, rulers and ruled, and, at broader levels of polarization, Western good and Eastern evil, ersatz civilization and Islamic barbarism, war and peace, plutocracy and democracy, north and south, west and east—all is upsidedownness.[1]

The Occupy Movement's attention in 2010 and 2011 to how Wall Street's direction of the economy works to bring greater monopoly concentration and social inequality wrought a good deal of public attention and considerable research on inequality.[2] Astounding figures dramatize that gross inequality is a global injustice. Just 8 people own as much wealth as half the world population, while the richest 1% owns more than the remaining 99% of the population. In the United States, distorted and lopsided "recovery" since the years of crisis has only brought growing

D.L. Johnson, *Social Inequality, Economic Decline, and Plutocracy,*
DOI 10.1007/978-3-319-49043-4_2

inequality of income and wealth. Continuing trends in income and wealth inequalities are the core of a pattern of market-driven development that creates a consumerist, throwaway commodity culture wherein resources and people are disposable factors of production. Capital relations create a culture of predation and hyper-exploitation of the environment and of people. Capital imposes a predatory society in the economic and social spheres, and the dictatorship of capital in the political realm. Capital imposes laws and policies that depend upon the political rule of plutocracy for maintenance of the system, and for repression of resistance at home and interventions abroad that feed the war machine and corporate profits. Capital fosters degenerative development in all the wrong sectors—in speculation, in wasteful, environmentally degrading, and socially destructive activities. There is no trickle down in an economy directed from Wall Street, only a flood up. Government fiscal policy favors only the special corporate interests. Monetary policy feeds speculative activity for the top dogs, driving up stock prices, taking toxic assets out of the balance sheets of the big banks at public expense, while social benefits are curtailed.

First, a review of the essentials on the class polarization inherent in the current phase of degenerative capitalist development—savage capitalism in its most vicious form.

ASTOUNDING FACTS ON POLARIZATION OF WEALTH AND POVERTY

The CIA rarely publishes truthful intelligence. An exception is some of the data in the *World Factbook*. The Gini Index, used conventionally and by the CIA, is a measurement of inequality. The United States, near the top among the wealthiest nations, ranks 45th in world inequality, on a par with several African nations, ahead of South Africa and Haiti, but way behind the countries of Japan, Canada, Australia, and Western Europe (even with the imposition of austerity by the financial oligarchy in Europe). Inequality is reflected in the ample data on the distribution of income and wealth, but also in social indices such as health and longevity, poverty rates, and educational attainments. The U.S.'s favorite adversary, Cuba, is near the top of the social well-being index; the United States is far down the list. There is also a decided reversal of previous trends opening some avenues of greater equality for race and ethnic groupings, and women, achieved by civil rights and women's movements.

There is a considerable amount of data on income disparities, a growing trend since the 1970s. The United States now ranks 93rd in the world in income inequality. Between 2002 and 2012, the top 5% of income earners increased their take from 27% to 38%, the top 20% increased from 53.4% to 61%, while the bottom 80% fell from 46.6% to 39%. The context is that stagnation tendencies since the 1970s were countered with policies fomenting "degenerative development," (defined in Chap. 3) moving alternately from recession to recovery to new cycles of the same, with overall slow economic growth. Maldistribution of income, beginning under the regime of Reagan in the 1980s, became pronounced during the economic expansion in the Clinton era, 1993–2000. For that period, the top 1% gained a 98.7% increase, the bottom 99% gained 20.3%, most of that to the top 10%. Modest economic gain in the 2000s was hoped to involve a trickle down but was, in fact, a rush up. With recovery from the 2001 recession and the Bush period expansion from 2002 to 2007, the top 1% garnered 65% of income growth. In the year leading up the 2007–2008 crash, one Wall Street oligarch, John Paulson, turned financial instruments into $10 million dollars in cash on a daily basis for most of 2007. The recovery from the great crash of 2008 meant that things got better for the big guys like Paulson, capturing, by 2012, 93% of income growth, apparently even a higher percentage in 2013–2014; the bottom 90% got next to nothing. This is a rather incredulous but repetitive story that one can follow either in short form in a succinct article by Emmanuel Saez or, in much astounding but belabored detail, in Piketty and in Joseph Stiglitz, as well as in Anthony Atkinson's book on inequality.[3]

Beyond the major works of Piketty, Stiglitz, and Atkinon (Atkinson), there are daily reports on facts and dimensions of inequality from on-line alternative news sources too numerous to cite. Here, I distill a few of these reports. Over time, and especially since the great bust, Americans work more and get less pay. Even vacation time from the drudgery of work is much less than in any European country—vacation days in Finland are 44, Italy 42, France 39… U.S. employees get 12 days. Productivity advances are not shared as they were from the 1950s to the 1970s, labor costs drop with technology applied to the labor process, and the gains go to the bosses. The index of productive gains from 1979 to 2007 indicates a rise from an index of 200 to 400, while the index of average hourly compensation remained static. Another study indicated that while productivity in the American economy doubled between 1973 and 2010, the real wages of workers declined by 7%. For college graduates in better-paid employment, there was also a relative stagnation of salary levels in relation to productivity gains. This capture by capital of the value of productivity gains is a main basis for growing inequality. During the "recovery" in 2013 and 2014, hourly wages of workers in real terms continued to decline, with black and Latino workers suffering greater deterioration than white employees. Significantly, the greatest decline in real incomes in 2013 and 2014 was among those with college degrees. The Pew Research Center examined low- and middle-income households in different metropolitan areas for the period 1999 to 2014. Average income in poor neighborhoods dropped from $26,373 to $23,811 in 2014. Middle-income averages fell from $77.898 to $72.919 in that period. The 10% that gained from the 2008 to 2014 recovery are clearly the beneficiaries and controllers of who wins and who loses in the vicious game of inequality.

Several studies also show that racial and ethnic disparities in wealth are pronounced. In 2011, white households had $111,146 in accumulated wealth, compared with $7,113 for blacks and $8,348 for Latinos. This is mainly accounted for by home ownership; over 70% of whites have home assets but home ownership by blacks and Latinos is much less. Inequalities by race are also evident in educational attainments: 34% of whites have college degrees compared with 20% for blacks and 13% for Latinos. According to Forbes magazine, the 400 wealthiest Americans have more assets than 150 million Americans. The Walton family, owners of Walmart, have as much wealth as the bottom one-third of Americans. According to Oxfam at the 2017 World Economic Forum, the 8 wealthiest people have as many assets as 50% of the world's population, 3.6 billion people. Oxfam announced that the global 1% has more net worth than the rest of the world combined.

Today, millions of Americans materially exist below the official poverty line. Forty percent of households earn incomes near or below the poverty line; for a family of five, Social Security considers $28,410 annual income the poverty line. Fifty-one percent of workers earned less than $30,000 annually, 62% less than $40,000, and 71 % less than $50,000. The federal minimum wage is now less than $8 per hour—for a full-time worker, less than $15,000 annually. The 2015–2016 campaign to raise the minimum wage to $15 per hour would result, when and if implemented, in a full-time wage of $600/week, $2500/month, $31,000/year. This is near to the poverty level for a family of five. Increasing the minimum wage would ameliorate the situation of those employed as full-time workers, but many jobs are part-time, millions are being pushed toward destitution with job loss, social services are curtailed, health coverage problematic ("Obamacare," a give-away to insurance companies, was nevertheless helping some), homes foreclosed, pensions gobbled up by Wall Street malfeasance, and millions more face a similar fate as a stagnant economy stumbles along. Many public pension funds were, and remain, managed by Wall Street firms. The funds took big hits in the crisis. Today, these funds are paying up to $10 billion a year in management fees, while there is pressure to slash contractual benefits.

While reported unemployment has fallen from 11% in 2009 to around 5% in 2016, this is not reflected in the share of income accorded the working class. Official figures ignore hidden unemployment and underemployment. One out of four workers has a job that pays less than $10 an hour and the United States has a higher percentage of workers doing low-waged work than other industrialized countries. Of course, unemployment is at higher levels in the periphery of southern and eastern Europe, and most of the world. That does not mean that U.S. workers are much better off. Wage levels for those still employed are being forced downward while benefits are cut; unions, where they still exist, are under attack and unable to protect jobs and benefits; income inequalities between the rich and their higher-paid staff and the middle- and working-classes, increasing since the 1970s, are now at record levels. American corporations close down their U.S. plants and shift their investments to low-waged countries; technical jobs are outsourced abroad; millions of home owners had their mortgages foreclosed; families, cities, and states are facing bankruptcy. And the political response is more of the same neo-liberalism that created the problems— cut government spending for any and all social services; use tax revenues to go to war; strengthen the repressive apparatus of the state; build more prisons and turn them over to private control as profitable businesses; curtail civil liberties and spy on citizens; play the racist card and discriminate against, jail, and deport immigrants; create anti-Muslim hysteria; license the corporate media to shut out critical viewpoints and incite an incipient neo-fascism; vigorously pursue the imperial vision with endless military interventions. Prosperity for the 10%, austerity for the 90%, repression for those who protest at home and war against supposed enemies abroad. Of these responses, the repressive is almost as notable under Obama as it was with Bush, with prolonged war, assassination of presumed foreign enemies, curbing the civil liberties of American citizens, clubbing and gassing demonstrators, and imprisoning millions of persons whose crime is being poor, black, or Latino. This will get much worse under Trump.

Undocumented immigrants are thrown into privatized detention camps and then deported (this was moderated somewhat by Obama executive action in 2014, but faced legal challenge and the Supreme Court agreed that the action was illegal). America has, by far, the highest incarceration rate in the world. The weight of the criminal justice system falls heaviest on the African-American population. There are more blacks in prison or under probationary control than there were slaves on plantations in 1860. In the police-contained ghettos, four out of five of black youth get in trouble with the law. In California, one of the more enlightened states, the number of inmates of all races has increased eight times faster than the population growth. Prisons are increasingly privatized, so that private capital profits at state expense. Once freed from prison, ex-cons have few rights and lack employment opportunity, being marginalized into the underclass permanently. With Trump's anti-immigrant and racist policies, America is in serious trouble and most Democrats are not of a mind, or in a political position, to do anything about it. What the 90% do have today is powerlessness and the mobilization questions are how to convert powerlessness to strength.

Gross inequality drives millions of Americans to abject destitution. By 2010, 50 million people turned to food stamps to eat, while congressional Republicans worked to curtail this and other programs, such as Medicaid, that provide a social net for people to live a minimal existence. Planned parenthood is being crippled by a vicious smear campaign to the disadvantage of poor women. Twenty-four percent of households with children do not have enough money to buy sufficient food. Thirteen million families had lost their homes by 2014, with millions more in the process of foreclosure. More than 15 million youth live in dire poverty, drop out of school, and hustle a street living, many to be incarcerated by having resorted to petty crime in order to eat. Of course, the burden of unemployment and hopelessness falls most heavily on people of color. In 2010, among young Latinos unemployment was 37% and youthful blacks 35%.

The ethics of social amelioration disappears in an orgy of social Darwinism; in capital speak, the poor can exercise their individual freedom by self-help, by personal responsibility. As politics is redefined as the freedom of capital to impose injustice, inequality, and indignity, the semblance of a politics of the common good withers in the face of formal concealment of authoritarian inhumanity. Obama, Clinton, and the Democrats play the political game according to rules defined by plutocracy. But their most serious failure is not accommodation to the power game, but the ignoring and demobilization of the millions who voted for change in 2008—only people's mobilizations can constrain the worst from happening. The 2016 Sander's campaign that mobilized such energy was subject to demobilization.

The imposed cultures of demeaning insecurity, fear, and social Darwinism drive people to mental distress. According to the World Health Organization, one in four U.S. citizens suffers from chronic anxiety, depression, or other mental disorder. Millions are addicted to opioids and thousands die of overdoses. Asylum America!

America Inc. is the worst of all comparable nations in a range of social and economic indicators. James Speth, in an internet publication, reveals some of these terms:

> The highest poverty rate, both generally and for children; the greatest inequality of incomes; the lowest government spending as a percentage of GDP on social programs for the disadvantaged; the lowest number of paid holiday, annual and maternity leaves; the lowest score on the United Nations' index of "material well-being of children"; the worst score on the United Nations' gender inequality index; the lowest social mobility; the highest public and private expenditure on health care as a portion of GDP; the highest infant mortality rate; prevalence of mental health problems; obesity rate; portion of people going without health care due to cost; low-birth-weight children per capita (except for Japan); consumption of antidepressants per capita; the shortest life expectancy at birth (except for Denmark and Portugal); the highest carbon dioxide emissions and water consumption per capita; the lowest score on the World Economic Forum's environmental performance index (except for Belgium) and the largest ecological footprint per capita (except for Belgium and Denmark); the highest rate of failing to ratify international agreements; the lowest spending on international development and humanitarian assistance as a percentage of GDP; the highest military spending as a portion of GDP; the largest international arms sales; the most negative balance of payments (except New Zealand, Spain and Portugal); the lowest scores for student performance in math (except for Portugal and Italy) (and far from the top in both science and reading); the highest high school dropout rate (except for Spain); the highest homicide rate; and the largest prison population per capita. Now, this is a pretty sorry score sheet for our country - which used to excel in many of these categories.

This is an important read; see also more on inequality in endnote 3, where the internet link to Speth is cited.

In these circumstances, the dream of the downtrodden for dignity, freedom, and democracy becomes a nightmare of despair. Individual freedom is redefined as the right of corporations to do what they will. Democracy becomes a meaningless ritual of vote casting in rigged elections. The principles of democracy are invoked to legitimize the opposite, authoritarian class rule. Defense of democracy is wrapped in a discourse of fear and insecurity, justifying repressive rule and tightening of the insecurity apparatus. Fortress America then exports its democratic principles by unleashing its sophisticated weaponry against barbarian hordes in the Middle East. Henry Giroux, always insightful and elegant, states: "If the first rule of robber baron politics is to make power invisible, the second is to make it unaccountable and the third rule is to give as much power as possible to those who revel in barbaric greed, social irresponsibility, unconscionable economic inequity, corrupt politics, resurgent monopolies and an unapologetic racism..."[4]

Elsewhere in the world, fortunately, people are rising up with demands for real democracy and social justice. In Greece, Spain, Italy, and Portugal, people are in revolt. While the Arab Spring has largely fizzled, in parts of Latin America progressive governments are departing from the policies of neo-liberalism and globalization. In May 2012, the French elected a socialist president who, at least rhetorically, promised to tax the plutocrats, save social programs, and reject austerity in favor of growth policies. Did not happen, just the opposite. In response to the January 2015 and November 2015 attacks by Islamic extremists, France went solidly behind the American inspired war on terrorism and France supports the austerity policies of the European Union under the sway of German, French, and Swiss finance capital (perhaps with more tolerance of Greek deviance than Germany). So far (but with some hopes for change under 2016 labor movements and popular pressures), the European socialists have continued their role as guardians of the status quo of roll-back of the social democratic state. The left-wing of the British Labour Party gained control after the conservative electoral victory in 2015, was challenged by the popular vote to leave the European Union, but stayed in control.

In October 2012, Venezuelans reelected Hugo Chavez to his third term as president to further the progress toward "socialism of the 21st century." What a contrast to the American elections! In Venezuela, the National Electoral Commission managed to register 96% of eligible persons, as compared with 65% in the U.S. 2012 election. The voter turnout was massive and Chavez won by a wide margin. Voting there is electronic, with paper ballots receipts reviewed by partisans of all parties. There is no miscounting or procedures that turn away voters. Ex-President Jimmy Carter, who heads a vote monitoring organization, referred to Venezuela's system as "the best in the world." What was more impressive, however, is that Venezuelans, unlike American citizens, had a real choice, one candidate promising to do even better in advancing the nation, the opposition candidate offering a return to neo-liberalism and the country's subservience to U.S. regional dominance. Unfortunately Chavez died, opening up opportunity for right-wing thugs, encouraged and financed by the United States, to create havoc in a 2014 unsuccessful attempt to bring down the government, and 2015 plots to kill President Maduro and install a military regime. The privileged elements and business interests unleashed economic chaos that led to right-wing gains in the legislature in December 2015. This violent oppositional uprising and their campaign of sabotaging the economy is reminiscent of the 1973 events that led to the September 11, 1973, military intervention in Chile against the elected socialist government and the subsequent brutal military dictatorship that featured neo-liberal policies enforced by violence. (Right-wing thugs supported by the United States and European Union also played a key role in overthrowing the Ukraine government in 2014 and the violent conflict that ensued together with a new cold war against Russia).

THE DOMINANT CLASS

Capitalist societies tend to be ruled economically, socially, and politically by those who own and control productive property, the circulation of commodities, and the flow of money. There is, historically, a leading sector that exercises predominant power. In nineteenth- and early twentieth-century America, it was the "robber barons"; in the decades after World War II, large industrial corporations; by the 1970s, conglomerates of diverse enterprises and the U.S.-based transnational corporations spreading activity worldwide; in the 1980s, the energy companies and the defense contractors; and, by the late 1990s down to the present times, the banksters and financiers, with the armaments industry, the transnational corporate giants, big oil, and the privatized complex surrounding the State of National Insecurity solidly behind them. It is this leading sector of oligarchs, finance capital, that now holds predominant control in the economy—and, in the political sphere, the dominant class as a whole rules as plutocracy. Wall Street is the center of this control, but it extends to Europe as well, and to much of the rest of world. German, Swiss, British, and French bankers and financiers are part of the oligarchic center, as are German and French finance ministers, and those who head up the European Central Bank, the International Monetary Fund, and the World Bank, and central banks in many countries. It is also this fraction of the larger dominant class of capitalists that has been engaged for several decades in a hegemonic project to remake the United States and Europe, and world society, into a savage capitalism in which their vested interests and class privilege are sacrosanct.

In the original version of this book I included a number of lengthy verses, but the publisher said no, so I state only a few lines of one here:

> Human evolution took a wrong turn.
> The Neanderthals are back!
> Zombies risen from the grave of history,
> Now chasing Homo Sapiens with their big sticks,
> Clubbing every social advance of human kind,
> Torturing and killing non-white peoples in distant lands,
> Jailing and deporting those considered aliens in Zombie heartland.

The financial oligarchy is the core of the Modern Neanderthals that have disentombed all the zombies that inhabit and pervert the current political culture.

The wealthy dominate the U.S. Congress. In 2007, 45% of representatives and 67% of senators were millionaires, and their wealth increased 11% during the crisis years 2008–2011. In addition, they regularly get payments for services rendered to lobbyists. Politics steps carefully in the footprints of economics. All of Obama's appointments to the Federal Reserve, Treasury Department, and the Department of Commerce were oligarchs drawn from Wall Street, and all the members of his Council of Economic Advisors were trained in neo-liberal orthodoxy. The American state today is as close as any time in history to the dictatorship of capital, totalitarianism striving to appear as benevolent democracy with a velvet lining but freely employing the iron fist to maximize its advantage in engaging a fierce class war against the 90% while drumming up terror, interventionism, and war abroad. Obama and the Democrats, and certainly President Trump, are not willing or able to face that reality; they are its cultivated instruments. It is up to the movement to reshape the political landscape. To do so effectively we must face the formidable and brutal power of the State of National Insecurity, a historically unprecedented concentration of the means of subjugation in the repressive apparatus.

But we have always to keep in mind that there is apparently no current serious division within the dominant class as a whole, the 1% is united behind the tenants of the 0.001%, the oligarchs of the financier center, the zombie speak of social Darwinist ideology, neo-liberal policy, and austerity—and, in the United States, hailing the religion of Republicanism, even though sectors have covered their bases by contributions to the Democrats. This is not to say that there are not tactical disagreements among the Fractions of capital about how to best maintain and manage the system. There appeared to be a serious divide among plutocrats in 2015–2016 with regard to Republican presidential candidates; some are fearful of Trump and searched for an alternative. Divergence among business sectors was revealed in the campaign contributions in the 2012 election, with money flowing in almost equal proportion to Obama and Democratic coffers, as compared with Republican funding. On the essentials that the state is destined to oversee the smoothest possible reproduction of the system of capitalism, there appears to be no significant division between industrial and financial capital; between big, medium, and smaller business; or between American-based capital and the national capitals of other countries. They coalesce in their view of salvation as reconstituting and extending the "neo-liberal" project (to be analyzed in depth later). However, this coalescence is unlikely to be an enduring situation. Crisis and stagnation, and the dominance of finance capital create a situation where sectors of capital become structurally disadvantaged and subordinated. And Trump and his social base of angry people will likely further divide the sectors of business.

The United States is a nation in which the economy is predominantly controlled by finance capital, the 0.001% among the 1%, and the moneyed elite at the head of big banks and Wall Street investment firms hold positions on the boards of directors of the major corporations in all sectors. They also have very substantial political power with unrestricted funds to pollute the political environment and to bribe politicians. Mitt Romney's 2012 top campaign contributors were Wall Street investment firms and big banks, with Goldman Sachs, Bank of America, and JPMorgan Chase at the top of the list, which also included Credit Suisse and his own Bain Capital. In contrast, Barack Obama's chief contributors were technology companies such as Microsoft, Google, and IBM, as well as universities. (Reflecting a divergence among the fractions of capital.) These lists do not include the many millions raised by the super-pacs organized by corporations and the wealthy, most supporting attack ads and activity supportive of Romney. The plutocrats most likely forgave Obama his reference to Wall Street "fat cats" as long as his actions remained consistent with their interests, as they faithfully did.

Two statistical references illustrate the increased dominance of the financial sector within the U.S. economy and financial oligarchs within the dominant class. During the decade of the 1960s, financial profits as a percentage of total corporate profits averaged 15%. This percentage increased in the 1970s, hovering around 20%. The proportionate increase in financial profits rocketed from 1985 to 1995 to over 30%, dipped a little in the economic difficulties of the late 1990s, to again take off in the 2000s, ascending to 40% of the corporate take in 2005–2007, increasing with the "recovery" from 2010 to 2015. The corollary to this tendency is the long-term decline since 1985 in non-residential fixed investment as a percentage of gross domestic product (GDP). During the 1970s, productive investment averaged over 4% of GDP—a low figure reflecting the long-term stagnation tendency of the U.S. economy—but, by 2005–2007, productive investment had fallen to 2.7%. Excess productive capacity of U.S. industry has steadily increased, while American industrial corporations, often with financing and consultative services from the big banks, shifted their investments to China, and to countries where labor is cheap and the investment climate good. Even the prosperous armaments industry, ever more generously subsidized by war and counter-terror spending, off-shores some of its business to firms in Israel and other countries. (Israel is the biggest world exporter of drone aircraft). Thus, the modest growth of the U.S. economy since 1985, but especially in the 2000s, has been mainly due to activity in military spending on the one hand, and most saliently the financial sector on the other hand—not in the "real economy", not in the production of useful goods and services that provide jobs and income to consumers. A financialized economy does not make useful products, it creates and markets transactions and financial instruments that have no net positive impact on the economy, serving only to divert surplus to financial oligarchs. With their ill-gotten gains they turn to gobbling up smaller or weaker companies and organize conglomerates. They pounce as vultures on weaker prey. There is a great deal of money floating around in America Inc., but oligarchs have absconded with it. It is said that they hold two trillion in cash alone—nice to have petty cash to gamble with. Financiers are essentially rentiers, the landlords of America Inc. Raking in rents makes nothing grow. The gain game balances at the sum of zero. Rent leaves the renter poorer, the landlord richer.

ECONOMY, SOCIETY, CULTURE, AND POLITY: THE FOUR PRINCIPAL MEANS OF PLUTOCRATIC RULE

In Chap. 3, the financialization of the economy is considered in relation to crisis and stagnation, and in Chap. 4 the restructuring of class relations is explored. In subsequent chapters, how the ruling class rules is considered in some depth. In summary, stated here: The dominant class prevails with diverse mechanisms. First, they instill their class-privileged ideology in the populace. This is explored extensively in Chap. 5, more theoretically in relation to the dialectics of counter-hegemony projects in Chap. 10, and the strategic programs outlined in Chaps. 11 and 12. Second, they subjugate agencies of state to their agenda, mostly argued in Chap. 6, with strategic considerations for undermining the omnipotence of state power in the final chapter. Third, they divide and conquer, by stratifying the population into competitive strata. The transformation of the social structure into subordinated classes and social groupings is analyzed in Chap. 7 on divide and conquer strategies. Faced with social divisions based on race, ethnicity, national origin, sex, and hierarchical stratifications within classes, the movement strategy is to celebrate diversity while forging class unity. Fourth, they use force, repression, and war. This is the really scary part. We live with perpetual war and under the watchful eye of the State of National Insecurity (Chap. 8). One has to question whether the United States will not turn toward fascism, into Amerikka Inc. Each means of plutocratic rule will be addressed in turn and related to questions of Movement strategy in the final chapters.

NOTES

1. Eduardo Galeano, *Upsidedown: A Primer for The Looking Glass World*, Henry Holt, 2000. Galeano has many books published and translated to English and very worth the read.
2. Guy Standing, *The Precariat: The New Dangerous Class*, Bloomsbury Academic, 2013. Standing examines the emerging class of people facing job loss, insecurity, and lack of meaning to their lives. He argues that the Precariat is a "dangerous class" because they are divided, lacking agency, and could be mobilized for scapegoating campaigns and political extremism. This treatise is born out, at least in part, by the exit of Great Britain from the EU and by Trump's support of the U.S. working class. The history of the idea of

Precariousness is explored in R. Jamil Jonna and John Bellamy Foster, "Working-Class Precariousness," *Monthly Review*, Volume 67, April 2016. Thomas Piketty, *Capital in the Twenty-first Century*, Harvard University Press, 2014, provides a great deal of useful and truly impressive data on inequality in the distribution of both income and wealth, historically and cross-nationally. The problem with this approach is that it reduces social class to statistical artifacts of income categories and asset brackets. The "1%" is a catchy category, but it is not really a class, in the sense that the financial oligarchy is a fraction of the capitalist class. Deciles and centiles are indicators of class standing but they are not class. Classes are historical formations of living subjects engaged in social relations, the most central of which is the relation capital to labor, a social relation based on antagonisms that are engendered by exploitation and oppression. Classes are enmeshed in human relationships with people of their standing and with others differently situated in the dynamics of class relations that are constantly transforming the social structure. Class relations create divisions and stratifications within class. Some divisions are ascribed, such as race, ethnicity, and gender. Other stratifications are distributional, hierarchies of income gradations, education attainments, occupational categories, and so on. These are examined in Chap. 4 on class transformation and Chap. 7 on how the capitalist class uses social divisions and stratifications to divide and conquer.

3. Paulson was associated with the defunct Bear Stearns and formed his own hedge fund company Paulson and Co., making hundreds of millions of dollars just prior to the crash in credit default swaps and betting against the subprime mortgage bubble. Personally involved in creating then puncturing financial bubbles, he nevertheless emerged again in 2010 with another hedge fund that brought him $5 billion in that year—surely a fine record deserving of appointment to the Treasury Department. On inequality, there is a substantial literature. Piketty, cited in endnote 2, is the most detailed study. See also E. Saez at www.truth-out.org/new/item8533; and Joseph Stiglitz, *The Price of Inequality: How Today's Divided Society Endangers Our Future*, W.W. Norton, 2013. See also Anthony Atkinson, *Inequality: What Can Be Done*, 2015. Atkinson's methodsfor addressing inequality are, like Piketty's, Keynesian in nature, hardly currently in vogue. Similarly, Stiglitz neither recognizes that inequality can't be cured under the rule of capital, nor that inequality

is necessarily immoral; he argues that inequality is detrimental to the optimum functioning of the capitalist economy. A focus on wealth and power is the excellent book by Greg Palast, *Billionaires and Ballot Bandits*, view at www.BallotBandits.org Especially interesting is the chapter "Penny's from Heaven?" that deals with Obama's appointment of Penny Pritzker as Secretary of Commerce in 2013. The chapter explores how Obama was groomed for stardom, and servitude, by Chicago financiers. The data in Chap. 2 that compares the United States with other nations is from James Speth, "America, the Worst of all Comparable Nations," www.truth-out.org/american-exceptionalism/131467228.

4. Henry Giroux at www.truth-out.org/farewell-mon-amour-prospects-democracy-electoral-defeat64535.

CHAPTER 3

The Political Economy of Financialization and Its Consequences

Crisis

The current economic situation in the United States and the even worse disaster in Southern Europe is a result of the exhaustion or lack of efficacy of the historical sources for the accumulation of capital combined with the political power of plutocracy that cannot, or will not, do anything but exacerbate crisis and stagnation. Accumulation is the dynamic of capitalism, the wherewithal to invest and make more profits in new avenues of business development—when accumulation reaches limits, crises come about. Crisis can take different expressions—drastic falls in asset values, sharp decline in economic activity, steep rise in unemployment…as in the Great Depression of the 1930s and, again, in 2008–2009. More common is recession of several years' duration, as in periods in the 1980s, the 1990s, and the first years of the 2000s. Notably, these recessions have increased in frequency, length, and depth since the 1970s, reflecting a deepening stagnation of the economy. Rates of economic growth have steadily declined in the last decades, with GDP growth of over 4% in the 1950s and 1960s, to an average of 3% in the following three decades, falling to 2% from 2000 to the crisis of 2008. loThe mode of economic recovery in America and Europe since the latest crash has nothing to do with the opening of new avenues of economic development and everything to do with resurgence of speculative activity (financed at near zero interest by the Federal Reserve) that was the immediate root of the 2007–2009

© The Author(s) 2017

D.L. Johnson, *Social Inequality, Economic Decline, and Plutocracy,*

DOI 10.1007/978-3-319-49043-4_3

debacle, but with the backdrop of vast expenditures for war abroad, and "security" and repression at home, and, most of all, with the heightened exploitation of labor resulting in declining income and short-falls in effective demand.

Some refer to "savage capitalism" or, in reference to the centrality of Wall Street, "casino capitalism." I will explore the concept of "degenerative development"—an epoch of wasteful, economically useless, and environmentally and socially destructive activity. The "recovery" since 2010 has been based in good part on a rise in asset values, especially in corporate stock (90% of the earnings of the largest American corporations between 2010 and 2015 have gone for stock buybacks and dividends). This activity has no basis in production of useful goods and services, but has resulted in mergers into ever larger conglomerates and in speculative activity by financiers. The 1% has appropriated a growing share of income and wealth since the 1970s and almost the entirety of the value generated from 2010 to the present. To augment their profit, businesses move to appropriate an increased proportion of the fruits of labor, which seems always to end up in the pockets of CEOs and stockholders who then engage in financial speculation, extend financial controls in order to further centralize control, and invest in stocks to keep stock prices on the rise, generating asset appreciation. The Federal Reserve freely lends billions at near zero interest. The rise to record level stock indices by 2014 had little to do with economic health and viability, but everything to do with corporate directors buying up their own stock and that of other corporations to increase their value, gathering more funds for yet more speculative activity. This is likely to be a formula for another crash. The recovery from 2010 was also based, in part, on shifting public funds from economically productive and socially useful activity by government to spending on perpetual war, and the extension and buttressing of the State of National Insecurity, wherein the state is progressively reduced to the centrality of the repressive apparatus. There is no government fiscal policy or corporate interest in investing in much needed avenues of economic development—clean alternative energy, productive employment, improving the life situation of the population, education, economic alternatives that protect a threatened environment...or even repair of deteriorated infrastructure. But the crucial part of the recovery is the intensification of the means to subjugate labor and appropriate an increased proportion of the fruits of labor, and the transfer of that appropriation to the coffers of the oligarchs and CEOs that make up the 1%. And this, in turn, means more funds to speculate and carry on war and repression. In the Obama era, plutocratic environment of Republican obstructionism and "liberal" democrats' acquiescence to economic power, the Keynesian measures of government spending to increase aggregate demand, taxing the rich to transfer income to the needy to promote demand, or other developmental activity are not even considered, except, of course, there is massive investment to fire the war machine and to protect "national security". Thomas Piketty's idea of a progressive tax on individual wealth to promote a social state is a notable departure from pure Keynesian measures, an interesting idea that a movement for change could pose as "demand the impossible." Progressive Democrat Elizabeth Warren is promoting a tax on financial transactions, a good idea, but what is needed is the closure of all big banks, and the creation of community and state banks that finance sustainable development.

The U.S. balance of payments, each year, reaches increasingly negative levels as more goods are imported than exported. This is due to globalizing investment to countries with lower wages and what American capital considers good investment climates. And these countries, led by China and the oil exporters, with positive balance of payments transfer the funds to the United States principally in the purchase of Treasury certificates. The inflow of non-productive dollars appreciates the value of the dollar (in 2015–2016, edging toward par with the Euro), which, in turn, spirals to make U.S. exports more expensive and imports cheaper. Obama's answer is to fast track trade agreements to further the process of corporate global power and precipitate greater decline in the U.S. economy. (See Chap. 9, section "Free Trade Has a High Price.") One of the few positive steps by Trump might be to revise free trade policy, but this will be opposed by sectors of capital that are linked to globalization.

The crisis is not one of capitalism as such; the system is as consolidated as it ever was. The crisis is profoundly one of the economic and social consequences of financialization and the unrestrained rule of capital. It is a crisis of humanity. The experience, now more and more exacerbated as plutocracy tightens its grip, is a crisis of the life situation of peoples in America Inc. and throughout the world. The American population, in 2015, had an indebtedness of $11.86 trillion in mortgages, credit cards, and student loans, and this after a 36% drop in household worth since 2005. Value is appropriated by capital in the first instance, by reducing wage levels everywhere, then realizing a second appropriation of value in the sphere of consumption financed by debt. Worldwide, total debt reached $199 trillion in 2014, up $57 trillion since 2008, much to the benefit of the financial sector. These are the bases of a historically unprecedented stagnation and associated crises that continue the radical transformation of the relations of social class, which will be explored here and in later chapters.

FINANCIAL INSTRUMENTS, NOT JOBS, SCHOOLS, OR CLEAN ENERGY

Throughout his long tenure (1987–2006) as Chairman of the United States Federal Reserve, Alan Greenspan regularly appeared before Congress. The obsequious senators bowed to Lord Greenspan as if he were the messiah of the century illuminating the most profound words of wisdom, an appreciation enthusiastically shared by President Clinton in the 1990s and President Bush in the 2000s. The financial crisis devastatingly revealed that Chairman Greenspan was a blower of bubbles, a purveyor of obscurantism, a servant of Wall Street power, a charlatan, and an exalted example of the financial oligarchs now in the saddle of power.

In 2008, we expected more of a president who promised change. Yet, President Obama's appointments to the Federal Reserve and to the Treasury and Commerce Departments from 2008 onward, and the staff that surround them and the president, are all out of the same Wall Street mold—just as Obama's appointments to the Department of Defense, the National Security Agency, and the CIA were figures associated not only with the wars in Afghanistan and Iraq, but also the war crimes and crimes against humanity of the Bush era. In plutocracy, political office serves economic power.

Given the depth of the crisis and a generalized understanding of the debacle of 2007–2009, how can one understand the business-as-usual ambient that prevails in the United States, and in somewhat different circumstances in Europe? Financial speculation was the root cause of the crisis of 2007–2009. In a functioning economic system, the financial sector must be the facilitator of production, not a usurper of surplus and economic power. From the point of view of finance capital, the economy that produces real goods and services has the disadvantage of spreading income downward to employees and consumers in the economy, whereas financialization of the economy allows the siphoning of monies upward to the oligarchs without the proceeds having to be spread around the debt-burdened population. The debtors had a temporary fix to their increasing precarity since the 1990s by borrowing against increasing home equities and credit cards given to anyone who applied. They paid the lords a very high rent. The financial superstructure collapsed in 2007–2008—in the aftermath debtors paid not only the interest, but lost their homes, pensions, and jobs.

Economic growth of the U.S. economy over the years since 2000, much slower than in previous decades, was due largely to two factors, government military expenditures in armaments and war, and speculative financial bubbles in real estate mortgages and various asset derivatives. For many years, the United States has spent more on armaments than almost all other nations in the world combined! Arms exports are a very big business. In his 2015 speech to the U.S. Congress, Pope Francis denounced the horrific human consequences of the arms trade. Obama has approved more arms sales abroad than any U.S. administration since World War II. Obama, as arranged by Secretary of State Clinton, exported $30 billion more in arms in his first five years than Bush did in his full eight years. And this after the United States won the cold war and had the opportunity to engage peace. While vast "defense" expenditures provide employment to American workers, American consumers cannot eat bombs or live in the drone aircraft that have the sole purpose of killing people and spying on other countries. Meanwhile, big banks and Wall Street investment firms packaged home mortgages into collateralized debt obligations (CDO), invented derivatives and other aggregated assets to make them into marketable instruments, and then sold them throughout world financial markets. This precipitated an extreme appreciation of real estate and other asset values in the United States and elsewhere, especially Europe. Home values with a 1950 index of 100 slowly crept up to an index of around 110 until the year 2000. From that year to 2007, the index nearly doubled, skyrocketing to 200. This appreciation had no basis in costs of production—wood, cement, and construction labor costs only marginally increased. The appreciation was entirely due to bank financing liberally extended to cash starved homeowners trying to make ends meet and to Wall Street's packaging and marketing sub-prime mortgages. The Federal Reserve, largely deregulated from controls over banks under President Clinton, obligingly facilitated the real estate spiral and consumer debt by lowering the interest rate to historic lows in the 2000s. Consumers borrowed against equity in their homes and charged heavily against credit cards liberally advanced by the banks. Workers and middle-class employees, in total dependence on commodity markets, sought to compensate for declining incomes by borrowing to preserve their standard of living. Rising education costs and falling government subsidies to higher education forced students and their families to resort to loans that they may never be able to repay, potentially causing yet another bubble that may eventually pop. In 2007 and 2008, all the asset and derivative bubbles burst. But the financiers who created the world's greatest Ponzi schemes are still there doing business-as-usual, having been bailed out financially and reinstated politically, while they continue to engage in criminal activity (such as the 2012 Libor interest rate rigging scandal and HSBC drug money laundering, tax evasion for the wealthy, and commodity price fixing—all with impunity).[1]

Bursting bubbles did not inhibit banks and Wall Street firms from resurrecting the con game in the mortgage field. In the low interest environment created by the Federal Reserve since the crash, the mortgage market, with the recovery, is once again on the move. The banks extend home financing or refinancing (more judiciously, it is claimed), get Fannie Mae guarantees, and then turn around and sell the mortgages at a profit to Wall Street. Wall Street then packages mortgages as bonds and sells them at a profit. The Fed buys many of the bonds, taking potentially toxic assets off the balance sheets of these institutions, while driving bond prices higher. The Treasury Department helps some homeowners with larger mortgage balances than the current home market price to qualify for refinancing. The same old game that led to financial crisis, clearly overseen by the Fed. The ultimate fall guys are the federal deficit and the taxpayer if the scheme fails.

The banksters that reward themselves with stupendous annual bonuses for their dedicated work in bringing down the world economy and, along with the corporate rich in general, avoid paying taxes by stashing trillions of dollars—that is *trillions*, not billions or millions—in off-shore tax havens.[2] Oxfam says $7.6 trillion. President Bush and the Congress gave tax cuts, Obama extended the cuts and held open loopholes in the tax codes so that the rich can engage in financial speculation at even higher levels and hide yet more money off-shore. Americans with more than $10,000 in foreign bank accounts are required to file a reporting form, FATCA, with the Treasury Department. This will affect several million Americans living abroad, but is unlikely to reveal tax evasion, as the 2015 scandal concerning the Swiss subsidiary of HSBC, the big transnational bank, reveals. HSBC had not been reporting foreign holdings to the Treasury Department under U.S. requirements (called FBAR) and advised depositors in secret accounts how to avoid taxes in their home countries. Trump promises to cut corporate taxes even further.

An indication of the soft hand in dealing with big banks is the 2015-appointed Attorney General Loretta Lynch's 2011 handling of the biggest drug money laundering in history. At that time, Lynch was U.S. Attorney for the Eastern District of New York. She crafted a "soft touch, deferred prosecution" deal for HSBC. (Given the long history of impunity for bankster criminality by the Justice Department, we can expect that to continue).

Finance capital is now highly concentrated into conglomerate groups. The ten largest conglomerates hold more than 60% of U.S. financial assets, compared with 10% in 1990. These giants include JPMorgan Chase (caught up in yet another financial scandal in May 2012), Bank of America (major rip-off artist in home foreclosures), Wells Fargo (caught in a big consumer rip-off in 2016), Citigroup, and Goldman Sachs (Goldman Sachs is everywhere in the world, and is a principal bank in extending corporate rule through globalization, greatly facilitated by Hillary Clinton as Secretary of State—she and Bill Clinton got fat fees and contributions to the Clinton Foundation for talks to the bankers. This constellation—not established industrial giants such as General Motors or General Electric (though both industrial giants have their financial wings engaged in financial transactions), or the high-tech innovators such as Microsoft, are the center of economic power in the United States. The Wall Street financier, not Microsoft's Bill Gates, is the symbol of where money, systemic direction, and economic and political power now reside. Plutocracy rules economic policy; government is of, by, and for capital, and not just in Washington, but in the European Union as well. Finance has become a global criminal enterprise that operates with impunity for crimes of fraud, malfeasance in office, money laundering, tax evasion…and then collects from the public treasury even when its bubbles burst and its schemes are exposed. The Treasury and Federal Reserve continue to this day to subsidize financial entities. JPMorgan has been getting about $14 billion per year (more on the Fed in Chap. 9).

The plutocracy that governs prevents any political response to promote developmental projects, or ameliorate social conditions and provide employment. The Obama administration relied on the bankers of the Treasury, the FED, Commerce and Obama's team of orthodox economic advisors to steady the course of degenerative development. Republicans in Congress work to "starve the beast" of big government, privatizing infrastructure, and get state and local governments to partner with finance capital to issue private activity bonds that give the investors tax free returns. So much for fixing dilapidated infrastructure, funding education, promoting clean energy and environmental safeguarding, public works projects… any and all measures to create jobs and genuine economic development. Rest well Professor Keynes, you had your day. Now it is up to the people to find the way forward. The Occupy Movement's primary target of Wall Street was right on. Today's movements need to find ways to make that struggle current and take on this oligarchy. The long-term aim should be abolishing the Federal Reserve in favor of a central bank that coordinates monetary with development and fiscal policies; nationalization of big banks to eliminate them or totally change their function; and the socialization or establishment of publically controlled local, state, and federal banking systems that serve the ends of sustainable economic and social development that benefits people.

The Norm of Economic Stagnation

Subsequent to the Great Depression and the post-World War II expansion of the world economy, the problem of stagnation of the economies of the advanced industrial countries of North America and Europe came about in the 1970s and was combined with high rates of inflation, referred to in that period even by mainstream economists as "stagflation." The response to the economic situation from the 1980s onward was to embark on new strategies of accumulation and global development. The crisis caused in the United States and other countries by the "Volker Shock" of the 1980s, imposed by the Federal Reserve with high interest rates, introduced a new form of attempt to restructure a failing accumulation strategy. This took the form of "globalization" and the implementation of the policies of what came to be called "neo-liberalism".

Globalization of corporate and financial hegemony was quite successful as a principal source of new accumulation but encountered increasing limits, to be explored in Chaps. 10 and 11. A fundamental part of accumulation tendencies since the 1980s has been the shift of investment in the production of goods and services to cheap labor countries and financialization of the economies of the American and European centers. In center economies, due to the absence of productive investment alternatives for capital accumulated, corporations and the rich found shelter in tax havens abroad (estimated at $7.6 trillion, but could be more), stockholders received generous dividends, acquisitions and mergers abounded and monopolization proceeded apace, companies bought their own stock to drive up share prices, and speculation became the principle avenue of surplus absorption. This has resulted in an economy in which unproductive activity—such as in speculative finance resulting in bubbles and flow of capital to speculative activity in other countries, promotion of wasteful pursuits in a wide range of superfluous services and the sales effort, the promotion of cultural spectacles as products of mass consumption and diversion from social and economic realities, continuing activity degrading the environment, and socially destructive activity as in armaments and war—have become the principle means of generating profits, in short, *degenerative development*. These activities led directly to the financial and economic crisis of 2007–2008 and the same activities continue today.

Under the reign of increasing monopolistic concentration of capital in the hands of giant corporations absorbing their competitors and centralization of economic control, increasingly administered by the financial sector, the tendency for more surplus value to accrue than could find profitable investment outlets in useful and productive activity became ever deeper. The policy of undermining unions, using technology to displace labor and routinize work at lower wages, and reducing the real incomes of the working population added to short-term profits but put severe constraints on income available for consumption, so that effective demand dwindled. On top of shifting employment to cheap labor countries and using technology to reduce employment and cheapen labor, capital came up with yet another way to reduce costs and improve profitability—shift part of the labor costs to the consumer. Work is transferred from the production site, where it is paid, to the sphere of consumption. Consumers fill their own gas tanks, eat at self-service cafeterias, and shop at supermarkets with credit card checkout. Paid labor is displaced by the unpaid labor of consumers.

Export of jobs abroad, shortfalls in consumer demand, and slow growth created a considerable excess capacity of American industry. Even with the proclaimed recovery, 25% of industrial capacity was unutilized in 2014. Business does not invest when there is idle plant and equipment, depreciation reserves cover needed upkeep, and replacement of equipment tends to increase efficiency, expanding capacity for which there is lack of demand for output. "An indication of just how serious the whole problem of surplus absorption, in relation to investment opportunities in particular, has now become, is that over the last decade the net operating surplus (after most costs have been paid and depreciation accounted for) of private enterprises in the U.S. economy has averaged 24 percent of the GDP. In 2012 it came to over $4 trillion."[3] The profit imperative to enhance exploitation and corner profit engenders a deep contradiction. Economic growth transpires, or the system slips ever downward. In this context, speculation in particular and degenerative development in general guided by the financial sector came to be the only way out for the dominant sectors of capital. Financialization is much more than the concentration of economic power in the hands of a moneyed oligarchy. It leads to the tightening of plutocratic political rule, the restructuring of class relations and the further subordination of subaltern classes, and the imposition of a culture of domination and the deformation of consciousness among masses of the population.

What is often ignored or downplayed in economic analysis is that economic developments and shifts in the accumulation process are fundamentally transformations in the structure, life situation, and relations of social class. This focus is explored in a preliminary way in this chapter and extensively in Chap. 4.

A digression into theory and history is necessary for an understanding of the factors underlying the present structure and relations of class and crisis in respect of questions of strategy for bringing about fundamental change.[4] Historical studies of accumulation often view technological innovation as the main source of development. Capital puts its money, gained from the appropriation of value produced, into new technological sectors. The application of power to mechanical devices in the Industrial Revolution, the steam engine and railroads of the nineteenth century, and the automobile, electronics, and computers of the twentieth century were, indeed, "epoch-making" innovations. In recent times, especially since the 1980s there has been a great surge in technological innovation. To the degree that consumers have income, they spend on gadgetry that decreases in price quite rapidly. Cheaper gadgets are made possible both from increasing productivity enabled by technologies and from export of production activity to low-waged countries. Many young people walk around with an iPhone to their ear, then return home to play games on tablets, or sit at their PCs to access the internet and social media. No doubt these innovations and the generated consumer demand help to prop the economy. The high-tech sector however employs a very small proportion of the labor force, and much of the manufacturing and servicing ends are transferred abroad. (In 2013, Apple had only 80,000 employees worldwide, and all its production facilities were in China and other parts of Asia). How would investment in the technology of rapid transit to move people around cheaply and efficiently, or renewable energy to displace coal, oil, and fracked natural gas compare with the efficacy of gadgetry? To have real developmental possibilities, technology would need to have economy-wide implication and generate vast employment in useful activity. Instead, computer-driven technology is mainly used to substitute machines for labor (especially in robotics), reduce labor cost by "rationalizing" work activity, increase productivity and profits (without sharing productivity gains with workers), while applying a computer enabled "Fordism", thereby further degrading the labor process to enhance labor subordination. Information technology also allows ease and rapidity of global financial operations.

Historically speaking, there is one source of accumulation that is even more important than technical advance, or as a consequence of great innovations—the incorporation of increasing proportions of the population into the waged labor-to-capital social relation, a relation that allows capital directly to appropriate value produced in the form of profit. The cotton mills of early industrialism, the laying of railroad track and manufacture of trains, the automobile factories and the associated highways and sub-urbanization...none could have come into being without waged labor. Today's working class is a historical formation long in the making. (There are other sources of accumulation that rival technology advances in significance, to be shortly explored: the internationalization of capital and the growth of the modern state, both of which are also dependent on incorporation of labor, although in different ways than in the direct production of commodities that allow the appropriation by capital of profit on the value of goods produced by labor).

Without the production and appropriation of economic surplus that is reinvested in expanded production, there is no accumulation and economic development, the system regresses to stagnation and into recurrent crises. In the system that we have lived under for two centuries and more, this means that capital needed to be in a position to exploit labor directly for a portion of the value produced, or to appropriate surplus that is generated outside the capital-to-labor relation.

In the earlier stages of development, capitalism depended considerably on the appropriation of economic surplus through relations of unequal exchange with non-capitalist sectors, with colonized territories, or with dependent economies in Asia, Africa, and Latin America. For example, the slave plantation system of the Caribbean and the southern United States produced a considerable surplus that merchant capital, in those days the dominant fraction of the capitalist class, appropriated through a variety of mercantile mechanisms. Some of the surplus found its way into the accumulation process in industrial sectors, furthering industrial development, first, in England and, later, in the northern region of the United States, while also developing what later came to be called "underdevelopment in peripheral areas", structured to be exporters of raw materials and importers of manufacture products. With the growth of the monopoly form of industrial capitalism in the late nineteenth century and its accelerated rate in the twentieth century, the principal means of accumulation shifted from unequal exchange to the dispossession of independent producers and their incorporation by carrot or by stick into the waged labor-to-capital nexus. This permitted the subsumption, under the aegis of capital of production previously outside the sphere of capital, and the direct appropriation of value from a growing labor force subject to relations of exploitation and, often forceful, oppression. In the plantation areas, slave labor became waged labor on modern capitalist plantations. In America, the supply of exploitable labor was greatly increased by immigration. Through the course of the twentieth century, accumulation proceeded rapidly on a basis of dispossession and incorporation to waged labor, so that, today, the great majority of the population, (including, in recent decades, the majority of housewives, much more on this in a later discussion of the interrelations of class, sex, and race) has been transformed into a mass of dependent waged workers. They are, without alternative, fixed in the employment of capital; yet, to live and reproduce labor power workers and their families are entirely locked into the consumption of the marketed commodities they produce.[4]

The increasing appropriation of economic surplus can result in unbridled accumulation without opening avenues of productive investment, which is what is happening in the current phase of degenerative development. The increased subordination of labor and vast inequalities generated, in turn, exacerbate conditions of crisis and stagnation. In recent decades, workers and the population in general have become more and more dependent upon the financial sector. Paychecks are deposited in banks and bills are paid by check or, nowadays, by electronic transfer; pension savings are invested in the stock market; purchases made by bank credit card can't be paid on the due date; and, as income did not meet expenses, home equities became sources of financing the increasing cost of living in the face of declining income. The downward spiral in purchasing power of consumers was partially compensated by the abundance of cheap imports of consumer products produced by run-away shops exporting American jobs to low-waged countries. But the machinations of the financial sector came to a sudden, bitter end in 2007–2008. The expectation of the bankers to keep accumulation going—by extending credit to increasingly credit-unworthy consumers, taking on more debt to profit by creating asset bubbles, and financing industrial production abroad to keep the flow of cheap consumer goods flowing—was smashed.

The bubble phenomenon that brought down the big banks and Wall Street firms (until the trillions of dollar bail-outs) had a prehistory. The savings and loan bank crisis of the 1980s, the 2000 dot-com crash, and, with the growing coverage of the financial superstructure abroad, the 1990s Asian Financial Crises, the 1992 Japanese asset bubble, the 1994 Mexican crisis, all preceded the great collapse of 2007–2008, which then spread from America to Europe with global economic repercussions.

With financialization, money flowed upward to the financiers, not downward to the working population that would enable production of goods and services in the "real economy" to expand and to consumers to purchase the products produced. The main source of economic stagnation and the crisis of accumulation is the steady decline of the real wages of the working population, workers, and sectors of middle-class employees, such that there is insufficient demand for the goods and services produced, or potentially produced, by a willing and needy labor force. With real wages in decline, workers and middle-class employees sent more family members into the labor force and turned to borrowing money on home equities and credit cards as a means to maintain their standards of material existence and social status. The big banks packaged and repackaged all sorts of exotic instruments leveraged with mounting debt. Total debt in relation to GNP rose from 150% in 1980 to over 350% in 2007. The banksters, holding debt of 116% of GNP, took advantage of their in-charge control over the economy to the extent that debt levels became unsustainable and the financial system collapsed.

Stagnation of the economy, periodic crisis, financialization, and degenerative development reflect a new historical phase of capitalist development. In process since the mid-1970s, they reached their consolidation phase in the 1990s and 2000s. There are various features (to be explored in more depth in Chap. 9 on Globalization and Neo-liberalism). First, the financial sector shifts its functions from primarily extending credit to businesses to invest toward all manner of financial speculation. Industrial and commercial corporations now make most investments from retained monopoly profits and generate a growing proportion of their profit from non-productive financial activity, usually in coordination with Wall Street. Second, the incorporation of most of the population into waged labor and workers' heightened dependency on commodity markets to live, create opportunity for the financial sector to incorporate consumers as a principal source of managing huge sums of capital. The policies of the government that shifted public benefits in education, pensions, health care, housing, and so on to the private sector meant that finance controlled access to these necessities and could profit from them. Third, neo-liberal policies of privatization, cuts to or elimination of public benefits, deregulation of finance and business, corporate tax reductions—policies imposed by the rule of plutocracy—fully complemented the consolidation of finance as the leading sector of capital. Fourth, globalization extended financialization on an international scale.

Income/Wealth Distribution and Stagnation

The trend toward greater and greater inequalities in the distribution of income in the United States is striking, a trend also evidenced in Europe. This was covered amply in Chap. 2. I don't know how accurate this assertion is, but is surely a trend—8 wealthy individuals own more than the bottom half of the world's population, while the 1% is on the way to owning more assets than the 90% below. Obviously, the totally lop-sided distribution of income and wealth is a major factor in the stagnation of the U.S. economy, and in Europe and most other countries as well. If the bulk of the 90% are more and more hard pressed economically, they cannot accumulate assets and their ability to purchase the goods and services they produce is reduced. In the terms used by Keynesian economists, reduced real income depresses effective demand, and most of the 90% no longer have sufficient assets to draw upon. This, in turn, causes recession to deepen and extend for a longer period. Keynesian solutions in the Great Depression and since have involved government stimulus measures, tax reductions to spur consumer spending, public works projects, greater government involvement with giving direction to the economy…but the programs of very limited scope applied by the Obama administration proved ineffective and Republican intransigence prevented even mildly serious measures. The European Union had even less stimulus, only forced austerity policies that particularly affected Greece, Ireland, Portugal, Italy, and Spain.

The "interventionist" side of state activity is stymied by Republican intransigence, there are only private enterprise solutions, not public. Monetarist policies by the Treasury and the Federal Reserve unleashed vast sums, but did not accomplish developmental ends. As detailed in later analysis, the main stimulus from 2009 onward has been the Federal Reserve release of trillions of dollars to financial institutions in low-interest handouts and in exchange for bank holdings of bonds, mortgages, and other assets, some of them "toxic", and keeping interest rates near zero. These funds did not significantly result in credit being available for investment in the production of useful good and services, but the stimulus may have kept the system from a total crash. Monetary policies freed up funds that have, in the main, resulted in speculative investment in stocks pushing up indices; commodity futures spiraling prices for minerals, grains, and oil (until December 2014, when the Saudi's asserted their oil power and the 2015 decline in commodity prices due to international stagnation in the industrial sector); foreign short-term speculations appreciating foreign currencies in relation to the dollar; and other activities that do not have much impact on the productive investment needed to stimulate growth and employment.

In the current phase of degenerative development, the most unproductive, wasteful, environmentally degrading, and socially destructive activities are the principal sources of accumulation. Even in productive sectors such as energy, the future appears of dubious efficacy. The thrust in the United States is energy independence, limiting imports of foreign oil and producing energy from shale sands deposits, fracking for natural gas, and "clean coal." Solar, wind, and hydroelectric power, it is claimed, are too inefficient or expensive, although some activity in this sector is happening. Ignored is the cost of externalities by the environmental degradation caused by mining shale, constructing pipelines, fracking, and mining and burning coal that lead to environmental disaster in the form of global warning. Degenerative development privatizes profits while socializing risk. Investors misallocating capital in sectors such as coal and natural gas externalize the cost of environmental destruction. Degenerative development continues with government subsidies and tax breaks, as well as cheap access to public lands and resources. Under Trump, pro-energy company policies will be extended and the cost in environmental degradation is augmented. Treaties meant to slow down global warming will be ignored.

In terms of class formation in the phase of degenerative development, the composition of the working class shifts from sectors engaged in employment in the production of useful goods and services, to growing proportions of workers doing unproductive labor in armaments, commercial, financial, sales, services, and security activities—often at lower wages with fewer, if any, benefits. The fact that growing numbers of workers labor in unproductive, wasteful, or destructive activity does not change their class positioning as working class—but their unproductive function in the labor process can affect their consciousness and propensity to mobilize to demand change. The nature of their work is one more factor that divides, fractionalizes, and stratifies the working class, along with race, ethnicity, and gender. The function performed in the labor process and the other divisions matters but, ultimately, a young worker today may have a stint in the military when facing unemployment, and later drift to being a security guard, to supermarket clerk or fast-food attendant, or other low-waged work. In trying to survive, it is all the same misery to him or her.

So, American capitalism degenerates to having two main sources of profit and accumulation. The intensified exploitation of labor at all levels—the working class, the underclass, and growing sectors of what used to be a socially privileged middle class—and shifting the activity of capital from productive to unproductive and socially/environmentally harmful activity, war and financial speculation being in the forefront of this activity, along with pillage of the natural environment. In Chap. 4, class formation is examined in more depth.

NOTES

1. For an analysis of HSBC activities, see http://www.occupy.com/article/hsbc-bank-scandal-widens/ The situation of manipulating precious metal prices got so bad that the Commodity Futures Trading Commission and the Department of Justice initiated an investigation of ten big banks for price rigging. These include the big international conglomerates—HSBC, Barclays, Credit Suisse, Deutsche Bank, Goldman Sachs, JPMorgan Chase, Societe Generale, and others. Another volatile commodity is petroleum. In late 2014, in the context of a relatively stagnant world economy, the Saudís kept on flooding the market with their low production costs oil, causing a drastic decline in prices, the pleas of other OPEC producers unattended. Some speculate that the Saudis were worried about the U.S. goal of energy self-sufficiency with expensive pipelines, drilling, and fracking for natural gas. Maybe. But since Saudi Arabia

is a staunch ally of the United States, it is possible that there is collusion to drop oil prices to make things more difficult for U.S. oil producing enemies, Venezuela, Iran, and Russia, which has certainly been happening.

2. Heather Stewart of *The Guardian*, UK, has estimated that the global super-rich have as much as $21 trillion stashed in cross-border havens. "$21 Trillion Hoard Hidden From Taxman by Global Elite," http://readersupportednews.org/news-section2/320-80/ 12567 Other sources cite as much as $32 trillion, with some $280 billion in lost tax revenue.

3. Much of the analysis in this chapter draws upon the writings on crisis and stagnation that have appeared over the years in the journal *Monthly Review*. Noteworthy is Fred Magdoff and John Bellamy Foster, "Stagnation and Financialization: The Nature of the Contradiction," *Monthly Review*, vol. 66, May 2014, p. 15. I have extended the political economy of *Monthly Review* by a sociological view of the interrelations of the economic to the transformation of social classes, although some of this thinking was stimulated by Harry Braverman's classic, *Labor and Monopoly Capital*, published by Monthly Review Press in 1974. Every movement activist should have a subscription to *Monthly Review* and review the extensive list of the best books available at www.monthlyreviewpress.com On a personal note, my economics education began in 1960, as a graduate student in Sociology at Stanford University, with a subscription to *Monthly Review*, faithfully read cover to cover to this day. My first seminar in economics was with Stanford Professor Paul Baran, a *Monthly Review* author and the most noted Marxist economist of the time. Another good source is Costas Lapavitsas. *Profiting without Producing: How Finance Exploits Us All*, Verso Books, 2014.

4. The analysis of social class relations is drawn in part from Dale L. Johnson (ed.), *Class and Social Development: A New Theory of the Middle Class*, Sage Publications, 1982. The analysis of this book pertains mainly to the United States. A sequel extending class analysis to other parts of the world is Dale L. Johnson (ed.), *Middle Classes in Dependent Societies* Sage Publications, 1983. See also Dale L. Johnson, "Class Analysis and Dependency," and other chapters in Ronald H. Chilcote and Dale L. Johnson, (eds.) *Theories of Development*, Sage Publications, 1983.

CHAPTER 4

Degenerative Development and Class Transformation

In neo-classical economic theory, the distribution of income and wealth is a function of "marginal productivity;" higher economic rewards accrue to those that make a greater contribution to society, as determined by the workings of competitive markets and the laws of supply and demand. This theory originated back in the nineteenth century and persists in mainstream economics to this day, as though monopoly and class power were non-existent. Thomas Piketty comes out of the neo-classical school and his work certainly challenges central tenets of neo-classical theory. At the same time, Piketty equates his book title, *Capital*, with simply the existence of private wealth that allows holders to increase income and assets. He divorces capital from the social relation in which wealth and income is extracted, which is a central structural determinant of class. In this chapter, I examine the historical formation of social classes in American society, and the current relations and class situations in which the classes are enmeshed, explored in more depth in Chap. 7. I postpone further analysis of the divisions within the capitalist class, begun in previous chapters, until later in the relation to class power and globalization. In Chaps. 9 and 10 the disadvantaged sectors of capital are discussed.

To be clear at the outset, the designation of the 1%, the 10%, or any other percentile in the distribution of wealth or income, is not the same as identification of a social class. Nevertheless, the 1% can be viewed in a descriptive way as associated with social class. The 1% is a composed of

D.L. Johnson, *Social Inequality, Economic Decline, and Plutocracy,*
DOI 10.1007/978-3-319-49043-4_4

financial oligarchs, and CEOs, and directors of large conglomerates and transnational corporations that, together, constitute a plutocracy. They are the dominant class of capitalists. The next 9% are, in class terms, the staff and line of the 1% and upper level bureaucrats of the state apparatus—as I termed it, the privileged "hangers on" of the dominant class. But conceiving class in this way has limitations.

The term "social class" is too often understood as denoting empirical collectivities of occupational groupings positioned together through a common factor—wealth and poverty, income distribution, gradations of occupational prestige, or relationship to the means of production (a criterion that has more analytic power). Wealth, and income distribution, and invidious distinctions of different occupations are often, in conventional sociology, reduced to the designation of upper, middle, and lower classes. In Marxist conceptions, classes are bourgeoisie, petty bourgeoisie, and proletariat, analyzed as concrete groupings in conflictive relations. In all these conceptions, the numbers in each class can be counted from census data, their wealth or poverty statistically arrayed, their invidious social distinctions surveyed, their privileges or deprivations measured. Of course, it is necessary to use terms that have an empirical referent and to investigate attributes that define class situations. But this does not reach for a full understanding of class dynamics. In capitalist society, all is in a constant state of flux. The social division of labor shifts, the application of new technologies revamps social structures, income distribution is altered, wealth is concentrated, life situations of the different classes change, over time new classes are formed while established classes are restructured, and preexisting historical social formations dissolve. Purely empirical designations direct attention away from the dynamic quality of class. The study of changing class relations, of the transmutations of the capital/labor relation, leads to an understanding of economic and social development of historical change.

Social class is a dynamic, relational concept. Descriptive usages have their place, as long as they are not conceived as static situations. In the workings of capitalist societies, the empirical configurations of bourgeoisie and working class are of less interest than the social relation of capital to labor. We know through empirical observations and theoretical generalization that this relation presents a central antagonism. It is a relation based on exploitation, the appropriation by capital of a proportion of the value produced by labor. It is in the interest of capital to increase the level of value appropriated from labor. It is in the interest of labor to resist exploitation and to try to increase the proportion of value retained. It is in the interest of capital to see to the reproduction of the social relations that preserve its class privileges and enhance its ability to appropriate value. It is in the interest of labor to modify or revolutionize prevailing social relations. The reproduction of relations of exploitation requires a superstructure of forms of social domination by capital. On the side of the labor, it impels many and changing patterns of resistance. The forms of domination and resistance permeate the whole ensemble of capital/labor relations, manifested in antagonistic dichotomies: supervisor/worker, technician/detail worker, social worker/welfare recipient, teacher/student, merchant/consumer, minister/parishioner, functionary/supplicant, doctor/patient, judge/defendant, landlord/tenant, IRS auditor/taxpayer, professional/client, and others. The permeation proceeds further in the stratifications that divide: men/women, white/black, Anglo/Latino, Christian/Muslim, even family relationships of husband/ wife and parent/child are institutionalized as relations of inequality, of domination and subordination. In this book, I am particularly concerned with the dynamic of all these relationships during the phase of degenerative development, of stagnation and crisis, of the reign of finance capital, dating from the 1980s.

In the phase of degenerative development and recession-prone stagnation, the accumulation process, as discussed in Chap. 3, has quite distinct features from previous historical paths of development. But the generalization remains current that the main feature of capitalist development, since its infancy and until today, is the polarization of social classes as a determinant of a wide range of social phenomena. The accumulation of capital is a good deal more than the movement of productive forces through time and geographic space. Accumulation is an historical process of changing class relations, of the formation and dissolution of social classes. Historical development of the capitalist mode of production involves, at the one pole, the concentration and centralization of property and control, wealth and power, in the hands of a reduced class of capitalists; at the other pole, development propels an ever greater proportion of the population into the proletarian condition. Artisans, peasants and farmers, small businessmen, national minorities, women and other unpaid producers of use values, are dispossessed of alternative means of living and are irresistibly drawn into the orbit of capital—reduced to dependence on wages, relegated to the social position of producer of value appropriated by capital, and entirely dependent on commodity markets for subsistence. As historical development unwinds within nations and internationally, all social relations prevailing in world society are increasingly defined by the basic social relation—that between capital and labor, bosses and workers, exploiters and exploited, oppressors and oppressed. With degenerative development in the current phase, this polarization is more pronounced than ever in history. Since there are many social divisions that are in a continual process of transformation, we can generalize that capitalist development through its distinct stages and phases has been, and remains, characterized by a multi-class complex of class relations in a bi-polarizing structure.

A few brief illustrations of this thesis: In the transition to capitalism in seventeenth- and eighteenth-century Europe, the bourgeois/proletarian relation had not yet become the central axis of class relations and socio-economic development. These relations were still engulfed within, yet increasingly penetrating, those of the feudal order of lords, peasants, and guild artisans. The bourgeoisie remained village burgers, primarily a mercantile formation. The landed gentry only gradually, with the lure of commercial gain, underwent embourgeoisement. The working class was mainly a youthful and feminine appendage of the peasantry, forced to send their women and children into the new factories as their traditional way of life was being destroyed by the dispossession of the peasantry of their land and by the commercial and incipient industrial developments of the era. Yet, an imperative of capitalist accumulation, spearheaded by mercantile interests and facilitated by absolutist states, was restructuring all class relations. The central antagonism was not yet bourgeoisie and proletariat, but a systemic one of a decaying feudalism and an emerging international capitalism, crystallized in the merchant–aristocracy relation and colonial expansion. The structure of the totality of multi-class relations was eroding pre-capitalist relations and moving toward the salience of bi-polar relations of a capitalist nature.

During the nineteenth-century stage of competitive capitalism, an ample intermediate class —a petit bourgeoisie of independent farmers, craftsmen, store keepers, and professional practitioners—was formed as a result of the economic dynamic of the era and as a refuge for ex-peasants and former artisans facing proletarianization. The image of a Jeffersonian America had some grounding in nineteenth-century reality.

The forces of twentieth-century monopoly capitalism—the concentration and centralization of capital and the forceful corporate absorption of waged labor—all but destroyed this petit bourgeoisie. And the same unraveling of forces formed a new intermediate class, the salaried middle class. Indeed, the middle class of the twentieth century is mainly an expression of the class polarization process. The middle class of the epoch of monopoly capitalism though, unlike the bourgeoisie and working class, and like the old petite bourgeoisie, is a transitory formation. The internal structure and character of the dominant class change, and the fractionalization and composition of the working class, change with successive stages and phases of development. But, as long as there is capitalism the polar classes remain. The intermediate classes, on the other hand, do not simply change in structure; they are always in a process of fundamental transformation, of eclipse and eventual disappearance, or of becoming qualitatively new formations. This is why there is so much conceptual confusion about what to label the class in sociological analysis—the new middle class, new petty bourgeoisie, new class, new working class, professional-managerial class, intermediate formations, *capas media*, *couches intermediares*, or strata occupying contradictory locations in the social structure. Different analysts have mistaken specific forms of social relations in particular conjunctures for more generalized class phenomena.

THE WORKING CLASS TODAY

If America is to become a just and decent society, the working class must be at the forefront of a lengthy and militant class struggle. Here, we look at the general nature of the working class; later, I examine its class situation and its capacity for mobilization.

Workers are those that are employed by capital to produce value in the form of goods and services. The object of capital is to appropriate the maximum possible of the value produced and capture that value as profit. As explored in brief earlier, until the twentieth century a majority of the American population was not working class but, instead, independent producers—small farmers, craftsmen, independent practitioners, small businessmen. The essential history of capitalist development is the incorporation of ever increasing proportions of the population into the waged labor to capital social relation. The first to disappear were the independent producers, then former slaves found jobs in industry, and vast numbers of immigrants became American workers. As the twentieth century progressed, the universalization of the market became complete. (Harry Braverman is a must read; see endnote[1]). Universalization meant that families could only live by gainful employment in order to participate in the purchase of commodities. By the 1980s, women became incorporated, largely into subordinate positions at lower salaries, as working-class families could no longer live on one income.

Today, no politician in the United States talks of the deterioration of the situation of the working class; they lament the lack of jobs for the "middle class", as if the American dream had previously eliminated the working class. Even the head of the AFL-CIO won't talk about workers, but uses the term "middle class." I suppose that President Obama and union leaders fear that using proper terminology might lend credence to the Republican labeling of such proclamations as socialist. Neither of the current two progressive spokespersons for the Democrats, Elizabeth Warren and, to a lesser extent, Bernie Sanders, talks about the working class, only the declining position of the middle class. I have never read that Obama talked about workers, and certainly not the working class. This flows in all likelihood from the tired notion that the middle class is a force of stability in American society, eclipsing the class polarization of labor and capital. But that polarization is now greater than at any time in history. The vast majority of the American population is working-class subject to a sharply deteriorating class situation. Within the limits of a stagnant economy, the scope of this class is continually augmented; the more so as substantial sectors of the middle class are pushed downward in the social order, while other workers are forced into the abyss of immiserated existence. That there is so much verbiage in officialdom about the middle class and no mention of the working class evidences an ignorance of class dynamics. In the last **30** years or so, degenerative development has meant an historical eclipse of the salaried middle class and the augmenting, under very adverse conditions, of the working class.

If we exclude a significant proportion of the population characterized by exclusion from the economy and by extreme instability and poverty—here, termed the "underclass"—the working class in America Inc. is, today, around **69%** of the employed population. In 1920, with industrialization in full swing, workers comprised **59%** of the working population; there were in those days still many small farmers and businessmen, own-account craftsmen, and independently employed persons. These sectors reflecting the means of making a living declined such that, by 1970, workers constituted over **60%** of the working population. Jonna and Foster break down the occupation categories of the working class.[2] This breakdown is mainly descriptive, leaving the analytic aspects mainly aside for now.

- Basic Worker Occupations include operatives and laborers, employed craftsmen, clerical workers, and service and sales workers. These categories have decreased as a proportion of the labor force since 1960. In 2011, the 86.5 million workers were 56.2% of the employed population. The sector of the working class in these categories showing the greatest relative increase is service and sales workers, whereas operatives and laborers, craftsmen, and to a lesser extent clerical workers, have shown relative decline as a proportion of the working class. This is in good part due to the globalization of capital with its export of manufacturing to low-waged countries.
- Added to these occupations are what Jonna and Foster term the Growing Worker Occupations: low-level supervisory workers, marginal teachers and counselors, agricultural workers, sales workers in insurance/real estate/advertising, recreational workers, and the unemployed. All categories showed increased participation from 1960 to 2011. These 15.9 million workers now push the total working class to 65% of the labor force. These occupations have increased in numbers; have high unemployment rates, and low, stagnant, or declining wages.
- The authors add a category, Additional Labor Reserves. People here are not part of the officially defined labor force but are there to work if and when employment is available. These include the marginally attached, non-working poor, returning students, and the incarcerated, all of these categories have greatly increased, especially since 1980. For example, the non-working poor increased from 900,000 in 1960 to 4.94 million in 2011. In all, the labor reserves total 19.6 million, 11% of the labor force. When included in the working class, the number of workers in 2011 was 121.9 million and 68.9% of the labor force. I will have more to say about the "reserve army labor" in a following analysis of immiseration of vast sectors of the working class such that the term "under class" might be appropriate and the numbers properly included within the working class would be proportionally reduced.

I note that the authors do not include teacher's employment as within the working class, and it is not clear whether health workers are included in the service category. This does not make good sense to me, the reasons for which are stated later in the commentary on education. Their inclusion would push the working class to upward of 70% of the population. However, we have to subtract from that percentage those who have been locked out and pushed into the immiserated underclass. The much celebrated middle class would then be less than 20% of the labor force.

While almost all workers are subject to forces causing a deterioration of their class situation, in America the working class is also divided—the many forced out of waged employment into what I hesitantly term the "underclass", and the more stable elements of the working class are stratified in social hierarchies and divided by their function in the labor process. The divisions within the working class are based on race, ethnicity, gender, unionization, geographical factors, the nature of their work, and other factors. This has implications for what sectors can be mobilized in a movement for change and which groupings will present challenges to win over or to neutralize. This I will take a close look at later in a discussion in Chap. 7 of the need to celebrate diversity and combat system-induced division. Capital's class offensive is to maintain and enhance rule by divide, conquer, and immiserate.

The Underclass of Immiserated People

The marginalization of peoples from the mainstream of economic and social life is a long historical process but, in global capitalism, has become accelerated in recent decades. Today, a handful of plutocrats have cornered as much wealth as is possessed by the poorest 2.5 *billion* people on the planet! The process has degenerated from incorporating people into the waged labor to capital relation at wages increasing roughly in relation to advances in productivity, and is now being transformed into a process of dispossession of traditional means of livelihood and/or des-incorporation from the waged labor force. Waged workers in the industrial center and poor farmers in the periphery are being pushed out from places in the economy that allowed them to live, now forced into a world of helplessness and poverty. They survive as best they can with social service subsidies where available and in the informal economy of street vending, casual labor, drug pushing, and street crime; they occupy homeless shelters and eat from food stamps and charitable bread lines, where present. Marginalization from work is a process of leaving the misery of work that allows subsistence to immiseration of life, embodying the grossest of social injustice. Injustice creates bitter resentment. Brutal conditions of life can breed brutality and criminality among some of the victims that, in turn, feeds into the cultivation of a culture of fear among the general population, a free hand for police control and brutality, and an all-encompassing and highly repressive criminal justice system. The apologetic sociology of "the culture of poverty" focuses on "welfare queens," the breakdown of "lower-class" family life, and related nonsense that was used to justify President Clinton's reform of the welfare system and other measures. If a culture of poverty can be defined, it is based on the subjection of human beings to conditions of lack of opportunity, squalor, cultural situations of disdain and mistreatment, and legal conditions of powerlessness and police repression. This can result in dehumanization of the victims. Rather than treat poverty as a social problem, the official response is containment of poor communities and police repression. This is worldwide, but the United States goes much further than many other countries in failing to treat poverty as a social problem.

The social change involved in historical development has meant that human beings are constantly shuffled and reshuffled into different social classes. Independent producers and immigrants became industrial workers; sons of workers became white-collar workers; sons of white-collar employees became technicians and professionals; women work their traditional place as wife and mother but need family survival wages by "manning" office telephones. But development has also meant that some groupings change their place in the economy without changing their position at the bottom of the economic and social pile. African slaves became Negro sharecroppers and share-croppers became African-American unskilled laborers and urban service workers, while others are ghettoized without steady employment, and subjected to immiserated conditions. The underclass in America is disproportionately African-American, Latino, and other ethnic minority, although in the contemporary period increasing numbers of white people are forced into the underclass.

Marginality is a concept that has its origin in the age-old concern for the plight of the poor urban groupings throughout the world that are uprooted from rural subsistence by economic forces and subjected to the vicissitudes of life as "marginal," "surplus population," "lumpen proletariat," "masses," "reserve army of labor," "colonized peoples" populations of a "dual society" where one sector is developed and the other underdeveloped, or simply the "poor who have always been with us." These are descriptive terms that do not have much analytical value (except the reserve army of labor, a tool in Marxist analysis of capitalism). Marginality as an analytic construct has its limitations. But so, too, does the "reserve army of labor" in an epoch in which fewer persons are incorporated to waged labor and those who were incorporated are pushed out of their jobs or into casual work that keeps them in utter poverty due to stagnation.

Underclasses are structural groupings created by economic changes. Groupings in American society include, now more than ever, those whose skills are superfluous to a technologically geared economy and consumer society that exports factory jobs and outsources employment abroad; then, there are the hard-core unemployed; those who find occasional employment in sweat shops; migrant agricultural labor; peoples trapped in rural and mining communities in which the local economy is shut down; minorities locked out and living slum life due to race and ethnic discrimination; the large populations in urban industrial centers that have been destroyed by plant closures; the formerly incarcerated locked out of employment; and many of the aged and infirm from physical or mental incapacity. I cannot find statistics that enumerate the changes in scope of the underclass in America. The closest are those that cite the proportion of the population earning below the official line of poverty. Sixty million Americans subsist as best they can below the official poverty line, around 18% of the population. Since official poverty is really destitution, it is fair to say that 40% of American families now have incomes near or below the poverty line. This does not mean that 40% are underclass, some hold regular jobs at minimum wages that don't meet even the family poverty level, but are still regularly employed persons of the working class. The struggle for a living minimum wage is a reform that is difficult but not impossible to achieve in America Inc., where plutocracy rules and the media use zombie speak. A higher minimum wage could lift millions out of destitution to minimum survival levels. However, even a $15 per hour minimum wage of full-time employment results only in $30,000 per year, still inadequate for a family to live with a reasonable level of material existence.

The cited article by Jonna and Foster utilizes the concept of a reserve army of labor, the potentially available labor force in the United States not captured in official unemployment statistics (categories stated earlier), to indicate that these categories of locked out labor have increased from the late 1970s to 30% in 2013. They divide these categories into "floating," "stagnant," " pauperized," and "latent" that encompass about 52 million people, which is not far from the official designation of poverty of 60 million. This perspective has a good deal of analytic power. The members of this population are dispossessed of access to the means of production, have only labor power to sell, and are entirely dependent upon the purchase of commodities for their material existence.

However, it seems to me that the concept of underclass, together with the associated concepts of marginalization and immiseration, have a heuristic descriptive value of designating sectors of populations on a world scale that are now permanently locked out of the working class as such. The United States today has the greatest level of inequality of any advanced industrial economy, and that inequality is now greater than that of India or South Africa. This is a result of capital's war on labor and the conditions of employment that create a vast underclass in the heartland of what the American myth considered the exemplar of "middle-class society." This underclass, insofar as it functions as a reserve army of labor, is an important instrument for reducing the wage levels of the working class.

The immiseration or pauperization of peoples is an accelerating global process in the present period. An ever greater proportion of the population is marginalized from the mainstream of world society as stagnation and crisis persist and globalization extends to furthest reaches of our planet. In much of southern Europe, it is not just great sectors of the population that are marginalized—entire countries are pushed down into the abyss of deepening peripheralization. In America and Europe, programs of social services to the needy are reduced, redefined as more effective means of social control, privatized, or eliminated entirely. I will return to the potential role of marginalized people in social change in a later section on strategies of change for the movement.

The Formation of the Middle Class

The "blue collar" industrial sector of the working class is very much in demise, and all worker occupations are being subjected to what Braverman terms the "degradation of labor." So, too, is the vaunted middle class in decline as their labor is degraded through de-qualification and de-professionalization. There is a long history in the interrelationship between the accumulation process, class formation, and today's stagnation and crisis. While the formation of a class of waged laborers dependent on commodity production for jobs is central, concomitant with the formation of the working class, different segments of a qualitatively new intermediate class were formed in the context of the polarization between increasingly concentrated and centralized capital, and a growing mass of subordinated workers. Large-scale production employing new industrial techniques, such as "Fordism", greatly increased the productivity of the growing labor force and created a sharply rising demand for engineers, scientists, and experts in organizational work. Scientists and engineers designed new means of augmenting worker productivity; administrative experts reorganized the labor process to subordinate labor more effectively; workers were subjected to routinized, de-qualified work and whatever skills they once had as skilled craftsmen were separated from their work and transferred to the new experts. Control of the production process and labor became a central concern; supervisors proliferated. Reproduction of a labor force now entirely dependent on wages and commodity markets, one stripped of folk knowledge, and arts, and communal survival services of the previous era, became a problem; a growing army of professionals was formed to deliver babies and attend illness, provide schooling, produce culture as a commodity rather than folk art, and apply a presumed expertise to all manner of acute social problems.

Historically, there has been a shift from *extensive accumulation* via incorporation of peoples into the sphere of waged labor to *intensive accumulation* via reorganization of the labor process to extract a greater level of profit. The middle class was elevated to administer intensive accumulation. In recent decades, especially since the 1980s, extensive accumulation has shifted geographic location from North America and Europe to Asia and Latin America, and, to a lesser extent, Africa and the Middle East. Intensive accumulation has shifted from rationalization of the labor process to increase productivity to measures to reduce the real incomes of workers in order to increase profit rates. This shift now effects the class situation of segments of technical, administrative, and professional labor that were employed by capital for the purpose of intensive accumulation.

The Intermediate Class and Its Fractions

Intermediate class is a better term than middle class, as it expresses more precisely the role of various strata in the relations of production, but I will bow to convention on this nomenclature. The old middle class of *independent producers* or *petty bourgeoisie* has been largely eliminated, as the majority was forced into the waged labor force, while some elements, small businessmen in various sectors, became incorporated into the middle class. The "new" salaried middle class, formed over the course of the twentieth century, is composed of diverse components that do not directly produce value but serve in intermediary, mediating places between capital and labor. The middle class is composed of several occupational groupings:

- *The administrators,* including supervisors and middle-level bureaucratic functionaries. They perform the "line" authority functions in the technical division of labor and are directly enmeshed in the antagonisms of capital to labor. This fraction of the middle class in the present, degenerative phase of development is being bifurcated, with most being pushed into or in the direction of the working class, while some are being elevated to serve directly the upper echelons of managerial capital, governmental bureaucracies, and the repressive apparatus. In the private sector, their salaries and bonuses do not compare with those of the CEOs and banksters, but their class privileges are elevated. In the public sector, those administrating public services are facing budget cuts and layoffs, while those occupying positions in the security and repressive apparatus have generous budgets and increasing privileged employment. Security personnel, public and private, analysts at computers, and managers of the criminal justice system proliferate.
- *The semi-autonomous employees,* such as scientific and technical personnel, and many professionals—the "staff" of the managers—came to constitute a large sector of the middle class. The "semi-autonomy" refers to their place in the labor process, which has historically evolved to fragment and routinize "worker's work," while elevating coordinative and developmental activity to work conditions that are more creative, higher-paid, and freer of direct controls. The same process of de-qualification of labor functions that scientists and engineers evolved to subordinate labor is now being applied to the formerly semi-autonomous employees. There is ever greater fragmentation of technical work, such that much of what needs to be done can be outsourced to India, where employees need only English and computer literacy to earn their meager wages. The National Security Agency contracts even sensitive intelligence work to private corporations who hire analysts, such as Edward Snowden, who blow the whistle on the machinations of the State of National Insecurity.
- *The service professionals* are mainly state employees who produce use values in the sphere of social services, but also include private sector employees in health and other services. Obviously, the impact

of rolling back the services provided by government at all levels by greater bureaucratic centralization and control, by cutting budgets, by eliminating many of the social programs gained by workers' struggles over many decades, by fiscal restraints, and so on have deteriorated the class situation of service professionals. The process of transforming the older class of independent practitioners of the professions into government employees through a process of professionalization now has a contrary tendency, de-professionalization. Professionals are subject to the constraints imposed by bureaucratic centralization of control, and the cut-backs and privatization of public services. This process is strikingly evident in the teaching profession in public schools and universities; teachers are required to function as guardians and university courses are increasingly taught by adjunct instructors at minimum wages.

- *The self-employed.* The bulk of self-employed people are in the informal economy of street vending and casual labor in construction, sweat shops, and agriculture and related occasional employment; they are located in precarious conditions within the underclass. Self-employed craftsmen and small businessmen that could be considered middle-class by some criteria face economic conditions of stiff competition from larger businesses. Most small businesses fail within the first years, wiping out the savings that allowed the proprietors the hope of achieving a better existence, forcing them back into the working class or underclass. Medium-sized businesses, too, are relatively unstable in an economy where monopoly prevails and finance capital holds the upper hand. The proprietors of those that manage to hang on can be considered middle-class. Most proprietors of small and medium-sized businesses that succeed usually have an affinity for the ruling ideology of capital. They are in favor of capital's drive to reduce wages, cut taxes, eliminate government transfer programs; they view government and labor organizations as enemies. They are largely not allies in social struggles for change.

In relation to share of the national income, the middle class as a whole has been in decline for some time, gradually in the 1980s and 1990s. Then, in the period 2000–2010, middle-class income fell by 5% and their share of wealth in the form of assets decreased by 28%. The transformation of the middle class is so rapid and profound that it is now difficult to identify the class as a percentage of the population; it appears no more than about the 10% who are being elevated to the handymen of the dominant class, with perhaps another 10% trying to hold onto their privileges.

This process of professionalization/de-professionalization, as well as qualification/de-qualification of the administrative and semi-autonomous segments of the middle class, I will analyze in more depth and relate the tendencies in class transformation to questions of strategy for the movement. *Capitalist development is one of multi-class relations in a bi-polarizing structure.* Economic and political power is ever more concentrated under the control of the plutocracy, while the underclass and working class grow in numbers and decline in class situation, and the middle class bifurcates into elevated and downgraded segments. In the current phase of degenerative development, the context is a one-sided class struggle by the plutocracy and its cohorts against the classes that make up about 90% of the population in a situation of stagnation and economic crisis. This crisis is being utilized to further the striving for absolute hegemony by the dominant plutocracy. For this reason, it is important to determine the class relations in which the dominant class, workers, middle-class employees, and the immiserated of the underclass are enmeshed, and the class situation and mobilization potential of the classes and fractions of classes that make up the 90%.

Internationalization, Accumulation, and Class

The dynamic of the restructuring of social class relationships is the accumulation of capital in its various avenues. The internationalization of capital has constituted a principal source of accumulation. This has a long history, culminating in present day global capitalism guided by transnational corporations and administered by finance capital, united in promoting the dual process of globalization and neo-liberalism.

The development of England, Holland, and Spain as the first colonial powers depended upon the pillage of tangible wealth of the world. Later, relations of unequal exchange between primary production in the periphery and growing industrial activity in the industrializing center were established and the European continent and America began to rival England. Still later, the export of modern capital from the center, now emanating mainly from the United States, into the areas previously underdeveloped by colonialism and imperial subordination became a main source of accumulation. Plants are closed down in the industrial centers, forcing communities into decline and worker's wages downward, as capital employs intensive accumulation in the national economy and extensive accumulation by shifting its activities to countries with low wages, weak unions, and a friendly attitude toward foreign investment. U.S. capital's promulgation of "free trade" agreements is very much part of this decided globalization trend (discussed in Chap. 9).

The internationalization of the accumulation process has tended, particularly since the 1980s with the ascendance of transnational corporations and international finance, to internationalize class relations. Local business classes, a growing working class, intermediate classes, and vast underclasses of marginalized peoples are formed in the periphery under conditions of dependency that are structured by accumulation on a world scale. These classes are involved in rapidly changing relations within national contexts, and these relations are necessarily seen as fixed within an international dimension, but also have their own dynamic in the tumultuous events of Africa, Latin America, the Middle East, and Asia.[3]

The formation of the American middle class and, to a considerable degree, the class situation of the working class are necessarily analyzed in part as an outcome of the rise of U.S. corporations, complemented in recent decades by U.S. banks and international financial institutions, as the dominant economic forces on a world scale. During the post-World War II period, the United States became the technical and administrative center of transnational capital and "free world" empire; middle-class employees guided the administrative and technical apparatuses of the global reach of the transnationals, and banks, and the agencies of state (the Departments of State and Defense, the Treasury and Federal Reserve, intelligence agencies, U.S. AID, and other agencies of government) that preserve and expand empire. In more recent times, a growing proportion of the productive jobs that opened up were abroad, not in the United States, the administrative center, or Europe, and administrative jobs are increasingly outsourced.

Accumulation and the State

The internationalization of capital is related to another source of the accumulation of capital, the expansion of the modern state. The "imperial" or "warfare" dimension of the "warfare/interventionist/welfare" state is a source of employment of large numbers of administrative, technical, and professional employees. The "welfare" dimension of the modern state, now under severe roll-back pressure, has evolved in the context of the difficult social conditions produced by historical development and in relation to the level and complexity of social struggle accompanying development, especially since the Great Depression of the 1930s. The decline of necessary social services previously part of community life, the misery among urbanized workers and immiserated populations, and the social demands of worker unions and peoples' movements have required the state to provide a wide range of services.

The "interventionist" or "positive" dimension of the modern state came about in response to periodic crises and the need for regulatory, monetary, and fiscal policies that facilitate accumulation. In the most recent phase of degenerative development, the U.S. state's *deregulation* of the financial sector became the key factor in the inflation of assets and the bursting bubbles that are the proximate cause of the international economic crisis. This does not mean that laws reinstituting greater regulation of banking and finance will be an effective means of overcoming crisis. As long as the economic and political power of plutocracy is present, regulations will likely serve to enhance the power of the financial oligarchy.

The imperial or warfare side to the American state came about mainly in the period after World War II. The United States emerged from that war economically and militarily supreme, and engaged the cold war, and intervened whenever and wherever in the world social forces challenged hegemony and threatened change. With the collapse of the Soviet Union, the imperial design reemerged with oil fever and a war on terror. The growth of the security apparatus and military adventurism of the American state, the super rogue state, the State of National Insecurity, has resulted in a vast recruitment of security and military personnel, the promulgation of Executive orders and Congressional laws that curtail individual and collective freedoms, a culture of fear, and an entirely new agency, Homeland Security, that competes effectively with government social services for scarce budgetary resources.

The middle class, then, was formed in considerable part to fill the multiplying interstices of the welfare/interventionist/imperial state. The welfare and interventionist sides to state activity are now increasingly subordinated to the imperial side and its domestic extension. This means that middle-class public employees in social services—teachers and social workers, in particular—are being downgraded, while security personnel are on the ascendance. This has serious implications for the movement that will be examined later.

In summary, the accumulation of capital—while it has an economic appearance in investment decisions, capital movements, and paths of historical development—is fundamentally one of the formation of classes and transformation of relations between classes. To repeat: This is a process of multi-class relations in a bi-polarizing structure. Over the last decades, the rationalization of the labor process, institutional centralization, financialization, and technological innovation have contributed to a sharpening structural polarization between capital and labor. Intensive accumulation greatly effects the class situation of the working class and pushes more and more victims into the underclass. In this bi-polarization, the middle class is less and less in the middle and more and more bifurcated into an upper and lower strata, the one pulled closer to the dominant fractions of capital, the other pushed toward or into the working class.

NOTES

1. The classic and best work to date on the formation of the working class and the universalization of the market is Harry Braverman, *Labor and Monopoly Capital*, Monthly Review Press, 1974. An excellent updating of Braverman's pioneer work is R. Jamil Jonna and John Bellamy Foster, "Beyond the Degradation of Labor," *Monthly Review*, vol. 66, October 2014.
2. Jonna and Foster, Table 1, p.7.
3. Dale L. Johnson (ed.), *Middle Classes in Dependent Countries*, Sage Publications, 1983.

CHAPTER 5

Ideology as the Root of Plutocratic Rule

SUBVERTING CONSCIOUSNESS

Capital dominates and plutocracy prevails in good part through promulgation of ideas, vulgar notions that flow from its privileged class interests, but repeated often enough that they seem to become common sense and widely adopted. The media wing of the 1% creates an "information age" in which we are all machine-gunned by soft bullets of doctored news and TV serials with the end of obliterating consciousness. The media, what passes for political discourse, popular culture, in some ways the internet, in general every means of communicating ideas, is directed to indoctrination of citizens in the ruling ideology. Perhaps the most central element is social Darwinism, the "survival of the fittest" means a "war of all against all." This creates a society of viciousness that staggers along held together by doctrines that grossly contradict experienced reality, a smashed sociality of lived contradiction, a failed state that poses plutocracy as democracy and practices austerity as promoting the social good, a state in which war and repression with their ideological justifications are central. A frightened citizenry is overwhelmed by oppressive circumstances that create all sorts of social problems—high crime rates, violent behavior, alcohol and drug abuse, mental illness, suicide, early death rates, susceptibility to scapegoating, and political support for demagogues. The ideology fashions policy—"neo-liberalism" promotes free market fundamentalism, financial deregulation and monetary orthodoxy guarded by the oligarchs of high

D.L. Johnson, *Social Inequality, Economic Decline, and Plutocracy*,
DOI 10.1007/978-3-319-49043-4_5

finance, and labor "flexiblization." The twin of neo-liberalism, "globaliza-tion," is facilitated by "free trade" agreements that spread the doctrines worldwide while fostering imperial interventions and war everywhere.

The ruling ideology is a formula for social dissolution and a failed state. Social dissolution is a social world and a cultural environment in which people live the experience imposed by social Darwinism and related dog-mas institutionalized in the dynamics of the social structure. There is a generalization of a failed sociality in our culture. The ideological basis of the degenerative phase of capitalism fosters a war of all against all among all the classes and peoples struggling for survival. Morality, civic responsi-bility, human decency are submerged in a culture of fear. The culture seeks to crush souls in the religion of class privilege. If allowed to continue, this will represent the collective death of all that is worthy in the history of civilization. The movement has a difficult *long march* to change a failed sociality to one in which people are active subjects of their own liberation. This *long march* has difficult uphill inclines, steep precipices on both sides of the road, and road blocks, erected by the repressive forces, that must be hurdled.

The United States is a failed state, not in the way that Iraq is a failed state, having been violently torn apart by the American invasion and occu-pation, but by the American state, as such, being progressively stripped of its social content and reduced to its repressive apparatus (that I term the State of National Insecurity). In the established political sphere, nothing can be done except what is forced on us by the thinking, class interests, and policies of the 1%. There is no "change we can believe in" enunci-ated by politicians or emanating from a government that is captive of the plutocracy. Social programs, any sense of the common good, are rolled back, austerity practiced. A failed state leads to mounting repression of the victims and change activists. Under Obama, corporate Democrats administered governmental institutions on behalf of the plutocracy and were kept strictly in line by Republican intransigence. Many supporters of Trump's candidacy recognized this failed state and were taken in by the slogan "Make America Great Again." Trump policies will only deepen the failures. His demagoguery has already acerbated America's failed sociality. Hate, bigotry, and irrationality are now pervasive.

I am given to overstatement to try to make a polemical point. Of course, there are still shreds of decency and soulfulness in America that our his-tory and cultural legacy have produced. A current decided tendency is not today's lived reality, but it could be tomorrow's if we, as a people, do not find effective ways to resist and renew. The greatest threat in the United States to redemption of a decent sociality and a more democratic state is the religion of Republicanism (or what I sometimes term "zombyism", sometimes terming Republicans "mummies"). This religion suffered a setback in the election of November 2012, resurged in 2014, and, in 2016, went truly wild. By 2016, it was so bizarre that it appeared that human evolution had taken a wrong turn. The apparitions lining up on TV lacked any appearance of traits that could be considered human. Reverting to my polemical overstatement, I would say that the Neanderthals are back! They call themselves Republicans, but they are zombies risen from the grave of history. They now chase Homo Sapiens with their big sticks, clubbing every social advance of human kind; torturing and killing non-white peoples in distant lands. Greed, obfuscation, and force infuse their mentality. The Republican base among the petty privileged and those with threatened privilege give the plutocrats the opening to whip-up the worst of social ills for their political advantage. The tea toasters party the death of decency; the white-skinned machos revive racist creeds and denigrate womankind; the xenophobic wave flags, spread fear, spout hate; the arrogant boast American Exceptionalism and America First; the straight machos spout homophobia; the morally confused believe that a fertilized egg is sacred life, but favor cutting programs to feed hungry children—and celebrate killing a million people in Holy oil wars. All these elements rally to Donald Shrill Trumpet.

These demagogues, led by Trump, deceive their base of admirers, many of whom are victims of the system they defend. The ruling ideology converts system victimization to personal shortcomings of the victims, teaching that the common good is bad for America Inc., that "handout" is immoral, takes away personal responsibility, and makes people dependent and lazy. Too many of the downtrodden are taken in and strive for gain and social positioning, and, failing, their experience leads to guilt of failure, self-loathing, and loss of soul. The experience of adverse circumstances is also displaced to scapegoats, holding white males in line with cultivated hate of illegal immigrants, uppity women, queers, off-white populations, and Muslims. Demagogues such as Donald Trump appeal to this loss of soul to "Make America Great Again" by engendering irrationality, hate, and scapegoating—cultural forms that have a long history in America that have made the United States much less than great.

The fundamental of class domination is that the ruling class rules, first, by subverting, distorting, and obliterating consciousness of the reality of the actual experience of oppressive circumstances. The consciousness of individuals, communities, and social classes is formed in the varied experiences of daily life that are conditioned mainly by class positioning. Consciousness becomes "false" when actual experience is given distorted meaning by reifications that twist or obliterate the reality of life experiences, misdirecting and transforming thought and feelings to fit system maintenance, to reproduce the injustice of *what is*. We now live in an Orwellian world in which the populace is bombarded with tautologies. "War is peace" from Orwell is very current; "freedom is slavery" is now "freedom is capitalism;" "ignorance is strength" these days becomes "ignorance is patriotism." A new one is "austerity is abundance." All the instruments of what Chomsky terms "the manufacture of consent" issue from their Ministry of Truth message that "reality is whatever we say it is." So, the question becomes the strategic and tactical methods of generalizing an understanding of *what ought to be*. But, first, we need to understand *what is* in the sphere of ideology. In this regard, all the elements of the ruling ideology have become condensed in a fashioned culture of fear.

The Culture of Fear

In 1998, one of my favorite authors, Eduardo Galeano, a Uruguayan writer, published an insightful book *Upside Down. A Primer for A Looking Glass World*. In a discourse on "the teaching of fear" Galeano opens with a pertinent statement "In a world that prefers security to justice, there is loud applause whenever justice is sacrificed on the altar of security... It is a time of fear."[1] Galeano noted the many upsidedowners in Latin America, the main region of the world, for now, fearlessly trying to right things. Venezuela, Cuba, Bolivia, and Ecuador, each in their own way, strive for rightsideupness. Each—and the leader Venezuela, in particular—meets the determined efforts of U.S. agencies of intervention striving to push events back to fear-ridden upsidedownness. While Brazil, Argentina, and Uruguay were moving forward in the 2000s, it now appears that these nations are being pushed back into the darkness of neo-liberal rule and subordinate positioning in the system of global power (discussed in Chap. 10).

Shrink wrapping minds—the purging of rational capabilities and ethical standards—is more effective than head bashing. Effective social control by the "powers that be" is best achieved not by law and punishment for presumed misdeed (though that helps), but through imposing their ideology, a principle element of which is the creation of a generalized climate and cultivated culture of fear within the population. The causes evoked to instill fear may be spurious or grossly exaggerated; big lies; stories based on historical myth that persist; overt or subtle racism; or events brought about by our ruler's actions in response to these fears. The wars in Afghanistan and Iraq are examples of promulgation of fear and then acting to make these fears appear to have more grounding in reality. In the 1980s, the United States, in its cold war policies of fear of communism, intervened in Afghanistan to encourage and arm Islamic fundamentalists to drive out the Soviets, who were there to prop up a modernizing regime under threat from reactionary Islamic forces and to protect their southern border from increased penetration of Islamic terrorism. To take on the Soviets, the United States armed Islamic forces that later evolved into Al Qaeda, the Taliban, and extremist political Islam. In the same period, the United States gave hard support to the Israeli occupation of Palestine, even introducing Islamic fundamentalists to Bosnia in support of interventionist policy in the breakup of communist Yugoslavia. Then, when the Taliban gained power in Afghanistan, and was said to harbor terrorists, the United States and its allies invaded, creating a spiraling cycle of violence, and giving occupied and warred-upon peoples good cause to fight back in the best ways they could. By invading Afghanistan and Iraq; by sanctioning Iran; by bombing Libya, creating chaos and ISIS; by threatening Syria and arming Islamic rebels, there ending in a destroyed nation with millions of refugees; by arming the Saudis to create mayhem; by weaponising Israel to murder Palestinians; by drone attacks and acts of official terrorism of the super rogue state—a spiraling cycle of violence was created. Official terrorism gave warred-upon peoples good cause to fight back with the means available, that is, acts the aggressors and occupiers label "terrorism." In the prelude to the Iraq invasion, the official lies were perpetuated by a servile media. Saddam Hussein's regime had something to do with the terrorism of the events of 9/11 and had weapons of mass destruction. These were big lies based on manufactured intelligence that spread fear among the American population and then led to invasion, occupation, hundreds of thousands of Iraqi deaths, millions of Iraqis displaced, a totally failed state, and a society of fratricidal struggle and continuing violence. This greatly increased the fearful militancy of Islamic fundamentalists and resistance fighters throughout the world. And, by 2014–2015, it culminated in the extremist ISIS occupation of vast sectors of Iraq and Syria, and extending into Libya.

The multiple interventions of the 2000s, and Obama's special ops assassinating suspects and drone attacks, raise the question of counterproductive stupidity. Given that interventions consistently come back to bite the imperial ass, why? The answer seems to be because a war on terror is a never-ending cycle of creating terrorists, medieval and evil as they are. Evil begets evil to better serve the devil of empire. The war on Jihadist ghosts keeps the money flowing, and the culture of fear deepened. Murder creates for every martyr one hundred militants, the more to feed the death machine. It is hard to understand as stupidity. The blowback from Afghanistan, Iraq, Libya, Syria, and Palestine is more likely intended consequence. How else to cycle perpetual war, while fueling the fire of fear? The purity of American Exceptionalism justifies all actions.

CULTURAL MYTH AND FEAR

Central to promulgated myth is the idea that America is *Exceptional.* This is the title of Dick Cheney's 2015 book justifying the wars and torture that he sponsored. Yet, this is not just a myth fostered only by the "neoconservatives" of the Bush era; President Obama has reiterated this on repeated occasions. In speaking to the UN General Assembly in 2013, when U.S. policy against Cuba and foreign policy in general was under attack, he said: "Some may disagree, but I believe that America is exceptional." The term was repeated in his 2015 state of the union speech. Again, in April 2015, in making excuses for killing hostages in a drone strike in Pakistan, he said "one of the things that sets America apart from many other nations, one of the things that makes us exceptional, is our willingness to confront squarely our imperfections and to learn from our mistakes." Would that it were so!

The myth has it that God gave America a destiny, a miraculous instrumentality, an ordained providence, a manifest for destined exceptionalism. Early Puritans set the scriptured tone, God's grace did not apply to the heathen inhabitants of the colonized territory. The British colonialists sent their "white trash." The classes in America became the "better," "middling," and "meaner." If the better married the middling, the off-spring was "half-breeds." It was not long before Calvinist self-denial evolved to preaching the gospel of wealth and Christian eschatology equated to cultural chauvinism. The faithful burned their heretical witches. Righteousness glimmered out all dark motive. African slaves were brought in to harvest the tobacco and cotton that shaped American history in the ways of racism. Robber barons usurped land, pushed the frontiers ever westward, genociding the native population. The industrial barons lacking labor to exploit allowed a flood of immigrants under the guise of the American dream, each wave denigrated with racist labeling. In the sway of exceptionalism rules don't apply, we Americans are a force for good; it is us and them, we and they, white Christians and brown heathens, civilization righteously suppressing discontent. To the extent that exceptionalism has been eroded in the view of many, there is Trump's "Make America Great Again."

Of course, certain key labels applied to immigrants are no longer in politically correct usage, any more than is the term "nigger". The "redskins" ethnically cleansed are now "native Americans." The Mexican-Americans—the "spicks" and "wetbacks" of the 1940s and 1950s—are now just deportable "illegal immigrants"; the Irish are no longer "micks", nor the Italians "wops", the Poles "pollocks", the East Europeans "bojunks", the Chinese "chinks", the Japanese "japs", and the Vietnamese "gooks." In America, the successful Jews were once "kikes" involved in a conspiracy for world domination, as the Nazis proclaimed. Today, we have the "hajjis" and "ragheads."

The mick "typhoid Mary" spread fear of disease among the general population and the wops organized the machine gun toting Mafia. Over time, the Italians, the Irish and other white-skinned immigrants "made it" in the established stratification hierarchies, many into the middle reaches of a class structure that remains, in good part, based on white-skinned privilege. The orientals eventually became more accepted for their work ethic and respectability. Even the Jews became so well thought of that the United States protects Israel's oppression of Palestinians with its military and political power. Israel remains America's staunch ally against any resurgence of Arab nationalism. While vulgar labels are rarely used in public discourse, racist treatment of Afro-Americans and Latinos remains very much current. Now added to the demonized populations, both off-white, are illegal immigrants and Islamic terrorists—the latter encompassing almost any person of Muslim faith, as they are out to destroy the glorious American way of life. The success of this reversion to racist vilification draws upon not just the cultural persistence of racist ideology and fear of newcomers among the privileged classes and the less privileged emulators of the dream of social mobility. It depends, too, on the unthinking acceptance of ignorance and bold lies. The media is a willing accomplice to the promotion of vile propaganda, stupidity, intolerance, and lies. This is not confined just to the strident hysteria dished out by Fox News commentators, but is generalized to agencies of misinformation, CNN and the major networks, who feebly try to be objective by presenting a guest who does not wholly agree with the nonsense being promulgated. The print media that the right-wing mislabels "liberal media" is not much better; the *New York Times* works hand-in-hand with the Department of State and the military apparatus to form policies that promote the imperial vision. The Right agenda defines the issues for public discourse in the media and in politics, and frames dissidence from the official wisdom as beyond rationality and acceptability.

Another myth, complimentary to American exceptionalism, is that of the persistent notion of civilization and barbarism. In the broad sweep of history conception, one of the most persistent notions is the idea of civilization (Western, of course) and barbarism. In the article "Empire of Barbarism", Foster and Clark trace the concept of barbarism to its Greek and Roman origins. "The distinction between superior civilized peoples at the center of the world and inferior barbarians on the periphery was thus basic to Greek and Latin thought."[2] How familiar to today's conception of bringing democracy and civilization to the barbarous peoples who inhabit the Middle East! The authors link Marx's conception of barbarism, having mainly to do with the plunder of colonialism, and Rosa Luxemburg's idea of the barbarism of World Wars I and II: "cities are turned into shambles, whole countries into deserts, villages into cemeteries...wading in blood and dripping with filth...as a roaring beast, as an orgy of anarchy, as a pestilential breath, devastating culture and humanity...the ruins of imperialistic barbarism."[3] This has some relevance to today's civilizing approach to the perceived backward barbarism of Muslim peoples. One can only wonder how anyone could believe that war, occupation, death, and destruction bring modernity and democracy to the region. The barbarism of today does not reside as much in the East as in the West.

Violent inhumanity, barbarism, has a long history in European colonialism and American westward expansion, and post-World War II anti-communist interventions throughout the world. What is unique to the present era is that it is truly senseless. In its stage of ascendance, capitalism pursued its imperative to divide up the world into colonies; competing imperialisms inevitably led to two world wars; the United States, supreme after World War II, needed to consolidate its hegemony on a world scale. It fought wars in Korea and Vietnam, outspent the Soviet Union in preparation for a shift from cold to hot war and caused the Soviets to collapse, and they more or less successfully suppressed nationalist and revolutionary movements on a world scale. So that, by the 2000s, there was no imperial imperative to continue a course of barbarism. They had a choice to pursue a different, less violent strategy, but they pursued barbarism. Real enemies of the previous era, nationalist and revolutionary movements, were crushed or contained. Only spurious enemies remained, so America created Islamic terrorists, who respond to Western aggression with their own barbarous measures. To be sure, this policy of terror and war follows the imperial vision, but it is very narrow. There are viable alternatives to interventions posing as civilizing missions to bring Muslim peoples to modernity, to the big world headache caused by oil fever in the Middle East. The oil barons, the Wall Street financiers, the transnational corporations, the military-industrial interests, the state/private corporate complex surrounding the State of National Insecurity, and all their integrated cohorts of lesser scale simply act on their most narrow vested interests, blindly pursuing a path of global hegemony and degenerative development that can only lead to a continuation of barbarism. There is no end of the global war of official terrorism—until curtailed, then ended, by people's mobilizations.

FEAR AND SCAPEGOATING

The current campaign against "illegal immigrants" and Muslims reinforced by the slogans of Donald Shrill Trumpet in the 2015–2016 Republican campaign is a virulent resurrection of the vilest aspects of the legacies of fear and ethnic prejudice in America. It is designed to make those insecure of their small class privileges, eroding with the onslaught of the offensive of capital, to scapegoat those least able to defend their interests. Michael Kimmel in *Angry White Men* has an excellent analysis of how the insecurity and anxiety of white males of the middle and working classes being downgraded in the social structure is related to anger and hate expressed against scapegoats. Other good sources for understanding fear and scapegoating are Whitlock and Bronski, *Considering Hate*, and Stephen Eric Bronner, *The Bigot*.[4] In the first week after Trump's election, there were 300 hate crimes, as defined by the Department of Justice, against Muslims, the primary target, but also blacks, Latinos and gays. During the 2015–2016 campaign, hate crimes peaked from previous levels. In the three weeks after the November election, 90% of schools reported increased cases of bullying.

Fearful barbarians, these Islamic terrorists. And those illegal immigrants taking jobs away from hardworking Americans need to be forcefully shut out and those here deported. Build a secure wall, paid for by Mexico, a skyscraper-high Trump wall, to deter immigrants and shoot to kill those who attempt to scale it. And to top off things to fear, America in 2008, faced with the excesses of the Bush dynasty and a deteriorating economy, elected a black President who stood for change! There is perhaps no greater tribute to the effectiveness of the big lie and conspiratorial spinning than the fact that, according to polls, more than 20% of the American population believes that Obama was not eligible to be President because he was not born in the United States, no matter all the evidence to the contrary. Once in office, Obama was endowed with an added stigma, he is also a socialist! Yes, he did make an effort, feeble and unsuccessful as it was, to push toward a system of universal health care, which in the entire civilized world is a matter of public good not a marketed commodity. The vested interests did that in quickly enough, "Obamacare" is a big giveaway to the private insurance industry. Otherwise, Obama proclaimed some good things that the world was waiting to hear, that, unlike the preceding Bush period, under his administration the United States would abide by international law and become a respectable world citizen. For these utterances, he was decorated with the Nobel Peace Prize! Only to quickly turn to dirty deeds of official terrorism by drone attacks, war escalation in Afghanistan, yielding immunity for Bush era crimes, building up the spying capabilities of the National Security Agency, tightening up Homeland Security in the war on terror, supporting neo-Nazi thugs in the Ukraine, carrying out regime change in Libya, applying sanctions against countries who prefer to chart their own course. Nice rhetoric belied by actions. Obama has been a rather good servant of the system, although, in his last year or so, he did take some steps in a forward way by establishing diplomatic relations with Cuba, negotiating (imposing is a better term) a nuclear deal with Iran, backing off a bit on his statement that Venezuela is a "threat to the security of the U.S.", and even trying to initiate a reform of the bankrupt criminal justice system. Still, the drone attacks continue, the war machine marches on with the vigilance of high-flying hawks, and the FED and Treasury continue under the control of Wall Street. Trump's appointments to financial and military posts are even more extreme than Obama's.

In a world where some countries are not compliant with the norms of globalization and sectors of the home population are discontent, our rulers feel threatened and engage in destabilization of countries that resist, most recently Libya, Syria, Iran, Venezuela, Bolivia, and Ecuador, and look approvingly at the European Union's draconian impositions on Greece and austerity measures throughout the continent. And, in America Inc., they forge a campaign to mobilize the blissfully ignorant into the ranks of Republican voters. They strive to maintain the socially privileged and the gullible in confused bewilderment, to hold white males in line by resurrecting macho and racist creeds, and do all they can to misdirect the growing population of economically depressed people into abject fear so that they misunderstand the real source of the problem and redirect their resentments against those on their side. When necessary, they will mobilize the know-nothings on the fringe as their goon squads. Feels to me like a new face of Fascism agitating to become America's future (discussed in Chap. 8).

Fear, Endless Fear

More than a century of a system built upon fear. The denigrated immigrants, the early century anarchists, the "outside agitators," labor union militants, the un-American rabble, then, after World War II, the grand crusade against communism with endless interventions abroad and anti-communist hysteria at home—all elements, foreign and domestic, to fear. Four million "gooks" were napalmed, killed in counter-insurgency programs, and their crops, forests, and health decimated with Agent Orange. The communists and socialists who led the union struggles for social progress were purged from unions and, with McCarthyism, decent people disappeared from public life in all areas of a civilized society. The roots of anti-communist hysteria and its effects are dealt with in later discourses on imperial ambition and war, and the State of National Insecurity.

This sad history has led to the present where the Soviet " evil empire" has collapsed and terrorism is transformed from a police problem to propaganda and dirty deeds to justify war, occupation, rendition of suspects for torture and indefinite confinement; new laws facilitating state-sponsored terrorism; creation of new agencies of state such as Homeland Security, and more and more budgets for secret security agencies; presidential authority and use of it by presumably peace-minded President Obama to kidnap or assassinate any supposed enemy anywhere in the world, even perhaps within the homeland, without any legal constraints; impunity for American officials responsible for war crimes and crimes against humanity.

All this while, the National Security Agency (NSA) gathers intelligence by monitoring all phone calls and internet communications of Americans and electronically spies on U.S. allies. How useful to compile lists of Americans who don't go along with the conventional wisdom and know what supposed enemies and real allies are thinking and doing.

Torture is truly a fearsome measure. One has to wonder why the United States defied international law and treaties and America's own laws to institute torture and then to grant impunity to perpetrators. By 2008, official studies began to question if torture, thought to be a means of extracting useful intelligence by the CIA and Defense hawks, actually had efficacy. The conclusion was that torture does not work. After water boarding, a suspect will tell the interrogator whatever lie he wants to hear. Little doubt that torture does not work, but that also misses the point. Torture became state policy, not just because it was erroneously thought to work, but in order to spread fear, especially among Muslim populations. But the word gets around and everywhere people not directly affected can't help but view in awe the torture and immunity imposed by a lawless state. The same could be said of the intimidating value of the NSA spying, down to the routine inconvenience of silly airport security checks. The display of raw power merits respect—and fear. Before domestic secret renditions (such as those of Mayor Emmanuel's Chicago police) and gross violations of due process, if not torture, become routine in America Inc., it is time to leave aside fears and seriously confront at every opportunity the fearsome apparatuses of the State of National Insecurity (a state progressively reduced to the repressive apparatus explored in depth in Chap. 6). Obama did back off on torture but strengthened the repressive apparatus and Donald Trump will keep the State of National Insecurity moving ahead. Donald Trump is gung-ho for torture, asked "Would you authorize waterboarding?", he replied "you bet your ass I would."

THE SUBTLE SIDE OF FEAR

Generalized anxiety is also promulgated in more subtle ways. Americans are instilled with fear of crime, a serious social problem generated within the immiseration process of degenerative development, and citizens therefore should own weapons, even military killing instruments, for self-defense. Then, when home-grown fringe fanatics or people driven crazy, at least in part from the culture of fear, engage in massacres of innocents, no one knows what to do (weapon prohibition is beyond rational discussion) except become more afraid and go out and buy a more lethal weapon. The killing of school kids and movie goers by crazed gun-toters escalates to killings of Muslims, and the forced internment of "illegal immigrants," and massacres in a black Church by a kid waving a Confederate flag.

The June 2016 mass shooting of persons in a gay nightclub in Orlando, Florida, was clearly a hate crime inspired by the homophobia that infects the culture of masculinity. Still, Donald Trump and the media managed to turn this into an event inspired by Islamic terrorists, the better to contribute to generalized fear. Then, the Republicans in Congress would not consider even the most modest proposal for weapons control. The House Democrats staged a sit-in demanding action on the absurd minimal measures of barring persons on the "no fly" list or suspected of maybe being a terrorist from buying a weapon. None in officialdom considers the deep roots of a culture of violence and fear that make America tops in the world in mass murders and killings by guns. The National Rifle Association lobby is not the problem; the problem is the ideologies that buttress the system of capital and plutocracy. About the only other state in this world that permits the arming of the population with military weapons is ISIS.

This example of shooting, 49 gay people killed and 53 wounded, is beyond subtle fear but, in a society composed of fearful, competitive individuals, other persons become viewed with suspicion or as enemies, and this leads to embracing an ethic of dehumanization of the Other. This ethic extends to viewing the most vulnerable populations as disposable, be they gays or young people of color fit only to be contained and locked up, or shot and killed.

Subtle fear even touches campaigns for worthy causes that are parlayed into sources of fear, rather than problems to address—unsafe food, chemical contaminants, global warming causing natural catastrophes, and so on.[5] Floods, draughts, tsunamis, earthquakes, and gruesome killings and the like are always top news. Fear is incubated and promoted with the rhetoric of safety and security in overt and subliminal ways.

In a culture of fear, violence is promoted within media and political spheres as a distraction from reality, entertainment. TV serials, movies, the evening news, all filled with violence in the expectation that we will all become immune, take killing as a matter of routine, but still remain fearful of being a potential victim. In TV serials, the good guys justifiably kill the bad guys. Yet, in the same vein, perpetrators of violence in media and political promulgations are identified not as agents of the state—not the computer operatives of drone aircraft killing supposed militants, not the torturers in rendition prisons in Guantanamo and secret locations, nor the Justice Department lawyers who legitimate torture, and certainly not the higher-ups who order these measures—but as young people of color in schools and on the street fit only to be locked up in the booming, privatized prison industry, or shot down in the streets. It used to be that most movies had a point, even a moral theme that we could identify with. Now, we are smothered by the voyeurism of blood, explosions, and bodies. Moral themes shift to amorality, to nihilism. Hollywood produces what they consider the audience will tolerate, or even come to want, and will make money; visual drama with little content beyond violence. Network news devotes itself to producing retrograde ideology and the reproduction of *what is.*

Conditioned fear fits perfectly with a culture of individualism and social Darwinism. Competition replaces cooperation with fellow beings. Suspicion and distance replace respectful, trusting interaction and love for one's peers. Social isolation replaces social solidarity. Fearful skepticism and individual isolation translate into apathy to confront issues. Competition also takes a collective form. Sport teams and events inspire the ethic of win, win. It is also the case that sports involve men moved by and promoting the culture of masculinity. Recent news stories cite studies that link athletes in college and high school to higher rates of rape than non-athletes. The fact that football players and boxers frequently end up with brain injuries is well-studied, yet no one suggests ending brutal sports that injure participants as well as enshrine the machismo of violent tackles and knockouts.

Then, who promotes this culture of violence and fear? The media, the politicians, well-funded think-tanks, super-pacs, sadly even these days universities, and behind it all the class, the plutocracy, that benefits from keeping people subordinate to the existing system and strives for a thought hegemony in popular consciousness. I will have more to say about the perversion of the critical role of education and universities, institutions that properly should be countering this by imparting critical thinking, in the context of an analysis of students and youth as a principle base for social change.

The system produces and reproduces fear not just to keep people in line, but also to foster irrationality of thought, legitimize greed, create openness to corruption of thought and activity, obliterate consciousness of critical thinking and consideration of others, and poses gross immorality as human nature in a society of war of all against all where only the fittest are meant to benefit. The culture instills fear of failure, feelings of guilt and inadequacy, projection of personal troubles onto scapegoats, an acceptance of violence against any and all rulers identified as enemies. Popular consciousness riddled with fear is a priceless commodity that plutocrats and politicians buy at a low price—or perhaps better said, they turn a nice profit from the sale of fear. Violence is routinized, normalized; those who buy into it, dehumanized; and, in the cultural sphere, a commodity to be consumed for the profit of Hollywood movie moguls and the entertainment industry of popular culture, spectator sports owners, big business media, and ultimately the armaments industry. Social Darwinism does not mean that the fittest will survive and allow some trickle-down subsistence to the less fit; it means, if not curtailed by popular will and action, eventual collective suicide for all forms of social well-being. The spectacle and utterances of the 2016 crop of Republican presidential candidates illustrate the political path toward cultural-political suicide, toward which Donald Trump will lead the nation—unless resisted on every front by a revitalized movement.

CAPITALISM AND MORALITY

Later, I compare contemporary Republicanism with classic fascism, for now the term "savage capitalism" is a fitting summary of the nature of the beast. Fascism is the ultimate defense of savage capitalism. Racism, patriarchy and sexism, social Darwinism, denigration of immigrants, scapegoating, gross inequality, homophobia, and the instilled culture of fear create a social environment that shrink wraps minds and impels civil savagery. What is astoundingly unacceptable is that this is then passed off as morality. The 1980s was the beginning of golden age of "supply side economics," Reaganism/Thatcherism, neo-liberalism and globalization. A great number of apologists spewed out the idea that capitalism maximizes virtue and is guided by noble motive in propelling history. One philosopher of virtue and supply-side economist, George Gilder, an economic anthropologist, wrote a best-selling book, *Wealth and Poverty*, much quoted by Ronald Reagan, in which he argues that capitalism "calls forth, propagates, and relies upon the best and most generous of human qualities."[6]

For many centuries, there have been "scientific-based" ideologies to guide ignoble purpose in making history and doing evil—the genetic inferiority of women and blacks, the extension of evolutionary theory to the doctrine of the survival of the fittest in human society, and manifest destiny and the white man's civilizing burden in colonial conquest. The 1980s surpassed all previous metaphysics of capital in promulgating an irrational economic anthropology of the essential morality of capitalism. The 1980s was the dawn of the collapse of previous economic paradigms, especially Keynesianism, to replace demand-side economic theory with supply-side dogma and the vestiges of the idea of the commons to be replaced by the demolition of the welfare state. Gilder proclaimed that the system we endure is not based on self-interest, but, indeed, social giving; not the lure of profit, but noblesse oblige; not exploitation or class struggle. No, the guiding principle is altruism.

In a critique of Gilder in 1981, I stated:

> *"Among the aspiring noveau riche of our own primitive intellectual culture, the ceremony is turned inside out: ideas are accumulated and the rawest and juiciest sold to the highest bidder. For this category of entrepreneur, Say's Law (supply creates its own demand) works in reverse: the demand for moral justification of organized immorality has never been higher, and the supply is readily forthcoming.... There are those who defend the system by executing nuns, and there are those who defend the system by promulgating ideology. There are those who rape and torture persons as a prelude to death of the body, and there are those who rape and torture ideas as a prelude to death of the soul."[7]*

The murder of nuns was carried out by Ronald Reagan's henchmen in El Salvador in the 1980s. The torture was George Bush's doing to CIA sequestered prisoners in Guantanamo, in Cuba the symbol of liberation struggles. In 2015, former Vice-President Dick Cheney wrote a book *Exceptional,* co-authored with his daughter, Liz Cheney. Cheney is the contemporary proponent of American exceptionalism. He says America is "the greatest force for good the world has ever known." Cheney raped and tortured bodies with "enhanced interrogation," now he rapes and tortures ideas as a prelude to the death of America's soul. There is no end to ideological mystification and, with Trumpism, we can expect even more of it in highly vulgar terms. Much of the remainder of this book will continue the debunking of intellectual garbage and moral corruption.

CONFRONTING FEAR

At the heart of movements for change, there has to be a conception of reconstructing a world based on a moral vision of the common good. Broadly or dialectically speaking, a counter-hegemony that turns the principles of the ruling ideology into opposite principles is required. Minimally, in the present conjuncture, the movement needs constantly to purvey that it is wrong to deprive people of their homes; it is unjust to reduce worker's pay below a living wage, or to push them into the growing class of immiserated peoples; it is unacceptable to treat immiseration, poverty, and slum life as a police problem rather than a social problem; it is evil to kill people in foreign lands in the pursuit of oil and empire; it is outrageous obediently to put the interests of privileged classes above those of the majority—and individual interest over the collective good; it is sinful to treat people of diverse color and ethnicity, illegal immigrants, and women as inferiors. This culture allows the corruption of people, perhaps especially persons of white skin and male gender, to feel themselves superior and to suppress rational thinking and feeling compassion, because one holds a steady job and income to live on, has "made it" in the stratification hierarchies, in a word has class privilege—however petty, and now threatened, that privilege might be.

The system we are subordinate to is profoundly immoral and systemically reproduces and generalizes that immorality. At the same time, I may have, again, overstated my case. We are dealing with a tendency toward gross immorality in the phase of degenerative capitalism, not an absolute or immutable reality. There is a dialectical relationship between the historical gains of civilizing principles from the Enlightenment down to the UN Declaration of Human Rights, reflected in the nature of states as historical gains. In spite of the culture of fear, the regression to social Darwinism, the cult of individualism, and all the evils here described, most people (including many within the 90% taken in by the religion of Republicanism and the deceit of corporate Democrats) have at least a semblance of good sense and decency, and forceful appeals to their feelings of what is right and wrong, what is decent and indecent, what is in their interest and what is not, who is their enemy and who their friend, will, in time, have an impact on consciousness and where people will stand in relation to real social change. So, how do Americans—and there are millions and millions of humane, thinking, decent folk—fight the culture of fear, barbarism, dehumanization, racism and sexism, lies, perpetual war, and manipulations that are very real threats—the things deserving of genuine fear in America and throughout the world? Thinking critically helps, but only acts of mobilization for justice will make change possible.

In the late nineteenth and early twentieth centuries, it was movements outside the dominant parties that effected change. The anarchists, socialists, workers' movements, and progressives were champions of immigrant rights and working people's interests, and found their political base there. They faced fierce repression. The agitators, the un-American rabble, the denigrated immigrants, were eventually purged from public life with racist and anti-communist fear but, in their epoch, succeeded in mobilizing the working class and thinking people of all classes, and in achieving some progress. In the Great Depression, it was mainly the labor unions, socialists, and communists whose agitation and mobilization facilitated the New Deal. In the 1960s, the Civil Rights Movement forced Presidents Kennedy and Johnson to act and the clamors for justice found resonance in mainstream white America; former slaves are now African-Americans or blacks, not "niggers." "Spicks" are now Latinos, Chicanos or Mexican-Americans (except in Arizona and Texas, and among Republican presidential candidates and their political base). Yet, racism is, again, resurgent. The youth movement was instrumental in bringing an end to the imperial war in Vietnam; now we are back to perpetual war. The women's movement brought greater equality and dignity; gains only to be challenged by outrageous sexism in the present American environment.

We need to build on this progress, recognize the racist diversion inherent in the terms "illegal immigrant" and "Islamic Terrorist", act to end the nonsense, reject fears of diversity that are parlayed into social divisions, deny white-skinned privilege and male supremacy, denounce ideological inventions that cultivate fear and appeal to petty privilege even as those privileges are being eroded.

The pages so far have explored the first way in which the ruling class rules, by ideology, by filling people's heads with myth and with ideas that reflect and promote their class-based interests. Of course, the contrary side to imposition is resistance. I recently reread Howard Zinn's *A People's History of the United States*. This book, employing the methodology of "history from the bottom up," is a must-read for all movement militants. Zinn graphically and artfully portrays how the ideology of capitalism and class domination has, since the first English settlements in America, served to justify the grossest of inhumanity, beginning early on with genocide against the native population and slavery. The ruling ideology was always backed up with sheer force when the exploited and downtrodden revolted. Zinn describes the Haymarket event in 1886. A labor gathering demanding the eight-hour day in Chicago's Haymarket Square resulted in deaths. Organizers were wrongfully blamed, tried, and hanged. One of the martyrs, August Spies, told the judge: "If you think that by hanging us you can stamp out the labor movement…then hang us. Here you will tread upon a spark, but here, and there, and behind you, and in front of you and everywhere, the flames will blaze up. It is a subterranean fire. You cannot put it out. The ground is on fire upon which you stand". The Haymarket events inspired Mayday, celebrated throughout the world, except in America Inc., as the day to demand the rights of labor for dignity and justice. A complement to Zinn in the British context, where capitalism and imperialism first took deep root to be exported to America, is E.P. Thompson, *The Making of the English Working Class*.[8]

NOTES

1. Eduardo Galeano, *Upside Down*, p. 79.
2. John Bellamy Foster and Brett Clark, "Empire of Barbarism," *Monthly Review*, vol. 56, December 2004, p. 2. See also "Violence Today," *Socialist Register*, Monthly Review Press, 2009.
3. John Bellamy Foster and Brett Clark, "Empire of Barbarism," *Monthly Review*, vol. 56, December 2004, p. 2. See also "Violence Today," *Socialist Register*, Monthly Review Press, 2009.
4. Kay Whitlock and Michael Bronski, *Considering Hate: Violence, Goodness, and Justice in American Culture and Politics*, Beacon, 2015.
5. A highly overstated but challenging fictional depiction of the interrelation between the culture of fear and environmental organizations and campaigns against global warming is Michael Crichton, *State of Fear*, Harper Collins, 2004. Crichton, dubiously and exaggeratedly, does not take seriously the thesis of global warming. For a good analysis of film in inducing fear, see Philip Green, "On-Screen Barbarism: Violence in U.S. Visual Culture, " in *Violence Today*, edited by Leo Panitch and Colin Leys, *Socialist Register 2009*, Monthly Review Press, 2009.
6. George Gilder, *Wealth and Poverty*, Regnary Publishing, 1981.
7. Dale L. Johnson, "Ideologues and Executioners," *Society*, September–October 1981.

8. E.P. Thompson, *The Making of the English Working Class*, Pelican, 1963. Thompson's classic study has particular relevance to the examination of consciousness in Chapter Nine. Working-class consciousness comes from values of solidarity, collectivism, mutuality, and collective radical struggle. He is often quoted: "The working class makes itself as much as it is made." Thompson's purpose was to promote a vision of democratic socialism, in contrast to the Soviet version of statist socialism.

CHAPTER 6

The Ruling Class Rules by Subordinating Government to the Sway of Money

Plutocracy

One of the great myths of our time is that capitalism and democracy go together like bread and butter, *bratwurst und sauerkraut, arroz y frijoles.* From one historical situation to another, the norm of political rule in capitalist society is an authoritarian form of the state, most often posed as the ultimate in democracy, too often taking the form of military dictatorship. America is a plutocracy, not an absolute authoritarianism, but a state of formal democracy with withering substance, moving now to what I term an authoritarian State of National Insecurity. This is so because the system of capitalism requires a political institution that manages its structural prerequisites and ensures its reproduction (more on this in analysis of the interrelationship of class, patriarchy, and sexism in Chap. 7). The repressive apparatus of the state is central to governance of the whole. This derives from the social relation of capital's appropriation of value in the form of profit which, in turn, is transferred for enforcement from the purely economic sphere to the relations of force embodied in the state. The system of law codifies the norms of property and commodity relations of society. The centrality of the agencies of intelligence, police, and military forces can vary in their specific historical expression. The Spanish Republicans lost the civil water to the Franco fascists. The German socialists, communists, and unionists were annilated by Hitler's fascist forces. Stalin's dictatorship created a highly privileged elite of party bureaucrats

© The Author(s) 2017

D.L. Johnson, *Social Inequality, Economic Decline, and Plutocracy,*

DOI 10.1007/978-3-319-49043-4_6

and the enterprise managerial class that eventually decided that their wealth and privileges would be even more enhanced by a reversion to capitalism. This newly formed capitalist class in Russia and the various former socialist Republics today are only mildly less authoritarian than the Soviet regime that collapsed 25 years ago in 1991. In the 1960s to the 1980s, various Latin American countries responded to the class forces demanding fundamental changes with fierce military dictatorship. The regimes in Argentina, Uruguay, and Chile were the worst since European fascisms. In Central America, the death squads and U.S. interventions prevailed in upholding oligarchic rule, finally giving way to less repression and more formal democracy in the 2000s. Later, I explore to what extent the United States today approximates a fascist state.

While Europe in the 1930s succumbed to the fascist onslaught, the United States responded with economic and social reform, deepening substantive democracy and extending a greater degree of formal democracy from the 1960s. The successes of the civil rights, youth, and women's movements furthered the democratic order. These gains have been set back since the 1980s by the working of the economy and by political reversals. The gains are now precariously institutionalized in the American state and under real threat from Trump, the Republicans, and the corporate Democrats who will mostly flow with the wind. The repressive apparatuses have been greatly strengthened, and American military and political power of coercion is utilized to further the imperial ambition around the world. On the home front, government intelligence and police agencies are more and more strengthened by Patriotic Acts and Defense Authorization legislation. The next step could be targeted harassment or arrest—even assassination cannot be ruled out—of American citizens, if not by government forces directly then possibly by private, well-armed goon squads. Homeland Security is a massive agency with 400,000 employees. Police departments in all major cities are equipped by the feds with the latest technology and weaponry for the effective suppression of protest, and local police coordinate how to handle demonstrations and occupations with federal agencies. The FBI infiltrates agent provocateurs into protest groups. The media trivialize and denigrate Occupy and try to ignore other protests, such as Black Lives Matter, until they become explosive. In short, in America of the 1%, social gains and democratic rights are under pressure and the repressive apparatus is ever stronger and more effective.

The United States has become an authoritarian state, the best pseudo democracy that money can buy. The plutocrats buy politicians of both parties, and then portray government as corrupt, oppressive, and wasteful—only private enterprise can solve social and economic problems, so keep the budget balanced (except to finance wars), limit taxes, and deregulate business. What business wants is what the 90% get, curtailment of the common good. They plunge the system into crisis and blame government. Capitalism ruled by plutocrats is the vehicle for environmental suicide, political malfeasance, chronic economic crisis, and social decay, what I term "degenerative development." Yet, the only proper role of government is defense and security, and strict service to the class that buys the politicians. This is what the movement is up against and those that can be mobilized from the 90% will need effective strategies that advance democratic gains while not precipitating situations such as those in Spain, Italy, and Germany in the 1930s, or Chile and Argentina in more recent times.

Democratization was a major theme in the campaign of Bernie Sanders and found great resonance among youth and decent folk of all classes. But these forces do not have the clout that the Republicans wield. And if these politicians appear as clowns, they are not funny and are certainly very dangerous. What a lineup of astounding Republican characters for 2016. Disinterred zombies all, appearing as mummies. Like a pack of hungry wolves, they encircled the lost sheep. The whole party, it seems, is an insurrectionist party of the resurrected Confederacy. Each candidate aspiring to be Der Fuhrer, competing to mobilize a political base with the demagogy of racism, sexism, and anti-immigrant scapegoating. Ignorant of economics, they espoused upside down principles, spending money only for war abroad and repression at home. Ignorant of science, they deny global warming and suggest evil lies behind the theory of evolution. Apparently, they never learned anything but the neo-liberal gospel at Princeton, Yale, the University of Chicago, and Harvard. The Republican Party has transformed into the most extreme political force on the planet, to be safely guarded by the Great Wall of Trump on the Southern border. The "party of *No*". *No* compromise on fundamentalist principle. *No* respect for any law or program that protects the rights of citizens. *No* peace. *No* decency. In Zombieland, there is *no* ethics, *no* caring. For the victims, this means *no* jobs, *no* future, *no* hope. The blowhard Trumpet, the mouth that roars, displaying the bare rump of America to the consternation of the world, is a creation of decades of Republican stirring up of latent pathologies among sectors of the population—a cultivated culture of fear, racism, patriarchy and sexism, homophobia, ignorance, and irrationality. Some elites, even in the Republican establishment, view with alarm the vulgar manipulation of these pathologies by Donald Trump. The vote in Great Britain to exit the European Union in June 2016 was largely the work of nativist, Trump-like politicians.

STATE OF NATIONAL INSECURITY

The plutocracy has been rather successful in reducing the state in America Inc. to its essence, the security apparatus. Ostensibly, the system of law and the police, security, and military forces are subservient to the legislative, executive, and judicial branches of government. In the contemporary era, however, these branches respond to and generally do the bidding of the repressive apparatus. This apparatus is composed of an array of agencies: the Department of War, the Joint Chiefs of War Staff, Special Killing Forces, the Central Intelligence Assassins, the National Insecurity Agency, the National insecurity advisors surrounding the President, Homeland Insecurity, the Injustice Department, the Federal Bureau of Cointelpro, local trigger-happy police, and the National Guard Against Insurgency. The Senate Insecurity Committee green lights their activity, the Executive Branch guards their prerogatives, and the courts don't punish wrongdoings. Together, these agencies have spawned a vast complex of private contracting corporations that is well beyond the "military-industrial complex" that President Eisenhower warned against. In these days, it is not just big corporations producing weapons, now it is private contractors that do much of the dirty counter-terrorism work, the computer surveillance and sabotage work, the spy activity on foreign leaders and corporate competitors, secret mercenary squads that disrupt and kill. The shadow private complex takes in trillions with no oversight or accountability to executive, legislative, or judicial powers. We owe a debt of gratitude to the whistle-blower Edward Snowden for the release of documents revealing the extent of NSA spying on citizens.

The State of National Insecurity responds to the interests of the plutocracy. Its activities serve Wall Street, the oil barons, the multinational corporations, the drone makers, the network of private security contractors, the GMO inventors, big pharma profiting from fast-tracked free trade agreements, the insurance racketeers serving up sickness under "Obamacare," and all the lesser but well-rewarded staff of hangers-on. All these entities thinking that what the 1% want the 90% will get—the shaft, not even the trickle down. The terrorism of war lubricates the shaft, shoving it to any boogeyman foreign terrorist created, and any bold peacemaker in the homeland. This state has its homeland, Fortress America; it has its dogma, the war on terror; Its policy guidelines, neo-liberalism; its ideology to instill in the populace, social Darwinism. The State of National Insecurity has its creative think-tanks; its political action groups to spread millions around the electoral landscape; its means of avoiding accountability, a drawn curtain blocking heinous crimes.

The Lesser Evil

In a polity with a semblance of democracy, how is it that the plutocracy so thoroughly prevails in America Inc.? It is not through the exercise of brute force, although the potential for gestapo-like killing, arbitrary arrest, detention camps, and torture are certainly embedded in the repressive apparatus that is the heart of the State of National Insecurity. For now, war and official terrorism, sanctions and subversion, are reserved for those on the world periphery who try to challenge the pursuit of the imperial vision—Muslim populations in the Middle East and progressive forces in Latin America. In the homeland, killing is mainly confined to those defined as street thugs, especially black youth. Of course, whistle-blowers such as Private Manning are jailed—Edward Snowden, who exposed the NSA, and Julian, Assange, who wikileaked war crimes, reside in exile, hiding from charges of the most serious nature of criminal exposure of state secrets. It should be taken for granted that anyone who expounds dissident views on the internet or in a phone conversation is monitored and duly recorded by the National Security Agency, then forwarded to the FBI for placement on "the list." Homeland Security extends mission-creep from foreign terrorism to keeping track of domestic protest organizations, such as Black Lives Matter. For now, they are keeping track, with a semblance of the velvet glove still there. We need to make "the list" impossibly long and dissident groups multiply in preparation to make the iron fist harder to unglove.

So, what does the loyal opposition offer in response to crisis and stagnation and the religion of Republicanism? This goes to the essence of the second way that plutocracy rules, by subjugation of political parties and the state and its institutions to the will of the 1%, its allies among the 10%, and those taken in by the subversion of popular consciousness that is the first means of subjugation.

It rather pains me to write about the Democratic Party. In 2008, my hope drowned my usual skepticism and I was taken in enough to vote for Obama, (in prior elections I had voted for protest candidates, except for McGovern in 1972). After the experience of George Bush II, the downtrodden and decent folk wanted real change. Sadly, what we got was Obamabust. To the many among the disillusioned, Barack Obummer became viewed as a counterfeit progressive—duplicity, distortions, misrepresentations, absence of integrity, betrayer of idealistic voters; a silk-worded servant of big money and war lords; Commander-In-Chief of the National State of Insecurity. Perhaps Obama was preferable to the Republican alternatives and, in his last year, did a few good things, such as the Iran deal and opening relations with Cuba but, as a loyal servant of capital, he did an exemplary job.

Too many decent folk fail to recognize that America Inc. is the best ersatz democracy that money can buy. Sure, big money prefers the Republicans (at least until Trump came along). Still, those who steer plutocracy will settle for a president whose change the conditioned and naïve will vote for—and Democrats who understand that compliance is rewarded and defiance punished. Enter Hillary Clinton in 2016. We are expected to vote for the lesser of two evils—or, perhaps better said, the evil of two lessors.

In the last years, the Republicans became entrenched in obstructionism to any Obama program that had some semblance of reasonableness. Meanwhile, the President fingered Wall Street foxes to guard the Treasury. The Securities and Exchange Commission got a lawyer not believing in crime and punishment for Wall Street crooks, while the Attorney General yielded immunity to war crimes and crimes against humanity. The Attorney General, Eric Holdem, played his winning poker hand, took the revolving door back to his reserved Wall Street office. The Fed, governed by bankophiles, went on quantitatively easing the burden of the Street's toxic assets. Commerce got a deregulating Chicago rich lady, a female vulture herself implicated in commercial crime. For the appointment of Penny Bankster to Commerce, Obama's rating ought to have dropped to sub-prime, but on Wall Street rose to AAA+. The State of National Insecurity matured under Obama. The Department of War got its lackeys. The generals who guided Bush's wars, with a nod from the President and his National Security Staff, sharpened strategizing the imperial vision. The CIA Chief invented drone murders and devised new dirty tricks. The National Security Advisor is a sharp-taloned hawk, ready to shock and awe. The UN ambassador is not at all embarrassed to justify state-sponsored terrorism, be it American or Israeli. The Assistant Secretary of European Affairs is all for renewing the cold war with Russia, and applauds the neo-fascist Ukrainian thugs. The neo-con strategists hiding in the shadow of the National State of Insecurity smile approvingly at Secretary Kerry's continuation in the war paths of Hillary Clinton and Henry Kissinger. The State Department remains staffed by those who are bent on pursuing the imperial vision. Homeland Security bloats with more hands on board than there are crooks on Wall Street. The NSA continues to monitor private phone and email messages to keep tabs on us "terrorists."

How nice to have an African-American as President (especially if it were true that he was not born in America and that he is a secret Muslim and a socialist). Meanwhile, our colored President lamented the police murder of a young black man in Missouri that he says could have been him—perhaps before he dressed in his Harvard Law School suit; before he was groomed by establishment insiders to disguise deception in eloquent glibness.

In 2008, America voted for change with hope. In 2012, expectations of change soured, but dim hope lingered. In 2014, disaffected voters and non-voters recognized you can't govern a democracy with nothing to offer and deserted the Party. Two-thirds of voters abstained, many recognizing that Dems prostrate themselves before the Mecca of power, being paid to meekly lie down and enjoy rewarded defeat. So, what do they do for 2016—float a damsel, a lay-down kitten. As senator, she went onboard with Bush's war. As Secretary of State, Ms. Clinton guided the war machine, tried to outdo Henry Kissinger, sanctioned Iran, bombed Libya, and praised Qaddafi's murder ("we came, we saw, he died"); threatened Syria and sent Islamic terrorists there. For 2016, warriors and Wall Street, too, are sure, she is no "populist."

LIMITATIONS TO THE SUBJUGATION OF THE STATE TO PLUTOCRACY

The ruling class rules, first, by ideology and, second, by plutocratic control over the institutions, policies, and activities of government. The Socialist Parties of Western Europe and the Labour Party of the UK earlier posed as defenders of the rights of the working class. Then, they imposed neo-liberal policies on the populations and came down really hard in southern Europe with extremes of austerity policy. In America Inc., the Democratic Party has shifted from pronouncements of defense of the common man to (but only rhetorically) defense of the privileges of the middle class. It is abundantly clear that the Democratic Party is a faithful servant of established class power. The notion of middle-class society is the Democratic Party's version of ideological mystification. They can't abide the idea that there can be class struggle with the working class at the forefront. They appear to be defenders of middle-class well-being and, when campaigning, pursue identity politics with appeals to women and ethnics. Chris Hedges stated it well: "Obama, who professes to support core liberal values while carrying out policies that mock these values, mutes and disempowers liberals, progressives, and leftists. Environmental and anti-war groups, who plead with Obama to address their issues, are little more than ineffectual supplicants....The closure of the mechanisms within the power system that once made democratic reform possible means we stand together as the last thin line of defense between a civil society and its disintegration. If we do not engage in open acts of defiance, we will empower a radical right-wing opposition that will replicate the violence and paranoia of the state. To refuse to defy in every way possible the corporate state is to be complicit in our strangulation."[1]

Still, let us work from the theoretical proposition that the state is an expression of class relations. This conception opens the way for changes in state policy (e.g., from neo-liberalism to Keynesianism) and the forms that a state can assume (variations of formal democracy and authoritarianism) that are brought about by social struggles for system preservation and enhancement, on the one hand, and for popular political, economic, and social gain, on the other hand.

I have oversimplified, especially in being a snapshot of *what is* in a particular moment in history. While it is true that plutocracy rules, it is more complex than a static view of power relations portrays. The state, conceived as government at all levels and the system of law, is not always, or even usually, an instrument of a ruling class to dictate at will their ends. The democratic state, as limited as it is in most nations to ersatz formal democracy—and, in the contemporary United States, a façade for hiding plutocracy—nevertheless reflects the social gains of centuries of struggles of colonized people for independence and by oppressed peoples for liberty, equality, and fraternity, the cherished cries of the French revolutionaries. The principles of the Declaration of Independence of the American Revolution and the Bill of Rights still have some meaning, although the Rule of Law mainly serves the rule of capital. The principles of human rights promulgated by the United Nations have universal bearing. While progressively weakened, laws governing the rights of labor to organize, the civil rights of minorities and women, social programs for the destitute and aged, and measures that have made our world more civilized are expressed and reflected in the modern state in the United States and many other nations.[2]

It is all these reflections and institutionalizations of social gains that are being challenged by capital's utilization of crisis, stagnation, ideological mystification, and political power to further their hegemonic project. Resistance to the programs of neo-liberalism is imperative. There needs to be massive resistance to the policies of Donald Trump. But defensive struggle does not, in itself, lead to new social gains. The struggle is not just against the programs the plutocracy is imposing, rather, it is for the necessity of transforming the system that produces injustice and reproduces plutocratic power. A broken system can be tinkered with but it cannot be effectively fixed, it needs to be transformed. The socio-pathology of *what is* can be eventually replaced with a substantive democracy based on justice, equality, and the common good. The idea is to broaden struggle from defense to offense, to free flow the imagination so that oppressed people realize their potential for social agency.

With sustained struggle, the state will begin to express changing class relations. These struggles occur within a context of multi-class relationships in a bi-polarizing structure. Here, and in Chap. 7, I examine some of the social divisions that are constituent to multi-class relations and the degree that expressions of protest, rebellion, and unity can impact upon the policies and form of the state.

The movements of peoples worldwide, the Indignados and the Podemos political formations in Spain and the anti-austerity activists of Greece forming the Greek Syriza government elected in January 2015, seem to be quite advanced—hopefully these formations will work out tactical activities that fit within a strategy of total change. So far, in Greece it appears that Syriza has capitulated to the coercive austerity of the European Union and its financial infrastructure. Perhaps it is better stated that Greece has been conquered by the German army, this time not Nazi, but an army of financiers heavily armed with euros and coercive institutional power. With determined resistance, this occupying army, too, can be evicted. As with the United States, the European Union is essentially administered by bankers, the European Commission in league with the International Monetary Fund, and the European Central Bank. The EU is a plutocracy that pushes austerity and all the policies of neo-liberalism, to the detriment of the population. NATO has been an integral part of the wars in the Middle East and Libya that have created a massive influx of desperate refugees. Brexit from the EU can be seen as a protest of EU imposed neo-liberal policies, the undermining of national sovereignty, and a nativist response to EU immigration policies.

In America, I consider here a few strategic considerations that can be considered fundamental. First, especially in the light of Trump's appeal to those who have legitimate grievances with the system and with Democrats who do not defend the interests of the downtrodden, we need to come to grips with the divisions that exist among the 90% and to understand which groupings are potential allies, which sectors can be neutralized in a developing struggle, and which elements are likely to line up in militant defense of the system. Second, in the United States in particular, the culture of fear that has been promulgated must be challenged and the generalized anxieties in the minds of so many of the 90% moderated, their justified anger directed toward the real sources of grievance. Third, there is the need to recognize fully and to act upon the fact that "Wall Street" is simply a short-hand manner of referring to a world system pursuing degenerative development that is given direction by the financial oligarchy but supported by all the fractions of capital and administered by compliant politicians and those sectors of the middle class elevated to be the line and staff functionaries of capital and within the repressive apparatus of the state. The United States is the administrative center of imperial ambition that resorts to fear and war as its chief instruments of domination. Fourth, working classes on a world scale, and certainly within the United States, are the main elements in the 90%. The marginalized and immiserated underclass is growing and the role of organized protest and rebellion by the most disadvantaged sectors has to be considered, supported, and joined by others to make poverty and racial and ethnic oppression class issues. Fifth, the union movements of the last century, the anarchist, socialist, communist, and trade union militants responsible for the historical gains of the past, are no longer there in America, and are declining too in Europe, and in America unions are not simply on the defensive, they are being destroyed. Support for unions to defend workers' interests and to shift bread-and-butter unionism and collaboration with bosses to class perspectives is essential. Finally, youth throughout history has been at the forefront of real social change. The situation of young people everywhere today is desperate, and they need to become, and likely will, the militants of our age. These considerations will be addressed in Chap. 7 on social divisions and the final chapters on movement strategy.

NOTES

1. "The Left Has Nowhere to Go", www.truthdig.com/report/item/the_left_has_nowhere_to_go_201100102.
2. I analyze in some depth the idea "the state as an expression of class relations" in Dale L. Johnson (ed.), *Middle Classes in Dependent Countries*, ch. 7, Sage Publications, 1983. The same book traces the roots of dictatorship that coincided with the initial spread of neo-liberalism through globalization as forms of political rule in Latin America, the West Indies, the Middle East, and the Soviet Union.

CHAPTER 7

Rule by Divide and Conquer

The third proposition is that the ruling class rules by creating divisions within and between social classes. In this divide and conquer strategy, the most important divisions played upon are those of social stratifications—the social divisions based on race, ethnicity, gender, and hierarchies within class. In the 2016 electoral campaign, Trump played upon these divisions with astounding vulgarity and the most serious damage to what remains of our civic culture.

The movement strategy should be to *celebrate diversity, combat division, and unite in struggle.*

Ideology and Class Relations: Allies and Enemies of Real Change

Income inequalities, the invidious distinctions of occupational prestige, differing educational attainments, ethnic and racial gradations, gender, distinct lifestyles, residential location, the difference between manual and mental labor, between blue-collar and white-collar work, or productive and unproductive labor, and other factors of function in the labor process and stratification of the population are, in people's daily experience, real social phenomena. At the same time, they are but divisional creations of the system that can, and do, turn people away from their existential interests to remain passively accepting of their place in the social order, or even

© The Author(s) 2017

D.L. Johnson, *Social Inequality, Economic Decline, and Plutocracy,*

DOI 10.1007/978-3-319-49043-4_7

to ally with the enemies of change. Stratifications are ideological manifestations of prevailing social inequalities, and they are perceived and acted on by people in daily life. These distinctions of social status are often mistaken by people (and by professional sociologists who specialize in ideological mystification) for social classes. Social classes are not based on gradations in income from upper to lower, or on the social prestige accorded different occupations. In the real world of social class relations, distributional and ascriptive inequalities, and invidious cultural and occupational attributes are integral to the social relations of exploitation and domination; they are facets of class relations in that the social meaning of stratifications systematically subordinates workers and serves to create divisions within the working class and to define boundaries in a social context between the working and middle classes, and between these classes and the underclass. These are mystifications of social differences that form ideological notions that serve to keep people divided, envious of one another, and create sentiments of competition and inferiority/superiority. The strongest of these ideologies in America of yesterday and today is racism, but sexism is on a parallel as a socially divisive ideology. Racism is adaptable as time changes, from directed against African-Americans, the ideology has shifted now to make Latinos, illegal immigrants, and Muslims, along with black people, the objects of prejudice and discrimination. "Women's place" is changing, too. So, let's look at that first.

PLUTOCRATS AND THEIR SERVANTS GET OFF ON SUBORDINATING WOMEN

Patriarchy is an ongoing social reality inherited in our times from a long-distant past. While recognizing that men in general perpetuate their manly power through clinging to the ideology of patriarchy, the class dynamic that capitalism produces is what is central to the perpetuation of patriarchy and the perverse culture of masculinity. Today, a supreme patriarch and vulgar sexist is President of the United States. The most radical and Marxist feminist studies are the most profoundly in touch with *what is*. This perspective begins with the tenet that women's traditional work—and, in good part, remaining so to our day—is to manage the reproduction of the labor force. Selma James states it succinctly:

"The ability to labor resides only in a human being whose life is consumed in the process of producing. First it must be nine months in the womb, must be fed,

clothed, and trained; then when it works its bed must be made, its floor swept, its lunchbox prepared, its sexuality not gratified but quietened, its dinner ready when it gets home, even if this is eight in the morning from the night shift. This is how labor power is produced and reproduced when it is daily consumed in the factory or the office. To describe its basic production and reproduction is to describe women's work.[1]

Of course, families reproduce not only labor power, but the *human species*. Yet, the organizational crux, in a capitalist society, is that capital expropriates unpaid labor, ideally, at the small cost of a single wage to maintain and reproduce labor power. Waged labor, on the one hand, and unpaid reproductive labor, on the other, is a material basis for antagonism between the sexes. In the contemporary era, male wages are increasingly insufficient to cover the costs of reproduction, so that mothers and housewives are increasingly incorporated into the waged labor force. This happens under discriminatory conditions such that women gain employment mainly in low-paid clerical and service activity, sectors expanding with the decline of male employment in productive enterprise and the expansion of work in servicing commodity circulation. When women are incorporated into previously male occupations, their pay is usually less than males performing the same job. The problem of maintaining a family life—that is, reproduction of labor—becomes more difficult and the cultural norm of masculinity too often means that women work a shift on the job and another one in the home.

The women's movement has achieved considerable successes since the 1970s, contributing no doubt to the current Republican campaign to put women back into their place, from restricting abortion to all kinds of new legislative initiatives. Legal strategies opening up admission to university and professional schools, and affirmative action programs had an impact and opened up some of the middle-class occupations to women, though much less so now, given the high and increasing cost of higher education. The pay differential of female to male wages increased from 59 cents per hour in the early 1960s to 77 cents in 2006, then went into a decline with the economic crisis from 2008. Women's participation in the labor force greatly increased to 60% in the 2000s. The campaigns of NOW and other feminist groups resulted in considerable social mobility of women into the managerial and professional groupings, 50% female in 2005—most, of course, in the teaching and health "helping" professions, with token CEOs here and there. (The only female Republican candidate,

Fiorina, was attacked for not doing a manly job as CEO of a large corporation). Nevertheless, the great bulk of women are in low-waged, insecure, working-class jobs.

Racial and ethnic discrimination prevail in female employment, with black and Hispanic women relegated to lower-paying jobs than white women, who, in turn, gain lower wages than white men. Hispanic women's wages are only 61.2% of those of white men. Black women earn 68.6% of white male wages. Both have lower wages than Hispanic or black men. Asian women fare somewhat better, but are far from on a par with white employees.[2] Women workers are concentrated in offices and in the caring and reproductive occupations that are 90% or more female: secretaries, nurses, bookkeeping, receptionists, child care, maids and housekeeping, teaching assistants, and preschool teachers. This employment has low rates of unionization except for teaching assistants. Elementary and middle-school teachers are 82% female and have the highest rate of unionization, 52.5%.[3] The work that women do in the labor force is mainly drudgery (except in some of the caring professions, such as teaching) but it does exchange dependency on the male breadwinner and family isolation for a degree of independence. Also, more and more men and older siblings are adapting and learning to share child care and household chores, important steps toward greater equality, denied in the larger inegalitarian system.

As women leave the home to work, they must turn to privatized child care or, when affordable, hire nannies and maids for their homes. This commodification of necessary tasks redistributes the work of reproduction to other women. This is no solution. Social reproduction must be a public good guaranteed by the state. At one point, a slogan in the feminist movement was "Wages for Housework." A good demand. The child tax credit given in the U.S. tax code is barely a first step. A movement demand should be minimally the kind of subsidies given in Scandinavian countries for maternity, child care, and family maintenance. In short, what is needed are demands that shift the identity of family life and child rearing from that of reproducing labor power to reproduction of the human species in a society in transition toward egalitarian social relations. Demand equal pay for equal work; parent-controlled child care centers; guaranteed income to live an adequate life for women and men, working or not, single or married. For a time, there was a movement for a global women's strike. Their demands are worthy guidelines: "Payment for all caring work—in wages, pensions, land and other resources. What is more valuable than raising children and caring for others? Invest in life and welfare, not military budgets and prisons." "Pay equity for all, women and men, in the global market." "Food security for all, starting with breastfeeding mothers, paid maternity leave and maternity breaks. Stop penalizing us for being women." "Accessible clean water, healthcare, housing, transport, literacy." "Nonpolluting energy and technology which shorten the hours we must work. We all need cookers, fridges, washing machines, computers, and time off!" "Protection and asylum from all violence and persecution, including by family members and those in positions of authority. Freedom of movement. Capital travels freely, why not people?"[4]

Stephanie Luce and Mark Brenner capture well the class aspect of women's work:

"As feminists, we want to see individual women succeed: to gain access to higher education, to have the opportunity for economic independence, and to find meaningful work. But it isn't enough for a few women, or even a lot of women, to succeed. Because under capitalism their success in leaving the class only means others are left behind. Under capitalism you can't have a manager without the managed, and you can't have a winner without a loser. And who is losing? It remains primarily women and people of color… the women who "win" under capitalism, as well as those who lose, have an incentive to build a cross-class women's movement to fight for a different model of production and social reproduction that allows us to construct our lives around human needs."[5]

To return more directly to the divide and conquer strategy of the dominant class and to the need to celebrate diversity and combat social divisions: In the cultural imposition fashioned by the contemporary media, the very concept of gender is formed, in part, by the images presented, women are sexualized to stroke the male libido. In other imaging women are portrayed as docile appendages of the family. Perhaps Hollywood is trying to be more politically correct, the industry's latest creations seem to be superwomen who can maim and kill as effectively as any superman.

Gender differentiation has a long history. The legacy of patriarchy, the ideology of sexism, and the cult of masculinity function to divide people and subvert consciousness of the place of the male population in the class order. It is no accident that the 2012 and 2014 Republican campaigns placed such a heavy emphasis on denying the rights of women, continuing with even fiercer pronouncements leading to the 2016 elections and the passage of numerous new pieces of state-level legislation restricting the rights of women. The Republicans are appealing to the white males who fetishize all things macho to mobilize them for right-wing reaction, along with the followers of fundamentalist Christian sects. In 2016, this long campaign by Republican zombies resulted in Trumpist misogyny.

Women's bodies are meant to be controlled by men who are the heads of families and therefore think they know best for women and children; by men who tote guns, drive big pick-ups, and like to push people around. Women's place is in the bedroom, the kitchen, the nursery, and the church pew, in America only lacking the hijab or head scarf in public. This is a worldwide thrust of the dominant ideology. In German, *Frau gehen um kinder und Küche.* In the pervasiveness of macho culture, *El lugar de la mujer es con los niños, en la cocina, y en la cama.* Secular America had been slowly moving away from strident machismo but, when males with macho self-conceptions are deprived of their class situational privilege and the power to bully by the workings of the system, the more fragile can become their masculinity and the display of their peacock feathers ever more pronounced. The privilege of being male, especially but not exclusively white male, can, and too often does, morally corrupt. And the symbols of masculine superiority are daily reinforced with the flip of the television control—women's roles are stereotyped; war and killing are celebrated as macho defense of the privileged homeland; the couch potatoes delight in spectator sports that are displays of violent aggression, that enshrine the glories of competition in which the strongest and best prevail, while the Mrs. cooks dinner. I don't want to over-generalize in putting down white males. Most are people who in their daily lives are good folk, and in interactions with women or people of different ethnic origin or sexual preferences are decent and tolerant. But we have to understand that, within the 90% who are objectively disadvantaged by the present system, too many don't see it that way, and a disproportionate number are white males. There are a lot of haters in America. They hate black people, illegal immigrants, Muslims, gays, women, liberals.... They like war, torture, guns, cops, authority.... They love Jesus, but have no idea that loving Jesus is out of sync with hate. They get enthusiastic about Donald Trump. Maybe some people are so hopelessly corrupted that we have to reduce our 90% disadvantaged estimate by a large percentage (estimated in the final chapter as 30%) to account for those who will forever stand by the system, perhaps the more so as white male privilege is continually eroded and as *what is* becomes seriously challenged.

Focusing on the divisions engendered by stratifications based on gender, race and ethnicity, and class positioning are central to understanding strategies of change. Any type of privilege that flows from the various social stratifications can divide, corrupt, and immobilize, and the most corrupting of all is class privilege, and more dangerously so as these privileges are threatened. The class dynamic of capitalism determines all the social stratifications. And today the white man, who all his life has gone to church, went off to war to serve his country, believed in the goodness of system, looses his job. His lifelong labors have come to nothing, his self-image threatened. Will he recognize that the convictions that guided his conduct and gave him his privileges have provided the basis for his personal failure? Will he understand that, in fact, it is not his personal failure, but that his lost privilege was built upon lies and that his belief system has been an accessory to his own demise? Many are enamored of Donald Trump, first, because he trumpets racism, sexism, and xenophobia, but also because he wants to right the wrongs of a system that has disadvantaged so many. Hopefully, in the long run, as the movement's messages permeate the culture, many men's heads will be turned around but, in the short run, our guy will more likely pin blame on scapegoats, "illegal immigrants," and Muslims, go home to beat his wife, and vote Trump and Republican.

In my moments of outrage, and they are perhaps too frequent, I view the subversion of consciousness by petty privilege as a rape perpetrated by the powerful. But, really, it is more like a gentile seduction of willing participants in mass culture. Or perhaps it is better said that we are all tempted to prostitute our minds and bodies for the pittance offered by the rich Johns.

Whether it is rape, seduction, or prostitution, the Republicans are the main thinkers of how to subvert popular consciousness. The Republicans know how to cultivate subtle racism, anti-immigrant resentment, sexism, the cult of masculinity, religious fundamentalist views on cultural issues, fear and insecurity—and to use these ideologies to snare the victims of the system they are determined to defend at any cost to the moral fabric of society. And the Democrats (with a few individual exceptions, such as Bernie Sanders) offer only mild platitudes, no serious critique or appealing ways out of moral decline and systemic crisis. In the culture of manufactured fear and scapegoating, perhaps our guy will even go to a gun show and bring back a powerful weapon to battle uncertainty with a sense of powerful certainty, the better to target the ghosts that have stolen his hopes. Mass shootings have increased every year in the United States, reaching daily occurrences in 2015. I don't want to stereotype as hopeless the white males who are tempted to cling to their white-skinned and patriarchal and class privilege even when they become deprived of the economic and social status bases for their feelings of superiority. But America certainly does have a problem in southern states with a legacy of racism, a macho culture, and pervasive religious fundamentalism. And something is not right in small-town and rural America, too, the denominated "red states". Moreover, Trump rallies and voters are disproportionately middle-class white males, although much is being said in the media that there are many white, working-class men supportive of Trump. That workers and poor people are attracted to Trumpism is, in good part, attributable to the Democrats, liberals, and progressives not addressing the needs of the lower reaches of society. It is also the case that those who are in life situations with little hope can be steered into hate. It will take the movement a great deal of time and patient work to convert those who now stand with the real enemies of change, first, to neutralize their reactionary assertions and, eventually, to win them over.

An indication of the stress produced by deteriorating class situations is a 2015 study that found that, among middle-aged white males, the death rate is rising at an alarming rate, largely accounted for by increasing death rates from drug and alcohol poisonings, suicide, and chronic liver diseases and cirrhosis. [6]

Sociologist Michael Kimmel has spent his academic career studying males and masculinity. His most recent book, *Angry White Men*, is an impressive work and a must-read for movement activists. Kimmel spent years suppressing his own indignation and interviewing white men that are part of the extensive groupings that constitute the extreme right wing in America Inc.

Large numbers of men feel emasculated, deprived of their rightful place in the social hierarchy to which they are entitled. Kimmel develops the concept of "aggrieved entitlement" to good effect. In the situation of being downgraded in the social order by the workings of the economy and in the face of perceived social gains by minorities and women, some white men come to believe that they are being deprived of the privileges that are rightfully theirs, by virtue of being white and male.

The reaction has been building up for years in the measure that the economy is going downhill to the detriment of white men—office workers, displaced workers, small farmers, shopkeepers, craftsmen, small business men—while America becomes more ethnically diverse and women have achieved more non-traditional places in society. Now, we see white males in the Tea Party, the Minutemen, the neo-Nazis, patriot organizations, anti-feminist organizations targeting "feminazis," the KKK and other white supremacists, the followers of radio talk shows that espouse hate, anti-Semite groupings, anti-immigration activists, and volunteer border patrols, Obama haters, hundreds of men's rights groups and websites, contempt for "tree huggers," father's rights for angry dads, men's clubs, and other hate groups.[7] These haters are stirred up by the big guys that Michael Moore in his book terms "Stupid White Men,"[8] and now comes Donald the Trumpet, sounding shrill notes the crowds want to hear. Some within the Republican establishment may have their reservations about Trump, but they have managed the system that has created a very substantial social basis for an incipient American-style fascism (More on parallels to classic fascism later).

According to the 2010 FBI report on violent crime, men committed 90% of 11,000 murders, 77% of aggravated assaults, 74% of offences against children and the family, mass shootings are almost entirely young white males, and, of course, 99% of rapes. Such violence is not due to male hormones, but to the corruption that male privilege entails.

STRATIFICATION OF THE WORKING CLASS

Again, it is workers who must be in the forefront of change. To be active subjects, people need to achieve consciousness of their positioning in the social structure and unite in struggle. Working-class occupations are subject to differing income levels, type of employment (as in producing useful goods versus employment in the repressive apparatus), degree of subjugation in the labor process, relative security or insecurity of employment, and other factors; they are stratified by race, national origin, legal and illegal labor, and gender. These change over time and with shifts in economic direction—in the current stage of degenerative development, toward employment in wasteful and socially and environmentally destructive activity, while also immersed in deeper divisions within the atomized and alienated population, and intensified ideological subversion of consciousness.

The official reformist discourse of the liberal thinkers is lamenting the decline of the middle class, the class situation of workers largely ignored, and the war on poverty a very distant memory. There is a multitude of social movements that arise from the segmented population, largely based on identity politics (race, ethnicity, sex, particular groupings of workers) as distinct from class politics. "Identity today is the ideological lens through which class conflicts and the effects of unfettered class power are refracted, understood, and fought…political discourses and practices have severed, in people's consciousness, the connection between experiences of oppression and exclusion, and the material conditions of these experiences."[9] There are class divisions within identity-based populations. For example, there are unemployed black slum dwellers, black workers, black professionals, black intellectuals that serve the movement, and a black bourgeoisie that serves the plutocracy. Similarly, there are impoverished single mothers, working-class women, middle-class women leading the feminist movement and others such as "anchormen" for Fox News and CNN, the privileged social set of the 10%, and the Hillary Clintons that play the game of established power. So, in too many ways identity serves to obscure class. The women's movement and the civil rights movement made great gains in breaking down preexisting discriminatory barriers and achieving formal civil rights, but the support of unions was all too hesitant. Neither movement has made great gains in changing the oppressed class position of the great majority of black and brown people and women. Indeed, the class situation of these groupings is worse now than in past decades. The task before the movement today is to unite forces and forge a class-based politics. If black, brown, and female persons of the more privileged sectors join in supportive struggles on the basis of identity politics, great.

One type of stratification within the working class is based on the blue-collar/white-collar distinction. Although a term no longer used much to differentiate working-class and middle-class employees, it still retains some invidious distinctions. Employment based on function in the labor process effects experience and consciousness, and it could be argued that a differentiation needs to be made between productive labor that produces value appropriated as profit by capital, the true proletariat experiencing direct exploitation, and unproductive labor that works in the sphere of circulation or distribution, where exploitation is more obscured. There has evolved in the culture status distinctions between service and office workers and industrial workers—part of the mythology of making it into the middle class involves "white-collar" employment. Certainly, office workers, service people, sales clerks, bank tellers, and the like, who labor in the sphere of distribution or the circulation of money, do not consume the fruits of productive labor. They produce a service not a physical product but, like a factory worker, they are hired so that their employer can gain or realize a profit. In our time, service workers are a growing sector of the working class and among the most downtrodden, with low wages, job insecurity, and limited benefits. It is unlikely that the distinction of white-collar, meaning middle-class privilege, is as pertinent as it once was. Most of these sectors of the working class are allies in the struggle for fundamental change.

We have to take into consideration the thrust of degenerative development and how that reshapes the life situation of the segments of the working and the intermediate classes. More and more of the labor force struggles along in low-paid service activity, underemployment, and unproductive employment in socially worthless work that nevertheless is indispensable for capital to realize profit. In previous analysis of degenerative development, I described the current thrust of accumulation in the clutch of recessionary stagnation and under the sway of financial oligarchy as "unproductive, speculative, wasteful, environmentally degrading, and socially destructive activity." More and more workers are employed in these leading sectors of the economy. They make their living in jobs such as keeping track of capital's money, the sale of superfluous commodities, building pipelines and fracking for natural gas, manufacturing drone aircraft, hacking computers for the NSA.... What impact does this have on the consciousness of these workers? I am not sure of the answer to that question. But it cannot possibly be rewarding work, in the sense of doing something useful, like growing food, building homes, nursing, or teaching. People in these positions surely suffer the extremes of alienation, not just in the sense of work activity, but any sense of fulfillment of human capacity. Surely living most of one's waking hours in degenerative work activity can lead to estrangement of self and from others. Capital has not only imposed antagonistic social relations between classes but also imposes alienative isolation, breaking out as competition and conflict between groupings and individuals, adverse conditions which can be internalized, affecting mental health. *Overcoming alienation and competition requires building consciousness through activity of transcendence. Demand meaningful work in producing socially useful goods and services in non-degrading conditions.*

Another related consideration is the link of changing investment patterns to the resurgence of the U.S. Southern Confederacy, where racism, sexism, and the most reactionary assertions prevail, now seemingly as much as they have since the days prior to the civil rights movement.

The "New South" began its path to a new type of merging of economic transformation and ideological shift to only slightly more subtle post-civil rights thinking some decades back. What were then called "runaway" shops from the northern states closed down plants in textiles and other sectors, and shifted new plants to the South where low wages and no unions prevailed. Atlanta became a successful industrial, commercial, and financial center of the New South. And Texas with its oil barons, vast oil refinery complexes, and racist history has, as its main product, reactionary ideology and national politicians. In recent times, the South has begun competing with other areas of the world with low wages and a friendly business environment, attracting investments within the U.S. marketing zone from Japan, Europe, and industrial areas of the United States in auto manufacturing, aerospace, and other activities. Unions don't fare well in the South, voting rights are suppressed, and the reactionary and racist thinking of the old Confederacy are resurrected in new form—and adopted by northern Republicans. America has, since its infancy, been two nations. These developments are bringing back the Confederacy in a new form, to the detriment of the entire population and the nation.

To return to questions of social stratification. When it comes to differentiating the working class and the middle class, function in the labor process has more relevance. Most employees generally considered middle-class do not engage directly in productive activity, that is, producing a good or service that capital appropriates a portion of as profit. But it is not the unproductive quality of work by supervisors, managers, professionals, and technical staff in corporate hierarchies that determines their location outside the working class—it is their function in the labor process. As drawn out in Chap. 4, class positioning has to do with place and role in the relations of production, with the relationship of different occupational groupings to the system of surplus appropriation and the class domination that sustains and reproduces that system. One of the most distinguishing features of advanced capitalist development has been the proliferation of employees retained to carry out the control functions of capital—control over the accumulation process—that is, over the system of surplus appropriation, and control over the labor process, that is, the means of control and exploitation of workers.

The livelihoods and personal class superiority of intermediate functionaries are rooted in hierarchically ordered systems of class domination. Historically, they have been involved directly in the middle of social relations of inherent antagonism to mediate those antagonisms. This is changing with the bifurcation of sectors of the intermediate groupings being pushed into or toward the working class, while other segments are elevated to higher management. I noted in Chap. 4 that, in the most recent phase of degenerative development, each of these groupings is subject to the same process of de-qualification of labor as was their role in relation to workers in the earlier phase of development. Their control function is fragmented and routinized, converted to de-qualified and de-professionalized tasks that appear more and more as worker's work. The corporations and institutions in which they work are centralized with administrative control at ever higher levels. More and more employees become small cogs in the giant machinery of corporate and governmental hierarchies, and are less and less the intermediate level functionaries of capital.

Whether or not middle-class persons being forced toward or into the working class are willing allies or enemies of the movement to be neutralized depends in part upon how forthrightly de-classed persons respond to changes in their situation and on the continuing strength or declining relevance of the divisive ideologies that the powerful promote. Among the most open to change are likely to be the service professionals being de-professionalized, teachers now defined as guardians rather than educators, social service workers who are forced to be bookkeepers and bureaucratic agents of social control, medical workers laboring in a seriously ill medical system dominated by insurance companies, hospital administrators and elite doctors.... The many technical employees, who once had some autonomy in their work, find that work fragmented and de-qualified by the very technology they invented, their pay cut or jobs outsourced, while the system analysts and top engineers are promoted to controlling staff positions.

It is those that work in the repressive apparatuses of the state that we have to worry most about. There is considerable selectivity in who becomes a service professional and those who look for work in police and security agencies. Teachers, social workers, and nurses, for the most part, tend to be women of a kind heart and gentle disposition who want a life's work in doing good. The profession of police work, on the other hand, can attract men who like exercising power over others, who get-off on bashing heads of young punks, although the great majority of police officers no doubt are decent persons trying to do a difficult job, at least in most instances, to protect social order when all is in social disorder. But the police murders, containment strategies in poor communities, arbitrary arrest and imprisonment…all must end with a total overhaul of the criminal justice system (discussed later).

The movement must find ways to neutralize the repressive forces, as the peace movement and American soldiers did in Vietnam. Which side are you on boys? For the hundreds of thousands who work in the expanding intelligence agencies, the FBI, and Homeland Security, whose job it is to monitor your internet communications, to infiltrate your organization, to put you and me on a list to be dealt with, to identify supposed terrorists for assassination, to plan and carry out all manner of dirty tricks, we can only hope for an occasional whistle-blower to expose their activities for public scrutiny—at least until their jobs are made impossible by the depth and mass of the movement.

Class-generated social hierarchies divide, but also generate specific social actions that express the antagonisms of divisional subjugation. The black movement is resurging with the protests since 2014 against police murder of blacks. The women's movement; the environmental movement; the Latino, and other minority organizations and protests; the jobless, the infirm, and the homeless who mobilize as they can…. The list keeps growing as the system does in more and more people and as they learn to act. *The movement questions are how to replace identity politics that arise from the system imperatives to divide and conquer to a transformative class perspective. The struggle is to come together in confronting division, celebrating diversity, and forming a class unity perspective.*

The response of a decadent system when challenged is to employ increasing levels of repression, and ever more frequent and more deadly recourse to pure force. Political paralysis caused by official political greed-lock prevents rulers from adopting sensible, system-saving solutions to the problems facing the multitudes that might contain protest or pacify discontent. Our rulers are clever and very efficient in applying the means of repression but, like Obama and most Democrats, inept in reform. They are distant, arrogant, or politically paralyzed. The movement cannot possibly win a shooting war against the most efficient repressive machine the world has ever seen—the movement can take advantage of official intransigence and do-nothing inertia, and win the struggle for hearts and minds, win-over the ambivalent, and neutralize the might of the repressive forces. Face fear with fearless determination. Tactics of disruption and obstruction will be faced with all manner of "riot" control technology, police tear gas, clubbing, arrest, and jailing. Some will be killed. For every repression of legitimate protest, popular indignation will grow and the repressive forces will be more hemmed in.

Immigrant Labor and Scapegoating

Why now all the hysteria about Illegal Immigrants and a renewed campaign against Islamic terrorism extended to the home front, even to presumed citizen sympathizers of terrorism? The campaign is mainly an attempt to displace anger against the system that has, since the 1980s, and grossly since 2008, severely eroded the class situation of millions of working and middle-class people. The degradation of work and insecurity of employment forced upon the working class and the downgrading of the middle class are real sources of fear within these classes, very convenient for a divide and conquer strategy. The blame for ills induced by the system is placed on innocent parties, these days Muslims and immigrants.

The context of scapegoating is within the larger framework of obliterated consciousness. When goodly sectors of the population cannot distinguish illusionary propaganda from the reality of private troubles, people can become mired in anguish and resentment, and direct their feelings against perceived targets that are also victimized by the system. Henry Giroux refers to a "civic illiteracy in which it becomes increasingly impossible to connect the everyday problems that people face with larger social forces—thus depoliticizing their own sense of agency…. Is it any wonder that politics is now mediated through a spectacle of anger, violence, humiliation and rage…? Paralyzing us in a sea of resentment waiting to be manipulated by extremists…." [10] This "civic illiteracy" meant millions of votes for Donald Trump.

There are 12 million people in the United States that are considered "illegal" or "undocumented" immigrants. Nearly all flee their countries of origin where conditions of life are impossible and are seeking opportunity. The largest number is from Mexico and Central America, but nearly every country on earth shifts some of its "surplus population" to America and Europe. In the United States, they find jobs in textile and apparel factories, agriculture, and services such as restaurants, household work, and gardening…. They constitute about 5% of the labor force and earn 41% of wage levels of native workers in the same occupations within the formal economy and have no benefits. Totally contrary to popular belief, undocumented workers do not have access to public benefits such as unemployment insurance, workmen's compensation if injured, food stamps, Medicaid, social security.… Many employers, fearing penalties for illegal employment, pay employment taxes, but the worker can never collect what is taken out of his or her pay. Proper identification is required for any of these benefits and the undocumented fear incarceration and deportation if they apply for benefits (The social security and Medicare funds are augmented by billions of dollars from this source). The sexual division of labor and pay discrimination in the social fabric is grossly reproduced in the informal sector. Immigrant women workers make well under than half of what undocumented men earn.

Throughout American history, immigration has been permitted, within legal guidelines, and with discriminatory and racist treatment as portrayed in Chap. 5. The guidelines were ignored whenever sectors of business needed a source of cheap labor in a precarious situation. In the 1980s, Congress and the Reagan administration passed legislation permitting the legalization of several million immigrants. Immigration since those years continued relatively unrestrained by increased border controls and harsh treatment of captured illegals. This was very convenient to sectors of industry and agriculture needing cheap and docile labor and to marginal small business trying to survive. Then, in the 2000s, immigration reform became politically impossible; more and more strident calls and policies for cracking down on immigrants became the norm. This really reached extreme forms with Republican candidate Donald Trump's sensationalist comments in July 2015 that Mexico sends its rapists, drug dealers, and murderers to the United States, with the other 2016 zombie candidates demurring a little but still falling into immigrant scapegoating. Nativism and anti-immigrant sentiments are increasingly evident throughout Europe, leading directly to the vote for British withdrawal from the European Union.

The Interconnections of Racism, Sexism, Scapegoating and Other Evils in the Reproduction of the System

Being white is an attitude that is taught through a process of socialization such that it becomes a system of privileged advantage that is not usually even consciously recognized. Being black or brown, on the other hand, is a social condition of oppression. Similarly with being male. Being male is an attitude of privilege, being female is a subordinated condition. Racist and sexist attitudes, and all the other dimensions of social stratification examined in preceding analysis, are built upon a system-created *structure* of inequality in access to employment, property, education, opportunity, and life chances. The white male elite act as guardians of the social divisions and use them to enhance their own class privileges, and to divide and conquer.

Today's demagogues are bitter about "political correctness." While direct bigotry is being resurrected to some extent in the political culture, it is not inflammatory remarks about blacks, women, Muslims, immigrants, and gays that is the problem—it is the economic forces and the political and social policies that structure inequality, discrimination, and subjugation that must be combated.

Combating racism, sexism, and artificial social divisions requires a pedagogy of the oppressed that teaches that whites and males have false privileges that are injurious to them as human beings. It requires a unity of class forces that welcomes diversity and fights battles on all fronts. Chris Crass addresses these issues in *Toward Collective Liberation: Anti-Racist Organizing, Feminist Praxis, and Movement Building Strategy.*[11]

NOTES

1. Selma James, *Sex, Race and Class*, PM Press, 2012, p. 51.
2. See publications of the Institute for Women's Policy Research for this kind of data and analysis of issues that affect women, www.iwpr.org
3. See the table of female occupations and unionization rates, p. 119 in Stephanie Luce and Mark Brenner, "Women and Class: What Has Happened in Forty Years?" in Michel D. Yates, *More Unequal: Aspects of Class in the United States*, Monthly Review Press, 2007.
4. From Selma James, *Sex, Race and Class*, p. 238.
5. Luce and Brenner, p. 130.
6. See Barbara Ehrenreich's analysis of the widely published study by Case and Denton of the spike in the death rate of white males and the critique of Ehrenreich by Schuman and Lui at http://www.portside.org, December 9, 2015.
7. Michael Kimmel, *Angry White Men*, Nation Books, 2013. See also Kay Whitlock and Michael Bronski, *Considering Hate: Violence, Goodness, and Justice in American Culture and Politics*, Beacon

Press, 2015. In the same vein as Kimmel is an excellent work by Stephen Eric Bronner, *The Bigot: Why Prejudice Persists*, Yale University Press, 2013.

8. Michael Moore, *Stupid White Men*, HarperCollins, 2001.
9. Martha E. Gimenez, "Back to Class: Reflections on the Dialectics of Class and Identity" in Michael Yates (ed.), *More Unequal: Aspects of Class in the United States*, Monthly Review Press, 2007.
10. Henry Giroux, "Zombie Politics and Culture in an Age of Casino Capitalism," www.truthout.org/HenryGiroux/
11. Chris Crass, *Toward Collective Liberation: Anti-racist Organizing, Feminist Praxis, and Movement Building Strategy*, PM Press, 2013.

CHAPTER 8

The Ultimate Means of the Rule of Capital: Repression, Terror, and War

Red Alert, Deadly Virus, WMASP

Dangerous Organism Poses Continuing Threat to World Health. In 2014, the World Health Organization drafted a Red Alert for a virus more deadly than Ebola, WMASPV, White Male Anglo Saxon Protestant Virus. The symptoms of those infected are propensity to violence and war, often cloaked in xenophobia and ideologies of racism and sexism, and exaggerated feelings of privilege. The virus infects mostly males in areas of the world where privilege and power are most entrenched. Research has determined that the virus induces an elevated level of testosterone, a stifling of cognitive rationality, a curtailment of moral judgment to distinguish right from wrong, and unrestrained greed. Some women of the privileged classes also become infected by intimate relations with the male species of their class. WMASPV is thought to have originated in Western Europe centuries ago and transmitted through the centuries like the plague. In the twentieth century, a particularly virulent outbreak occurred in Europe in the 1930s and 1940s. Competition for control of empire went together with racism, xenophobia, glorification of the master race and the omnipotent state. Millions were annihilated in death camps. Twenty million Russians died by infestation from WMASPV spread by the invading German army. Through early colonization by the heavily infected British imperialists, WMASPV became established in North America, where today it is the most entrenched and vicious in its manifestations. Today, the American variant of WMASPV is engaged in a violent struggle with a

© The Author(s) 2017

D.L. Johnson, *Social Inequality, Economic Decline, and Plutocracy,*
DOI 10.1007/978-3-319-49043-4_8

mutant of the virus, MMFV, Male Muslim Fanaticism Virus, endogenous to the Middle Eastern sector of the world, with African variants. It is hypothesized that MMFV first developed as a resistant antibody, then to be mutated into a rival organism. Only the most determined and firm measures will succeed in eventual control of these most dangerous organisms.

The Fourth means, but no means the least that the ruling class rules is by force and violence.

IMPERIAL AMBITION AND WAR

America has a penchant for declaring war on intractable problems. Wars are embarked on whatever occurs to the powers that be that are viewed as problematic. The 1960s war on poverty, designed to counterbalance the war on Vietnam, has been long-abandoned in favor of neo-liberal poverty creation and a war on the poor. The social programs of the 1960s, in the domestic context of cold war and associated counter-insurgency wars, were superseded by the war on drugs (derived from strategies of the war on the poor and the war on crime in America, and counter-insurgency wars abroad), war on Afghanistan, war on Iraq, and the most intractable of all, the war on terror.

None of these wars has actually been won and fighting the wars creates more problems than are solved. War on one country in the Middle East works to extend conflict to other countries. The war on drugs has been entirely counter-productive. No czar heading the Drug Enforcement Agency seems to realize that the problem of drugs is not one to war against in Colombia and Mexico; demand in the U.S. market creates supply abroad, but starts with large sectors of the U.S. population seeking chemical relief from their life situation and the anomie of social dissolution. In May 2016, CNN broadcast a program on the use of opioids in the United States. The United States is only 5% of the world's population but consumes 80% of world opioids. Millions of Americans are addicted and thousands die from overdoses. The pharmaceuticals that manufacture the prescription opioids probably get their opium from Afghanistan. The social dissolution that induces drug use in the United States produces not only crime, but also the war on crime, putting millions of people in prison—and narco-states in Mexico and Colombia, and corruption and enrichment of American puppets in Afghanistan.

War on Afghanistan began with the 1980s U.S. cold war worry about Afghan secularist attempts to modernize and the supportive Soviet intervention. The CIA created and armed the future Islamic militants. There is always a war prelude of beat the drums loudly. "The Reds are in Afghanistan." In Afghanistan, anti-communist intervention led naturally to the beginnings of Islamic extremism. The Iraq War was preceded by official lies about non-existent weapons of mass destruction. When war becomes a mindset, there is no debate, questions are answered before they are asked, the strategy and tactics are defined by declaration—military force, drone attacks, secret renditions, invasion and occupation abroad. On the home front, the complement is NSA spying on citizens, FBI harassment, creation of a culture of fear, police containment and repression of ghettos and poor communities, construction of more and more prisons.... There is no endpoint, only deepening chaos, engendered counter-violence of the warred upon, and escalation of the war effort to ever wider theaters with deeper thrusts.

Let's begin with Iraq. Prior to the 2003 invasion, the regime of Saddam Hussein was portrayed as a rogue state. Iraq was an authoritarian regime with nationalist ambitions, but hardly a threat to neighboring countries after the defeats in Iran and Kuwait, and certainly no direct menace to the United States, only to the neo-Conservative fashioned vision of a new world order. What the United States wanted specifically was the oil that Iraq sits on, to remove an insubordinate nationalist from the scene, and, more generally, to situate Iraq as an example to all nations that resist being incorporated into the Bush Family and Associates Inc. dream of the new world order, an order fired by oil fever and based on neo-liberalism in the extreme, implemented by imperial power. The coercive power of the institutions that enforce globalization and neo-liberal policies—the IMF, the World Bank, the WTO, the UN, the Treasury and Fed, and Wall Street— are not sufficient to insure conformity. Enforcement requires coercion and military force exercised by the United States.

In the American construction of a new world (dis)order, in the aftermath of 9/11 the United States drew upon the experience of 60 years of anti-communist and anti-nationalist interventions throughout the world and became a super rogue state.

The hypocrisy of the cries of the wounded giant after 9/11, hiding the imperial design since 2001 in a war on terror, was once concealed in the rhetoric of the cold war. Communism, which came to be defined as almost any threat of change to the established order, nationalism especially, had to be, and was, fought by any means necessary. In Indonesia in the early 1960s, the United States fully backed a military coup that overthrew the nationalist government and killed 500,000 persons said to be communists. The torture of political prisoners was not unique to the Bush era; it had its origin in CIA programs in Latin America under President Kennedy in the early 1960s. During the 1962 Cuban missile crisis, Kennedy brought the world to the edge of nuclear holocaust by attempts to turn back the Cuban revolution with the Bay of Pigs invasion, the embargo, sponsoring terrorist strikes within Cuba, and the real threat in 1962 of American military intervention that the Russian missiles prevented. The fiery explosions that destroyed the World Trade Center appear as mere candles in comparison with the napalm that cremated untold numbers of Vietnamese. In the counter-insurgency war, 1.7 million National Liberation Front fighters were killed, with more than two million civilian casualties in Vietnam, not including victims in Cambodia and Laos. The dead constituted 21% of the population, and 5.3 million more were wounded. Nine thousand Vietnamese villages were destroyed, North Vietnamese targets were carpet-bombed, and 19 million gallons of herbicide poisoned the land and the people. These were war crimes paralleling those of Nazi Germany.

While facing ignoble defeat in Vietnam, the United States was successful in Latin America. The overthrow of democratic governments by right-wing military dictatorships in the 1960s and 1970s, as in Argentina, Brazil, Uruguay and Chile—Chile, the first 9/11, 1973 bombing of the Presidential Palace and the death of President Allende and the nation's democracy—stemmed the socialist tide by disappearing socialists. The generals and death squads in Guatemala and El Salvador, with the blessings and aid of Ronald Reagan, kept the guerrilla insurgents in check through village massacres and brutal repression. The U.S.-armed Contra forces smashed any hope for the Nicaraguan people. Fifty years of embargo and attempts to overthrow the Castro government kept the revolution isolated on one small island. (They even tried to get Fidel to smoke an exploding cigar and doused a gift of a wetsuit with lethal chemicals.) Congress finally banned assassination as a legitimate foreign policy tool, but the word later became Bin Laden and Qaddafi, and any presumed terrorist anywhere, dead or alive, preferably dead.

The dark side of neo-liberal ideology and policy that guides globalization in today's world is the resort to interventionism and militarism. As an integrated operating system of assumptions and policy prescriptions, neo-liberalism (explored in depth in Chap. 9) is imposed by the extension of market relations worldwide; as a set of policies by international financial institutions; in "free trade;" as an ideology by the promulgation of thought hegemony. It is imperial thinking in its most sophisticated and modern expression. Thought is backed by force, historically in the age of classic imperialism, and in the present era of globalization.

The Spanish colonization of America was based on brutal conquest. The British fleet and armies carved up Asia and Africa. In the twentieth century, competing colonial powers—British, Dutch, Belgian, German— wrought total havoc in Africa and Asia, and led directly to World War I, in its essence a war of competing imperialisms. In the 1930s and 1940s, Japan entered the scene in Asia and the Pacific, and Nazi Germany conquered Western Europe and surged into Eastern Europe and the Soviet Union. World War II was, again, fundamentally a war of competing impe- rialisms. The Japanese wanted to wrest control of the Pacific Rim from the United States and the British out of Asia. The Nazis wanted the British Empire and French, Dutch, and Belgian colonies. With American military and economic supremacy following World War II, most of the traditional imperialism of the British and Europeans was defeated, in the main by nationalist struggles for liberation. The British were forced out of India, the French out of Algeria and later from Indo China, the Belgians out of the Congo, and the Dutch out of Indonesia. (See my personal experiences in the U.S. military in the 1950s in endnote.[1])

The Americans went to war, cold war against the Soviets, hot wars against revolutionary forces in Korea and, later, Vietnam. In Latin America, efforts from mercenary invasion to terrorism and embargo failed to destroy the Cuban revolution, but were successful in efforts to instill reactionary military regimes in South America and turn back insurgent forces in Central America. In short, world history since 1945 has been written by attempts to hold back threats to American supremacy by war and subversion, with occasional resort to diplomacy to facilitate domi- nation. Promoted as fomenting democracy and progress, magnanimous America was, in reality, better seen as sledge hammer America, or, as time went on, oil slick America.[2] Then, by the 1990s, the Soviet "evil empire" had collapsed and revolutionary movements were largely contained. The Soviet Union went down; its skull fragmented by continuous blows of the sledge hammer and the severed corpse of communism was claimed by neo- liberal internationalism. China successfully resisted the sledge hammer but was seduced by runaway shops seeking cheap labor. Vietnam turned the sledge hammer around to beat the aggressor into ignoble defeat, to then choose to integrate the nation from out of the flames of napalm into the global economy. Emulating the success of the state capitalism of China,

Vietnam now exports cheap manufactures and agricultural commodities, rice, fish, coffee. American focus shifted to oil fever and rolling back Arab nationalism. War and occupations of Afghanistan and Iraq and interventions everywhere in the Middle East created a fearsome new enemy, Islamic jihad.

Then, in 2014 and 2015, the United States stepped up its campaigns against its chief rivals, Russia and China. The campaigns included both economic and military measures. The stable rule of empire involves curtailing the power of potential rivals.

First, came the American support for the extreme right-wing coup in Ukraine. This led to the popular vote in the Crimea to dissociate from Ukraine and join Russia. Then, the ethnic Russians on the Eastern border with Russia revolted against the policies and repression unleased by the Kiev regime. Reputed Russian support of the rebels led to economic sanctions being imposed by the NATO countries on Russia. The Ukraine is now a key country in the NATO military encirclement of Russia. This was followed in October 2015 by virulent U.S. critiques of Russian military intervention in Syria, viewed as a prop for the Assad government. In 2016, there is some nominal Russian and American cooperation in a joint campaign against ISIS in Syria, but the United States maintains its goal of deposing Assad, continuing the established pattern of regime change of governments even remotely nationalist in orientation. The State Department staff of Clinton-type warriors in 2016 urged Obama to send troops fight Syrian government forces and establish no-fly zones, which would greatly enhance the cold war against Russia already in motion.

Washington is bent on trying to limit China's growing economic and political clout as a rival world power. U.S. military presence has been extended by a massive naval build-up in the South China Sea and extending armed forces agreements with Japan, the Philippines, and Australia. In the economic sphere, the Trans-Pacific Partnership (TPP) Agreement with Pacific nations is specifically promoted as a measure to open the Pacific region more fully to U.S. capital with the end of curtailing China's influence in the area. Edward Snowden released an NSA document that indicated extensive cyber-espionage of Chinese industries, while President Obama accused China of cyber-espionage just as President Xi Jinping was arriving in the United States to visit with U.S. high tech companies about cooperative agreements. This was anti-China sabotage that reflects the influence of the most militarist power configurations in Washington.

ON THE INFAMOUS, SATAN HUSSEIN

The United States war against Iraq has a familiar history, at least to those who follow historical events. The United States cultivates clients then, when they fail to achieve desired objectives or don't toe the line, deposes them or wages war. This was the case of Ngo Danh Diem in Vietnam, Ferdinand Marcos in the Philippines, and Manuel Noriega in Panama. All were American assets that later turned into liabilities. A stunning example of how the United States cultivates assets that later turn against imperial power is Afghanistan. There, the secular, modernizing democratic regime with a communist representation of the 1980s faced insurgency by Islamic tribesmen. The Russians came in to support the Afghan progressives. The CIA then organized and equipped with sophisticated weaponry the Mujahedeen and the most retrograde elements of Islamic character to take on the government and its Soviet supporters. Osama Bin Laden and Al Qaeda got started as American assets, and the Taliban rose out of the war against secularism, nationalism, and modernization. The insurgent reactionaries, strengthened with American military aid, drove out the Russians and hanged the head of state from a Kabul lamppost with his testicles stuffed in his mouth. (In Libya, the Islamic elements working with the United States and NATO murdered Qaddafi by sodomization with a bayonet).

In 1959, the CIA recruited Saddam Hussein at the age of 22 years to carry out an assassination against the leader of the anti-monarchical revolution. Hussein later came to prominence in the Baathist Party in 1968, a moderately secular and nationalist political party. Hussein was a main participant in the purge of Iraqi communist and other progressives who were arrested, executed, and exiled, leaving only the opposing Sunni and Shiite elements who fled to mosques. In 1979, the United States assisted their man in a palace coup in the expectation that Hussein would take on the Iranian clerical revolutionaries, which he obediently did in a fierce war debilitating to both oil producing countries, giving the Israeli's more breathing space. The United Stated supplied the "Good Saddam" regime with the technology to produce biological and chemical weapons to take on the revolt-minded Kurds as well as the Iranians. These weapons of mass destruction were destroyed after the first Iraq War, but the accusation of continued possession became a key justification for the 2003 invasion. In 1991, Saddam was an ambitious man and made a grab for Kuwait's oil deposits. The United States cannot tolerate disloyalty and nationalist ambition. "Saddam the Good" became "Satan Hussein," number one enemy of the "Empire of the Good", led by Father Bush, the Texas oilman. In this convoluted history, "Satan" got his due, but it took a while for the Central Agency of Godly Intelligence to find the former CIA-created "Good Osama Bin Laden" in the Afghan fight against the Soviets who had later become "Osama Evil Incarnate."

When nationalism in any form is defeated, be it Nasser in Egypt, Assad in Syria, Qaddafi in Libya, modernizing regimes in Lebanon and Turkey, or Saddam Hussein in Iraq, either you get military dictatorship subservient to U.S. power, or secular governments are replaced by hatred and violent actions of reactionary extremists and the chaos of religious and tribal warfare, resulting in national disintegration. The incorporation of Turkey into the global system in the 1980s meant a regime practicing neo-liberal economics, political despotism, and Islamist conservatism. Egypt is the fiercest military dictatorship in the world today. In Iraq, the occupation and internal strife has divided Turkomans from Kurds, Kurds war against Arabs, Sunnis fight Shias, one Shia faction is pitted against another, Baathist against all, and American clients in the puppet government repress insurgents. Syria and Libya are torn apart by militias armed by the United States. And now the fiercest of all insurgencies in Iraq and Syria, ISIS, extending into North Africa with Egyptian aircraft called upon to bomb ISIS targets in Libya. American interventions have now precipitated the greatest refugee crisis since World War II, with millions escaping for their lives from Syria, Iraq, and Libya. Neighboring Lebanon, a tiny nation of two million persons in 2013, has doubled in population with two million Syrian refugees. The massive refugee influx into Europe has there provoked a nativist response that is threatening to the future of Europe, beginning with the British exit from the European Union.

A Super Rogue State

In a never-ending campaign, the super rogue under Bush and continuing under Obama declares its right to use unilateral preemptive military means against whatever nation or political group or social movement is deemed to present a challenge to imperial design. With drone attacks, the executive branch, with Obama personally authorizing targets, used the terror of drone bombing to kill anyone anywhere at any time for any secretive reason based on classified intelligence gathered by a secret process and carried out by unidentified officials giving orders to anonymous computer technicians.

The super rogue uses economic and military aid to construct and fortify client rogues that pursue policies of official terrorism, Israel being a prime example but including allies such as Saudi Arabia, a country where the most retrograde Islamic culture flourishes and produces Islamic terrorists in great numbers. The super rogue uses terrorist means to wage a war on terrorism. The root causes of the terrorism of the desperate are totally ignored. Terrorists are to be exterminated, the horror of which incites resistance, initiating an escalating chain of violence.

The super rogue prefers working diplomatically to forge alliances with friendly nations but will strong-arm when necessary. It expects European allies to be, like Great Britain, vassals in the imperial system, and France takes the forefront from time to time, as in Libya and again in Syria after the Paris attacks of November 2015. The super rogue bribes and coerces lesser states to follow its dictates, or threatens them with sanctions, such as in Iraq prior to the invasion, and Iran, Libya, Syria, and Venezuela, when they exercise some independence. The super rogue works to dominate international institutions, successfully with the IMF, World Bank, and World Trade Organization and, when it does not get its way, seeks to undermine or to make institutions irrelevant to its actions, as in several UN agencies, even the UN itself. The super rogue violates international law, established treaties, and human rights at will and with impunity, and then celebrates these violations as bringing freedom and democracy. The super rogue fails to ratify internationally promulgated treaties on nuclear test bans and weapons, labor codes, economic and cultural rights of women and minorities, pollution, endangered species... name any worthy cause and the United States opposes or ignores the effort.

The construction of the super rogue state, initiated after the collapse of the Soviet Union, was made possible by the events of September 11, 2001. The Burning Bush needed his violent homologues, his mirror images, Osama Bin Laden and Saddam Hussein. Of course, there was the 1980s prelude of the CIA arming of the Islamic forces in Afghanistan. After the first Gulf War, the Father Bush and Clinton administrations got the U.N. to install a sanctions regime against Iraq. This devastated the social fabric of the nation and tightened the strong arm of Saddam Hussein. Imports of food and medicines were cut off and the mortality rate of children under five years increased from 56 per 1000 in 1990 to 131 per 1000 in the mid- to late 1990s. No one listened to Allah speak wisdom: "Feed thine Enemies," or "A Burning Bush will ignite the whole world, put it out," or "War is terrorism with a bigger budget."

Bush pushed his Iraq "shock and awe." In the first two months of the 2003 invasion, American bombers conducted over 29,000 air strikes, killing tens of thousands of non-combatants. One body count study found 46% of the victims were female and 39% children. Americans dropped the BVLU-82B 15,000 pound bombs with a blast radius of 5,000 feet, cremating everyone in that space. More than two million Iraqis fled to neighboring countries; 2.7 million left their homes for safer environs within Iraq. Half the world's refugees have proceeded from Iraq and Afghanistan, at least 5 million people. When Syria and Africa are included, the number of refugees in the recent period reaches more than 8 million escaping to other countries and four million internally displaced. This approaches the refugee problem during World War II. In Iraq, years of occupation followed, with torture in prisons, internecine killings, bombings by occupation resisters, mass displacement of millions of Iraqis, and the total sectarian fragmentation of the nation—which then opened the path for the extremist Islamic elements to form ISIS and carry on their brutal war of revenge.

The military-corporate complex of the State of National Insecurity saw to it that the war in Iraq became increasingly privatized; by 2007, there were 180,000 private contractors, outnumbering American troops even after the "surge" by 20,000. Many of these are mercenaries, some of whom, like Blackwater Inc., had no qualms about indiscriminately shooting down civilians. Apparently, neither the troops nor the mercenaries are very good shots, one study found that it took 250,000 rounds of ammunition for each insurgent killed. The yearly use of small-arms ammunition totaled 1.8 billion rounds in the mid-2000s, with many a bullet purchased from Israel.[3]

Fifteen years of intervention in Afghanistan and Iraq have resulted in at least 1.3 million deaths, quite possibly, according to Physicians for Social Responsibility, more than two million. And that does not count the casualties in Libya, Syria, and Yemen and in other areas where war now rages. In the war between ISIS and American-supported forces in Iraq in 2015, 8.2 million Iraqis were in need of emergency assistance of food and medical supplies and, in mid-2015, a gross humanitarian situation built up in Yemen as a result of Saudi air assaults with U.S. weaponry. The Americans got Turkey into the war against ISIS in 2015, but they preferred to ignore ISIS and war against the Kurds, the only sensible and effective force fighting in the devastated area, and shot down a Russian aircraft confronting ISIS. American and allied troop deaths are modest in comparison, around 8,000 killed, 50,000 wounded, 400,000 with post-traumatic stress syndrome—and large numbers of military personnel suicides. The military onslaught in Iraq was followed by an occupation designed to demolish a society and replace it with an economic order based on the policies of neo-liberalism—privatization, shock therapy to the economy, lay-off of 500,000 government employees, the confiscation of oil money and revamping of the oil industry to favor foreign interests; a social order transformed into a war of all against all; and a political system based on sectarianism, cronyism, and the corruption of officials placed in their government posts by the American occupiers.... Naturally, there was resistance, the occupiers and their Shiite puppets first took on the Saddam loyalists, then the Baathist remnants, and, finally, Sunni insurgents involving counter-insurgency killings, torture in prisons, and the dismantling of all democratic forms, seemingly perpetual internecine warfare....

Afghanistan is somewhat different than Iraq; there, the violence is less internecine than a scattered population against the occupiers and their corrupt American selected puppets. It has become clear that Afghans are very diverse peoples but have one thing in common—the will to resist. They resist in spite of tens of thousands of casualties, millions exiled to Pakistan or roaming the countryside homeless. All Afghans, except the graft-grabbers, the profiteers from opium, and the American puppets, are consigned to a subhuman existence of extreme deprivation. The asymmetry of power is awesome, sophisticated weaponry and long-crafted counter-insurgency tactics for 15 years against the resilience of the wretched of the earth. Surely, no imperial power in history, from Rome to the Ottomans to the British, has inflicted such violent oppression and suffering on peoples whose only desire is to be left in peace. America, having crushed secular nationalism as the way forward to more democratic societies, cannot defeat the resistance, the "terrorism," in Afghanistan or anywhere in the region, religiously motivated or not, because it has become the scream of the wretched and oppressed.

And the monetary toll foisted upon American taxpayers in these two wars? At least $4.4 trillion, not including interest on borrowed money to finance war budgets, another $7.9 trillion as the bonds mature. In 2014, 27% of tax receipts went to the military, with an additional 18% to cover past military actions. In the first year of the Obama administration, coinciding with Obama's receipt of the Nobel Peace Prize, war spending reached the highest level since World War II.

There is a growing literature on the Iraq and Afghanistan wars. Especially noteworthy are Michael Schwartz, *War Without End* and Jessica Stern, *Terror in the Name of God: Why Religious Militants Kill.*[4] On Muslim cultures and Islam, there is little published of worth. I wanted to include a section in this chapter on the region and the incitement to Islamic-phobia, but the literature is so corrupted by Western academic "orientalism," the "clash of civilizations," militaristic garbage, and related nonsense that I gave up trying to make the topic sensible to American readers. There is one source that I can highly recommend, the work of Aijaz Ahmad, a former colleague of mine at Rutgers University. Ahmad located in India for many years is now in exile at a University in the United States. Especially relevant to understanding this area of the world is "Islam, Islamisms and the West". Ahmad, an extraordinarily insightful cultural, sociological, and political analyst, has highly informative books and articles on related topics, and is a frequent contributor to the Indian English language journal, *Frontline*, on-line articles available at the journal website, www.frontline.com[5] Samir Amin is a good source to complement Ahmad, especially in dealing with Arab nationalism. Amin can be read as background to war on Libya and regional nationalism. A well-documented study of the way in which the CIA and the Pentagon foment Islamic insurgency is Horace Campbell on the NATO/U.S. attack in 2011–2012 on Libya.[6] The Libya situation will be analyzed shortly.

It is truly distressing to realize that a war on terror is being conducted with terrorist means far exceeding those for which the super rogue was the target on September 11, 2001. Two events on Mayday 2011 provoked my sense of outrage beyond its usual limits. Most days I can watch the news with a mild sense of disgust at the state of the world or dismay that any decent human being with normal intelligence could believe the deceitful propaganda passed on to the gullible as news. The first event was the NATO bombing of Qaddafi's family compound in Tripoli, killing his son and three grandchildren. It is obvious that this was a targeted assassination attempt against a head of state, reportedly carried out by the French contingent of NATO and certainly with a green light from the United States. The "get Qaddafi" pronouncements had been circulating in the United States for a time. The second event was the unprecedented late Sunday night May 1, 2011 gathering of the press at the White House for President Obama's proud announcement of the killing of Osama Bin Laden in Pakistan. Justifiable homicide? If we are to believe what we are told (mostly we should not), Bin Laden was the mastermind of the September 11, 2001 attack which killed over 3000 persons in the World Trade Center. This fugitive managed to hide out for ten years. And the Navy Seals, trained as a killing force, carried out the assassination reportedly without prior notification to Pakistan of a pending operation. (In mid-2015, there were news items that, in fact, Bin Laden's location had been known to Pakistani intelligence, even that they were holding him captive, and they finally gave him away.) Since the building was surrounded, one might think that a surrender order was appropriate, but no, the intent was to kill. I suppose that one could say that those who live by violence die that way. Should not we then understand the killing in September 2012 of the American Ambassador to Libya and several others in the Benghazi Consulate (which, in fact, was a CIA station) in the same light? The Republicans tried to smear Secretary Clinton with a scandalous cover-up of a Benghazi fiasco. But the Ambassador killed by insurgents was a U.S. point man directing the Libyan insurrection against Qaddafi and a CIA coordinator from Benghazi to send Libyan and other jihadists and armaments to Syrian insurgents. Later, I analyze in depth the Libya situation and Secretary Clinton's role. She lied to the House Committee investigating events at Benghazi. As seems always to be the case with top political figures, Clinton enjoyed immunity for instigating the Libya intervention and lying about her role to Congress. This is of far greater consequence than using her private email to send secret government messages, but it is not even an issue.

The war on terror is a gigantic fraud, a largely successful attempt to provide ideological justification for America's imperial ambition in the oil-rich Middle East, a strategic plan to demolish any form of Arab nationalism, a smoke screen for America's state sponsored "official" terrorism. This terrorism is exercised far in excess of anything that Islamic extremists have perpetrated, or have the capacity to do so. The term "terrorism" is a one-dimensional catchword, an ideological construct forged to instill fear, to encourage the flag wavers, and to build political consensus and popular support for violence and war. This allows plausibility for the official wisdom that invading another country—Afghanistan first, then Iraq, later NATO serving as surrogate in Libya, and now Syria and Yemen, and in the process cremating tens of thousands of civilians with bombs—is not terrorism. People being burned alive and blown to bits are acts of terrorism, whether this occurs in Baghdad or the Pakistani frontier, Tripoli, Kabul, or New York. Of course, this was not all Bush and Company and the Pentagon, it has a history—and a continuation under the president the majority elected in 2008, and with greater reluctance and skepticism again in 2012, to put a stop to wars, torture, and violations of international law and human rights. How does one characterize President Reagan's 1986 bombardment of Libya in an attempt to assassinate Qaddafi, an alleged promoter of state-sponsored terrorism, killing his daughter and many civilians? Or the deaths during Reagan's invasion of Grenada? Or the first Bush's invasion of Panama, killing hundreds, in the effort to extra-officially extradite a general who had the temerity to stop taking the CIA's money (from drug trafficking) and not be very supportive of American-sponsored violent counter-insurgency in Central America? Or Clinton's human devastation in Iraq with sanctions and no-fly edicts. Let's call the military interventions of the Americans for what they are: *official terrorism*. A long history of official terrorism is the root cause of the suicide bombings and other terrible acts of the terrorism of the occupied, the oppressed, the victims, and the desperate. Were the United States to end all forms of official terrorism, become a good world citizen practicing non-intervention, the terrorism of the desperate would diminish, if not disappear.

And what of the official terrorism of the client states set-up or supported and armed to the teeth by the United States? The nasty confrontation between the United States and the Islamic State of Iran had a great deal to do with American support for their client, the repressive regime of the Shah. Iran had good reason to develop deterrent weaponry, given the U.S. nudge to Iraq invading Iran in 1979, followed by Israeli threats to bomb Iran and all manner of hostile actions designed to isolate and bring down the Iranian government. After many years of crippling economic sanctions, finally the United States and its allies applied the extreme of coercion to get Iran to agree not to develop nuclear weapons, much to the consternation of the American warriors and Israel. But nuclear disarmament by the big powers that hold such weapons, and Israel, Pakistan, and India, is not on the agenda. Finally, Obama did something sensible, only to be attacked by the war crowd. Perhaps Trump will pull back on the 2015 deal between the United States and other powers on Iran's nuclear program. There is little doubt that there will be further war on Syria. Both are countries that resist as best they can to being incorporated into the global empire. In April 2016, President Obama dispatched an additional 250 Special Forces to Syria and there is talk of further U.S. intervention.

Saddam Hussein got his due in 2003 but the chaos left from the invasion and occupation leaves open to question whether the Americans will have their perpetual access to the region's coveted oil deposits. The Philippines, too, had a great deal of trouble with Islamic rebels. The origins of this conflict go back to the years of the corrupt dictator Marcos, kept in power with American military and economic aid. Indonesia can be considered one of these violent client states, the demise of nationalism there began with the slaughter of a half million communists. Israel, a nation that engages in state-sponsored terrorism in the extreme, has received more American military and economic aid than any country in the world, allowing the continuation of the Palestine occupation and violent repression of the resistance. Withholding that aid will likely end Palestinian attacks on Israel, establish a Palestinian state alongside Israel, and go a long way toward making a more peaceful region. Instead, in 2016 Obama negotiated the largest ever military aid program to Israel.

The machinations of the United States in the Middle East, its endless pursuit of the war on terror, reach points of the truly absurd. I received an email one day with a blurb on absurdity, no author identified:

Clear as Mud

"Are you confused by what is going on the Middle East? Let me explain. We support the Iraqi government in the fight against Islamic State. We don't like IS, but IS is supported by Saudi Arabia, whom we do like. We don't like President Assad in Syria. We support the fight against him, but not IS, which is also fighting against him. We don't like Iran, but Iran supports the Iraqi government against IS. So some of our friends support our enemies and some of our enemies are our friends, and some of our enemies are fighting against our other enemies, whom we want to lose, but we don't want our enemies who are fighting our enemies to win. If the people we want to defeat are defeated, they might be replaced by people we like even less. And all this was started by us invading a country to drive out terrorists who weren't actually there until we went in to drive them out. Do you understand now?" (Insightful author not identified).

The Directorate of National Insecurity knows that a war on terror is a never-ending cycle of creating terrorists, medieval and evil as they are. Evil begets evil, the better to serve the devil of empire. One wonders, what other country than America Inc. could be so stupid as to spend trillions of dollars in wars in Afghanistan and Iraq against lightly armed insurgents and gain nothing but chaos? But the blowback is predictable, if not intended. The war on jihadist ghosts keeps the money flowing and the culture of fear deepened. Are war and official terrorism in the Middle East a theatre of the absurd? Indeed. Stupidity? Maybe. Designed chaos? More likely than stupidity. Who benefits from violence and war is cogently addressed by Pilisuk and Rountree.[7]

LIBYA: ONE NATIONALIST DOWN, A NATION DESTROYED, ISIS UP

In the first months of 2011, popular revolts in Tunisia and Egypt sparked what came to be called the "Arab Spring." With a quite different character to the insurgency against established regimes, revolts spread to Libya and Syria. An armed rebellion occurred in the oil-rich Libyan province of Benghazi. The Libyan government of Qaddafi responded with threatened force. The United States, Britain, and France rushed a resolution through the UN Security Council on the "responsibility to protect" in reference to the Benghazi rebels facing the Libyan armed forces. As so often happens with UN interventions instigated by world powers, the resolution was forcefully extended far beyond its stated purpose. To "protect" insurgents, NATO aircraft unleased more than 9000 strike sorties, many against civilian targets. Uranium-laced warheads were used. Qaddafi's family was killed by bombs, and his Tripoli home and headquarters were destroyed. The Qaddafi strongholds of Misurata and Sirte were carpet-bombed. Up to 30,000 civilians died in bombardments and killings by insurgent militias, most of them of Islamist character. The NATO/U.S. air campaign to "protect" rebels in Benghazi became a campaign for regime change, the destruction of the Libyan state, dissolution of society, and the killing of Qaddafi.

The 2011 effort to "get Qaddafi" had a long history. Libya is rich in oil and natural gas, has potential for electric energy from the southern desert, and a vast underground source of water to be tapped. Libya was also the most socially developed country in Africa, with a top rating on the Human Development Index. Fewer people lived below the poverty line in Libya than in the Netherlands and Libya had the lowest infant mortality rate in Africa. Shortly after achieving power in 1969, Qaddafi forced the United States out of Wheeling Air Base. In the 1970s, Libya nationalized its very substantial oil industry and became a firm supporter of OPEC. This was an inspiration for Iranian nationalization of oil in 1979 and Saudi Arabia's takeover of Aramco in the mid-1980s. In this timeframe, Kuwait, Iraq, Venezuela, Nigeria, Qatar, and the United Arab Emirates fully nationalized Western oil companies. In 1977, the United States ranked Libya high on the list of enemies. In April 1986, President Reagan ordered a bomb attack on Qaddafi's family residence in Tripoli in an unsuccessful attempt at assassination, a terrorist attack not that much different than the "terrorism" that Reagan *et al.* had accused Libya of perpetrating.

From the 1970s (until the 1990s when sanctions became too debilitating), Qaddafi had been a firm supporter of progressive and nationalist movements. Libya was important as foreign support for South Africa's African National Congress against the racist regime and diverse African liberation movements, as well as the Palestinian cause. The period 1977 to 1988 was one of confrontation with Western power. Then the sanctions hit hard. Ostensibly, the sanctions imposed from 1989 were related to the terrorist downing of a civilian aircraft over Lockerbie Scotland in 1988. Libya was accused of sending agents to do the dirty deed, although there was no credible evidence to support that accusation. The real reason for sanctions, of course, was quite different: to punish misdeeds as defined by Western powers and to curtail nationalist assertions and Libya's support for African and Middle Eastern causes. This was one part of a larger, successful war against Arab nationalism in any form. In 1996, British intelligence and the Libyan Islamic Fighting Group were foiled in a plot to assassinate Qaddafi, one of a number of attempts against his life. However, the sanctions worked, Qaddafi capitulated, and Libya was brought back more into the Western fold with opening of the oil industry and adoption of neo-liberal reforms. Nelson Mandela mediated with Britain and the United States to lift the sanctions and this was accomplished in steps from 1999 to 2004 once Libyan nationals as suspects were handed over for trial in a Netherlands Court and compensation paid by Libya to victims killed in the airliner attack. Doubts were raised whether the two convicted terrorists, imprisoned in Britain, had any affiliation with the Qaddafi government or anything to do with the explosion of the aircraft. Qaddafi and Libyan authorities were conspicuously quiet about the U.S. invasions of Afghanistan and Iraq, even offering ingratiating support for the U.S. war on terror. Establishing its anti-terrorist credentials, the government went after the Islamist opposition within Libya. Qaddafi's son Saif al-Islam emerged as the influential moderate element in the government. And young Libyans trained in the economic orthodoxy at the London School of Economics were promoted in the Libyan National Oil Corporation and state bureaucracy, introducing market reforms.

During the years prior to the NATO 2011 bombardment, Qaddafi began to depart from his prior capitulation to sanctions in search of greater economic and political independence. His most audacious move, in the eyes of the United States and British and French oil powers, was his proposal to African oil producers to shift away from petro-dollars toward another trading currency. He moved to underwrite a common African currency backed by gold to establish an African bank promoting economic union. In the financial sphere, the former role of Goldman Sachs in Libya (Libya lost $1.3 billion in 2008 in the collapse of Goldman Sachs) became threatened when the Central Bank of Libya financed the Bahrain-based Arab Banking Corporation, moving it away from the Central Bank's former servile position to Western finance capital. Secretary Clinton had close ties to Goldman Sachs and one can surmise that this had something to do with Clinton's enthusiasm to wage war and kill Qaddafi. While the prior period of liberalization had allowed foreign oil companies to participate with the Libyan National Oil Corporation, Qaddafi thought it prudent to pluralize participation. Exploration and production sharing agreements were extended to include Brazilian Petrobras, Petro China, Sinopec, and other emerging oil giants. By 2010, China became the top investor in Libya in diverse sectors. By 2011, it had proved very dangerous for Libya to engage in activities perceived as threatening both to Western financial and oil interests. Qaddafi paid with his life; the Libyan people were rewarded with violence, destitution, and the surrender of their future.

While France took the lead in the first air strike immediately after the UN "protect" resolution, the U.S. military was still in a bit of a quandary about what to do. But American NATO-based military assets to gather intelligence, conduct surveillance, and refuel French and British aircraft were quickly in place. Hundreds of air reconnaissance flights were made daily and thousands of strike sorties decimated all targets; the Blitzkrieg was total. The mission to protect civilians killed them instead. France and Britain had a political problem with other NATO contingents; Germany and Poland, skeptical of French President Sarkozy's ambitions to recolonize North Africa, flatly refused to participate and other NATO contingents held back. Only 8 of the 28 NATO countries finally participated in the war, all but France, Britain, and the United States in a pro forma fashion. Secretary of Defense Robert Gates and the Obama administration with Secretary Clinton were fully on board by June 2011, unsuccessfully pressuring the Germans and other NATO countries to participate. The aggressors could not agree on a command structure so the United States put up AFRICOM as a front and called the assault "Operation Odyssey Dawn." The land, sea, and air attack on Tripoli was called "Dawn Mermaid." The African Union made efforts to achieve a settlement and got Qaddafi to agree to step down. To head off a negotiated settlement, NATO asked the International Criminal Court (ICC) to indict Qaddafi for crimes against humanity. That says a great deal about the politically subservient nature of the ICC. Would that the ICC would try NATO leaders for war crimes in Libya, up to 50,000 dead in a war to protect, along with the Bush era criminals and the Israeli militarists slaughtering Palestinians!

Qaddafi, overwhelmed by the bombings and the well-armed Islamic insurgency, went into hiding. Located by NATO Special Forces with their technology, Sitre where he was in hiding was carpet bombed. Mercenary militants were called in and killed him by sodomization with a bayonet. America's Diplomat-In-Chief, Hillary Clinton, busy advocating taking care next of Syria's Assad and overseeing the arming of Islamic militants there, took a moment to be sage: "We came, we saw, he died." And this person who celebrates murder of a head of state was designated to be the next President of America Inc.! The results of the Libya attack, like Afghanistan, Iraq, Syria, and Somalia, is a country, no longer a nation, in total sectarian conflict of armed groupings, political stalemate, and social disarray, with Islamic extremists the dominant forces. The provisional central government, manned by neo-liberal technocrats, is impotent. During 2011, there were 1700 armed militia groups operating in different regions and communities in Libya, fighting each other, and out to kill Qaddafi. The militias committed gross violations of human rights with killings and the imprisonment and torture of many thousands. Black Africans were shot down. Government coffers with billions of dollars were impounded. The NATO-established central provisional government to this day has no control of Libyan territory or events. That government, insofar as it can do anything at all, is forced to follow the neo-liberal conditions over dispersal of government funds (which come almost entirely from oil exports that recovered after Western oil companies rushed in to divide up the spoils of war). Conditionality over use of funds is required by the IMF and World Bank. The neo-liberal policies of international finance are more easily imposed in situations of chaos. (Which is what the intransigence of financial institutions has been bringing about in Greece?)

As analyzed in Chaps. 2 and 3, the heart of the dominant class in America Inc. and extending into Europe and globally, is the oligarchy of finance, now more or less merging with international oil companies with a growing financialization of the oil business. The financiers and oilmen groom intimate relations with the American military, CIA, and the corporate contractor complex surrounding the repressive apparatus of the State of National Insecurity. Top Generals and CIA directors and operatives are intertwined in a concerted effort to forge the "New American Century." The Libyan Central Bank's establishment of the Arab Banking Corporation threatened American financial capital speculating in derivatives that depended on the recycling of petrodollars. In 2010, these interests managed to get the Treasury Department to freeze $30 billion in Libyan assets. With the support of the National Security Advisor to Obama, Samantha Powers, these interests came to the conclusion that Qaddafi had to go; Secretary Clinton gave the nod, although the Pentagon was not yet onboard.

The Benghazi event of the killing by insurgents of the American diplomat Christopher Stevens on September 11, 2012, revealed how the NATO/U.S. intervention had been transformed from saving lives to death and destruction, the dismembering of the nation, the murder of the head of state, and regime change. Stevens was no "diplomat," he was an intelligence operative headquartered not in the Tripoli Embassy as Ambassador but in Benghazi as the chief American intelligence operative. Stevens was in touch with the many militias in the area, and his death was the result of inter-militia warfare. Stevens had been appointed Ambassador to Libya in January 2012, but had been on the ground to coordinate the American presence with NATO activity and the NATO-constituted Libyan Transitional National Council from March to November 2011. Before that, Stevens had served as Chief of Mission in Libya from 2007 to 2009. Stevens' duties in Benghazi included liaisons with the area militias, the provision of material aid and weaponry to the domestic insurgency, and the sending of Islamic militants to fight the Assad government in Syria (at least 3000 were deployed there by Stevens), and, most of all, the coordination of a web of intelligence operatives and private contractors serving the CIA, military intelligence, and the oil companies. The identities of the three others killed with Stevens were first believed to be Special Forces security personnel, or private military contractors, but questions were later raised that they were more likely CIA operatives.

Republicans in Congress tried to embarrass President Obama and Secretary Clinton for lack of security at the "Consulate," but the issue became somewhat muted when some truths about the true nature of the "Consulate" began to emerge, although there was, in 2015, still a Republican-controlled Congressional Investigative Committee out to embarrass Hillary Clinton. Clinton defended herself in October 2015 Committee hearings. The charges about lax security were the focus, but Republican Representative Mike Pompeo got to the heart of real issues. He asked Clinton: "Were you aware or are you aware of any U.S. efforts by the U.S. government in Libya to provide any weapons, directly or indirectly, or through a cutout, to any Syrian rebels or militias or opposition to Syrian forces?" Clinton's answer: "No." Pompeo continued, "Were you aware or are you away of any efforts by the U.S. government in Libya to facilitate or support the provision of weapons to any opposition of Gadhafi's forces, Libyan rebels or militias through a third party of country?" Clinton: "No." These are outright lies. So why is Clinton not cited for lying to Congress? And now Pompeo has been appointed by Trump to be the Director of the CIA.

More truth emerged after the forced resignation of American generals and CIA Director David Petraeus. In late 2012, the Obama administration, rather embarrassed by the fiasco of Libya, decided to purge some of the most recalcitrant military officers linked to the neo-conservatives of the Bush era. General Carter Ham was replaced as head of AFRICOM and his side-kick, General William Ward, was demoted. AFRICOM is the U.S. military apparatus for the African continent and the front for the NATO attack. Then Navy Rear Admiral Charles Gaouette was reassigned out of a key naval strike group. The most dramatic exit was four-star General David Petraeus, who was forced to resign as head of the CIA.

The personal career of Petraeus is revealing. The General, responsible in different years for administration of the occupations in Iraq and Afghanistan, became a key figure in the build-up of a military-intelligence community cabal to form the policy of imperial war and the war on terror in coordination with financial and oil interests. Military generals together with CIA and military intelligence agents launched a "New Crusade" associated with the Project for a New American Century of Bush, Cheney, Rumsfeld and Company to promote the American way of life and a crusade for Christian values. On the home front, the crusade included indoctrination programs in Christian fundamentalism at the military academies, but the most serious of the crusading efforts were in the Middle East. General Petraeus became a key figure in this faction of crusaders. In the 2000s, Petraeus held the highest posts in the U.S. Army: Commander of the International Security Assistance Force, the Multi-National Force in Iraq, the U.S. Central Command, and U.S. Forces in Afghanistan. In spite of his crusader reputation, Obama appointed him as Director of the CIA in September 2011, where he oversaw the Libya War. In December 2016, Petraeus was in Trump's lineup for an important position, such as Secretary of State. In his thoroughly researched and insightful book on the Libya war, Horace Campbell states "General David Petraeus had come up inside the military in the heyday of the neoconservatives and had sought to mobilize their propaganda techniques and strategies to advance his own career and the fortunes of the branch of U.S. capital that was in ascendancy. Under the intellectual and ideological vision of General Petraeus, the convergence of the dark capital of financialization and the dark forces of covert wars had merged when he was elevated to become Commander of U.S. Central Command and later left the military to head the CIA."[8] Petraeus was finally forced to resign the CIA, ostensibly because he provided classified information to his mistress who was writing a book lauding his career as American's greatest general (Paula Broadwell, *All In: The Education of General David Petraeus*). The real reason for his dismissal, though, appears to be that the CIA and military intelligence were making decisions independent of the civilian executive branch. The Justice Department recommended felony charges for providing classified information to his biographer but, as always with high-level criminals, immunity prevailed and charges were reduced to a misdemeanor of mishandling classified information. Hillary Clinton is not charged with any crime for her private email messages or for lying to Congress. Would that Chelsea Manning, Edward Snowden, and WikiLeaks people be granted such immunity!

Among the warring militias in Libya, ISIS seems to be on the rise. Now, we have U.S. supplied Egyptian aircraft bombing ISIS strongholds in Libya. With the rise of ISIS in Iraq and Syria, the U.S. capitol building became a haven for hysteria purveyors, a virtual terror pulpit. South Carolina Senator Gramcracker and others of his ilk warned of the eventual black flag of ISIS over the White House and Capitol unless drastic measures were undertaken. Supposedly liberal Senator Feinstein, Chair of the Senate Security Committee stated, "the threat of ISIS poses cannot be overstated." The media covered all this with solemn attention. But not a word about the turn of events in Egypt. American military aid to Egypt has been around $1 billion annually, going back decades since the engineered demise of Egyptian nationalism and accommodation with Israel. First, the long term of Mubarak, finally deposed as a result of the popular uprising in the Arab Spring of 2011. The military and security forces killed thousands of demonstrators, but relented to sponsor elections that went 70% to the Muslim Brotherhood for the parliament and the election of a Muslim president. (The Brotherhood is a moderate force, not Islamic militants). The military, displeased with the electoral results, shut down the parliament, arrested the President, now sentenced to death with 547 others, and continues to violently suppress the secular opposition. There is no U.S. curtailment of military assistance, no action against overthrow of an elected government and gross violations of human rights. Only U.S. requests to bomb insurgent elements created by the NATO/U.S. assault on Qaddafi's Libya.

NATO knew full well that their intervention depended upon working with Al Qaeda and other Islamic extremists groups, and bringing 5000 Arabic-speaking NATO-trained Special Forces from Qatar to do the dirty work. Black immigrants working in the Sirte region were ethnically cleansed, the city of Sirte bombed to rubble, and 50,000 or more civilians were killed by bombings and shootings on the ground by militias and foreign mercenaries. Now ISIS is gaining strength and slaughtering Coptic Christians. What next, another NATO/U.S. intervention in Libya in a, no doubt futile, war against fanatical elements they created? One analysis in truth-out.org summed up the machinations well: "NATO attacked Libya to counter and manipulate a general Arab uprising that took the rulers of the world by surprise. Unlike his neighbors, Qaddafi had come to power by denying Western control of his country's natural wealth. For this, he was never forgiven and the opportunity for his demise was seized in the usual manner, as history shows...Since the Second World War, the United States has crushed or subverted liberation movement in 20 countries and attempted to overthrow more than 50 governments, many of them democratic and dropped bombs on 30 countries and attempted to assassinate more than 50 foreign leaders."[9]

As always in such events, the American and international press based their reporting on Libya on the material fed to them by the directors of war. The alternative media reporting on Libya events was scattered and not greatly informed. The full story never became known, and then only to a select audience, until the publication of the incredible compilation of facts and analyses by Horace Campbell, *Global NATO and the Catastrophic Failure in Libya*. This book is a must-read for those who would follow the intricate path of imperial ambition, revealing not only the folly of Libya, but also what is behind global war and official terrorism.

DEATH SQUADS

They are called Special Forces, and include the Navy Seals that took out Bin Laden. The old Green Berets of the Vietnam era are apparently now reorganized as Special Operations forces that include Rangers, Navy Seals, Delta Force commandos, specialized helicopter crews, boat teams, and other military or privatized death squads organized by the Special Operations Command (SOCOM). (Privatized forces include Blackwater Inc. convicted in a U.S. court of the indiscriminate killing of civilians in Iraq, now reorganized with a different name and said to be participating in coup attempts in Venezuela.) Special Forces are now deployed in 147 countries, up under Obama from 60 at the end of the Bush era, and moving toward more deployment. SOCAM coordinates the actions of 72,000 personnel with a budget of $10.4 billion. In all, the United States maintains 865 military bases in 80 nations from which Special Forces can be deployed, plus the stationing of Special Forces and military trainers in still more countries. The bases cost at least $80 billion each year. At the last count after withdrawals from Iraq, leaving behind total chaos, there were 190,000 troops stationed in other countries, plus large numbers of civilian security personnel under contract with the Pentagon and CIA-favored companies. In Iraq and Afghanistan, during the occupation period the Pentagon retained 225,000 private contractors. The number of additional CIA and NSA contractors is classified information. The cost of these military and security forces is enough to lift every American and many in the world out of poverty. The vast military spending, of course, creates federal budget deficits. Military spending cuts are taboo—they only increase. Facing insolvency, tax increases on those who can pay are not considered—impossible under the rule of money. The economy could be seriously stimulated with fiscal policy in the Keynesian style—not consistent with recessionary stagnation, degenerative development, and reduction of the state to the repressive apparatus. The end result is spending cuts in the provision of social services and public programs—a nice fit for the regime of capital.

The organization or sponsorship of death squads by the United States has been in effect since the 1960s, when President Kennedy let loose the CIA to counter pressures for revolutionary change in Latin America. Their greatest success was the assassination of Che Guevara in Bolivia in 1968. A striking case is Colombia, a country with a long history of oligarchic, repressive rule and human rights violations that was countered by the organization more than 50 years ago of the Fuerzas Armadas Revolucionarias de Colombia (FARC) that successfully has occupied extensive rural areas of the country. The Pentagon began advising Colombia on counter-insurgency in the 1960s. Under President Clinton, Plan Colombia was instituted and the Drug Enforcement Administration's (DEA's) war on drugs took on a central role in Colombia, as well as Mexico. The FARC was later joined by the Ejercito de Liberación Nacional (ELN). Military forces, unable to contain the FARC and ELN, in the early 1990s, organized private death squads (Autodefensas Unidas de Colombia—AUC) to carry out extra-legal village massacres and assassinations. The AUC became affiliated with the narcotics trade, and hired itself out to big landowners and foreign agri-business companies to "protect" them against labor agitators and to expand landholdings into peasant villages after people fled for their lives. One company that dealt with the AUC was Chiquita, a U.S.-headquartered agri-business transnational with holdings in 70 countries that operated a large banana plantation in Colombia. The 4000 victims and family survivors of the repression sued Chiquita in a U.S. court and achieved a guilty verdict for financing AUC with $1.7 million between 1997 and 2004. Chiquita was fined $25 million. However, the Supreme Court voided the verdict in 2015, ruling that the Colombian victims had no standing in U.S. courts.

Fascism, American-style

Labeling is often misused to evoke an exaggerated image. A term such as "fascism" should be used judiciously. I do so here in stating that America Inc. is moving in the direction of what has historically been portrayed as fascism—in effect, a new face of fascism. The classic cases of fascism are Nazi Germany, Mussolini's Italy, Franco's Spain, and Imperial Japan. The regimes came about in an essentially dual context from the early twentieth century through World Wars I and II. One context was the very strong assertion of class struggle and socialist movements in Europe and the Russian Revolution. The other context was the competition of nations for empire. Great Britain, France, and Belgium became challenged by Germany and Italy, leading to both World Wars, and Japanese militarism and expansionism rose to take on European colonialism in Asia and the American sway over the Pacific region.

The main features of fascism were:

- A highly authoritarian state which used extreme repression to liquidate all challenges to the existing order
- A political regime that uncompromisingly represented the interests of the economically dominant class
- A violent assertion of expansionist ambitions for control of territory
- The mobilization of civilian goon squads to deal with dissidents and create an environment of fear
- Ideological proclamation to create a conception of nationalism as the superiority of the nation and its people over all other nations and peoples; as a corollary to nationalism, racist conceptions of manifest destiny to suppress, conquer, or eliminate inferior races.

Fascist movements were evident throughout Europe during the 1930s, in Germany, Italy, Spain, France, and England especially. Today, these movements are still alive in the form of extreme right-wing anti-immigrant forces throughout Europe, especially in France, Austria, and Eastern Europe. Germany still has its neo-Nazis. The British exit from the European Union was, in good part, inspired by nativist demagogues. The main political/military force in the Ukraine today is neo-Nazi.

Fascism was not confined to Europe and Japan. There are the numerous post-World War II regimes of an extremely brutal nature, the South American military dictatorships, for example. The term "clerical fascism" was applied to the post-1979 Iranian regime with its imposition of Islamic rule. However, the Iranian revolution was to demolish the prior regime of the Shah and its business associates, not to cement the power of a dominant economic class. Moreover, it is clear that Iran has moved away from clerical rule toward greater secularism and democratic forms of governance. One wonders if the current Islamic extremist elements, such as ISIS with the violent imposition of religious fundamentalism, might also be considered fascist in nature, although most of the features of classic fascism are absent. Apart from the United States, the closest proximity to classic fascism today is Israel. Given the historical oppression of Jews and Nazi extermination it is really, really sad to have to recognize that the historical victims of fascism have become victimizers and purveyors of similar doctrines. Indeed, Zionism can be construed as fascism. The Israeli state oppresses Arab populations within Israel, practices apartheid, colonizes and occupies neighboring territories, threatens other countries, repeatedly resorts to violence and official terrorism, and declares war on its neighbors.[10] So, how does the United States measure up to the features of fascism?

The Authoritarian State and Repression FBI surveillance, infiltration of dissident organizations, framing leaders and other machinations, is sustained and effective. The FBI spent $5.3 billion, 54% of its budget in 2015, in war on terror activity. The Agency engaged in 440 "terror disruptions" in 2015, but there were only 60 terror-related arrests. Presumably where terrorists don't actually exist they have to be invented then "disrupted." Given that Homeland Security, the National Security Agency, and other police forces also endlessly search out terrorist ghosts and keep tabs on dissidents, this is a formidable, repressive activity. Comparable to the Nazi Gestapo? No, at least not yet. Perhaps one cannot say the same for the CIA and its renditions and torture programs. Beyond violent repression, all fascist regimes had their propaganda ministry attacking any and all opponents and intelligence and security forces staying on top of the population. In America Inc. we have the State of National Insecurity. The technology of the security apparatus is much more efficient than the Nazis could even envision, but is not yet used for the extremes of repression. The main difference is that the Nazis faced serious challenges in consolidating power from communists, socialists, and democrats of moderate persuasion, so they unleashed violent repression against all enemies of the state. Given that the internal opposition to the American state is, at this time, not a mobilized and serious threat, there is no present need to have a Gestapo or to let loose the militias, but the 2016–2017 political climate is moving in that direction. Trumpism has elements of the main features of an incipient fascism and one is "law and order," the strengthening of the repressive forces.

A Political Regime that Reflects the Interests and Pursues the Policies of the Economically Dominant Class What else is the rigged formal democracy of America Inc. than unrestrained plutocracy, the political rule of capital? For now, only weakly challenged. Classic fascism expounded that the state is the embodiment of a national spirit and stands above society to impose the dominant class's idea of what is good. This appears to be how plutocracy views the role of the state in today's America Inc. Those who question American exceptionalism and America First, or who lack enthusiasm for "Make America Great Again" are un-American enemies of the state. The greater the degree of system impingement on the situation of the population, the more social privilege is eroded, the greater the culture of fear and scapegoatism is promoted, we can only expect that resistance will be labeled as seditious and that the forces of official and extra-official repression unleashed.

Capitulation by Obama and the Democrats slightly eased the proximate danger of an American-style fascism that the privileged interests would impose when and if necessary. Why be nasty when you can get a nice guy or, were Clinton elected, a compliant lady to do what you want him or her to do by proper grooming and intransigence if he or she steps a little out of line? Most Democrats represent no progressive ideas, so plutocratic interests are better served by less extreme means. But that current of know-nothing extremism in defense of indefensible interests is ever present. Many plutocrats don't think rationally about what might make America great again. Some are hesitant about Trump, but incipient fascism can only be dealt with by a resurgence of social and political movements demanding justice, decency, and real change to a system that fosters injustice, indecency, and violent repression on a world scale. Still, the resurgence of a popular movement as it gains strength may, in fact, precipitate escalating repression, even perhaps the formation of death squads. The Justice Department, the Alcohol, Tobacco, and Firearms Agency, and the FBI will likely not seriously investigate intimidation and killings of movement people, and, as with other crimes the state fosters or tolerates, the perpetrators will be immune to prosecution. The FBI may well, as in CONTERINPOL of the 1960s, be part of organizing violent repression. In other parts of the world, American agencies of state actively promote death squads; it is not improbable that they may decide to bring the war home. The movement must act proactively and militantly to defeat fascism before it is fully upon us.

Expansionist Ambitions The Nazis invaded Europe, the Italians North Africa, the Japanese Asia and the Pacific with the ends of challenging competing imperialisms and occupied vast territories. Since the end of World War II, the United States as supreme world power has engaged in endless interventions and war throughout the world. It continues that interventionism today with invasion, occupation, or meddling throughout the oil-rich Middle East. A main purpose of the State of National Insecurity is the pursuit of empire by whatever means necessary. This is militaristic expansionism unparalleled since World War II. Official terror and war are always there to back the worldwide institutional control of capital with its globalization power of neo-liberal policy. Trump and Putin, it appears, have a mutual admiration pact. If so, this might cool down the cold war. But armed interventions in the Middle East will continue on most likely a wider scale, and perhaps be extended to Venezuela.

Right-Wing Social Movements, Domestic Violence, and Fear Today's Republican Party is evidently inextricably tied to what it considers its base in extremist elements such as the Tea Party, anti-abortion groups, fundamentalist Christians, right-wing libertarians, white supremacists, violent hate groups, and all manner of groupings of an extremist character. Exit polls at rallies indicated that many Trump supporters are middle- and higher-income, middle-class, white males, although the media cite white working-class people as adherents.

What is ever present is a cultivated culture of fear, as examined in detail in Chap. 5. Fear is generalized through the war on terror and by media controlled by plutocracy. This incites the social base of these groups that espouse a more classic fascist ideology. There is evidently a split within the power block forging capital's hegemonic project fully to consolidate and institutionalize the unquestioned rule of capital. The lineup of Republican candidates all aspired to be Der Fuhrer with racist, chauvinist, xenophobic tirades that appeal to the white privileged and those losing their privileges by the workings of the system. This worries some of the establishment ideologues who used to control the Republican Party and successfully subordinated Democrats to their policy guidance. The moderate Republican elite (if, indeed, there is such a grouping) have not been able to control the outcome of Republican presidential candidate selection. The publicity given by all the media to Trump and the inability of a supposed Republican moderate establishment to promote an acceptable candidate, leads me to the conclusion that plutocracy was pursuing a dual strategy—promote and mobilize an extremist, essentially fascist base, while being quite willing to accept a trustworthy Hillary Clinton. Plutocrats put their money in Congressional races to retain Republican obstructionism to any domestic progressivism. The right-wing militias are reputed to be organized mainly for the violent resistance to government tyranny, as in the Oklahoma federal building bombing—domestic terrorism by "Vanilla ISIS" and "Yáll Qaeda" groupings. They may act as government goon squads at some point and movement activists can expect to be victimized by vigilantes filled with hate and out to defend the system with violence.

Ideology, Nationalism, and Visions of Superiority In this realm, indeed, America Inc. resides well within the legacy of fascism. This legacy, in turn, derives from many centuries of "scientific-based" ideologies that have guided ignoble purpose in making history and doing evil. The genetic inferiority of women and people of color, the extension of evolutionary theory to the social Darwinist doctrine of the survival of the fittest in human society, manifest destiny, and the white man's civilizing burden…all have their long histories and contemporary extensions. The Nazi view of the essence of Man's nature was a propensity for violence, as annunciated in a long Germanic philosophical tradition. Violence was a means to an end, but also an end it itself because it brings Man closer to his inner essence, war being an extension of human nature. Our rulers in America Inc. certainly have a propensity for violence and war, but this is attributable to class interests, not human nature. Their myth becomes the most twisted part of their consciousness. Nazi conception of Arian supremacy lead to the extermination of Jews, Gypsies, and others considered inferior beings, and was the crudest of racism. In the United States today, black people are not sent to the gas chambers; rather, they are shot down on the street daily and sent to prison in massive numbers. Immigrants are scapegoated, blamed for the ills of America, rounded up and placed in internment camps; all Muslims are maligned, and with even more repressive policies advocated by Trump. Black, brown, and red people suffer discrimination in employment and institutions, and are victimized by racism nurtured by extending the idea of privilege to the white-skinned population. Well beyond the entrenched racism of American society is the mystification enshrined by all the ideological apparatuses. Plutocracy becomes democracy, exported worldwide by intervention and force to save humanity, together with diffusion of the superiority of Western white Christian civilization over barbarism, the myth of American exceptionalism and American First, and Trump's version of decline from exceptionalism "Make America Great Again!", social Darwinism, the cult of individualism, the superiority of private enterprise and all the other tenants belabored in previous analysis.

Today's Republican Party, with its dual base in a mobilized, extremist grass roots, on the one hand, and the moneyed elite, on the other hand, approximate the main features of fascism. The base of the party that voted for Trump shows definite fascist characteristics. But I am not sure that we should label Donald Trump as a resurrected Mussolini, or that this incipient American fascism will be able to mature. But the movement must be intransigent at every turn in this direction.

We were faced with a political choice in 2016 between the lesser of two evils. Where is the good? There is only the evil of two lessors. Eduardo Galeano speaks of the "Theatre of Good and Evil." "In the struggle of Good against Evil, it's always the people who get killed...Eliminate Evil? What would Good be without Evil?...Good and evil, evil and good: the actors change masks, the heroes become monsters and the monsters heroes, in accord with the demands of the theatre's playwrights."[11] The different strains of murderers all have one thing in common: moral corruption. Immorality is conditioned by reduction of social, cultural, and political differences to military definition. Pursuing the great truth of good against evil, the new crusade, they kill before asking any question. The CIA torturers and assassins, the Special Ops mercenaries, the Pentagon warriors, the drone drivers, the higher echelons of the U.S. government that give the green light to official terrorism, the agents of Israel's Mossad and the Israeli High Command that orders genocidal bombardments, the jihadists that behead captives, bomb innocents, and ethnically cleanse...all are worshippers of death. The main difference is one of disproportionality. While the terrorism of the desperate may be viewed by them as the only option, it is only feeding the imperial beast what is needed to continue escalating the killing. Certainly, Islamic fundamentalism feeds practices abhorrent to the secular mentality, but so do Christian and Jewish fundamentalism. We have supported, and can continue to support, forward-looking movements toward a better future in the global South. We can't root for the good guys in the current Middle East strife. There are some forward-looking Kurdish groups, but for now it appears there aren't many Middle Eastern progressive forces; they have mostly been murdered. Wholesale killing of any peoples is morally unacceptable. Let the advance of secular culture drown fundamentalism.

NOTES

1. A personal note on the Dutch in Indonesia and related cold war misadventures: As a young man in the early 1950s, I faced the draft, so to avoid foot-soldiering in another Korea, I joined the U.S. Air Force. First, I was trained as a bombardier. From Mather Air Force Base in Sacramento, CA, I perfected dropping atomic bombs on the Mark Hopkins Hotel in San Francisco. My near score was less than 100 yards. Fortunately, I was transferred out of the Strategic Air Command to be a Reconnaissance officer, that is,

a spy. After a brief stint in West Palm Beach, Florida, in a squadron triangulating North America with Greenland and Europe electronically, in order that nuclear weapons could accurately hit Moscow, I was transferred to Japan. During my stay at a base near Tokyo, a red alert was issued to all American forces in Japan to prepare to intervene on behalf of the Dutch in Indonesia. It never happened, but it made me wonder. As a country boy, I had little patience for military hierarchy, so my friends were enlisted men and I refused to join the (elitist) officers club. I also wondered aloud why my squadron had lost 5 of 16 aircraft in the year prior to my arrival, shot down by Russian defense over "international waters" (actually Siberia, the squadron mission was intelligence reconnaissance). My squadron was then in transition from propeller-driven aircraft, easy targets, to the high flying jet, B-58, so fortunately I did not have to spy. The B-58 was the first version of the U-2 shot down over Moscow in 1958. In the 18 months I spent in Japan, I had to do little flying, so I had time to learn Japanese and explore the country. On the airbase, to whoever would listen, I said that I did not feel comfortable being a spy and risking getting shot down. My squadron commander called me in one day and said "Johnson you insubordinate son of a bitch, I am transferring you out of here." The next day, I was ordered to appear at the Mapping and Charting Room for all targets in the Pacific Theatre to be Officer in Charge. This required upgrading my security status to Top Secret. I was duly checked out in my new duties. Reporting to work one day, I was met by a red-faced major who ordered me to report to the Office of Special Investigation immediately. There, another major escorted me to a cubicle where he read to me charges—that I was a member of the Communist Party. Since I never even had met a communist in my life, it kind of surprised me. It turned out during investigation for Top Secret clearance that I had once attended a debate between a Democrat and a Socialist in passing through San Francisco, at which apparently the FBI or military intelligence had photographed attendees and compared with the time of my brief stay in San Francisco. Pretty efficient surveillance for those early days before the NSA. I was taken to the debate by my brother-in-law, a prominent Trotskyist in the International Longshoreman's Union. I suspect that my genuinely subversive relative by marriage worried them a lot. So, not long after, I was given a discharge "For the Convenience of the Government." In 1959, I entered the graduate sociology program at Stanford University where I became a 1960s student activist. Still a member of the USAF Reserve, I was subject for several years to repeated visits by military officers demanding that I sign a loyalty oath. I refused. They threatened me with dishonorable discharge. The American Civil Liberties Union managed to act on my behalf for an honorable discharge. In the 1970s, I requested my FBI file under the Freedom of Information Act. I got a much redacted 200-plus page document chronicling all my subversive activities, the Fair Play for Cuba Committee, the civil rights movement, and Vietnam anti-war activities. My Department chairperson informed me that the FBI had approached the Sociology Department and the University administration to stop my financial aid. To Stanford's credit, they did not. I was astounded that the FBI spent so much time and trouble keeping track of a minor activist, when they were so busy with the Conterinpol program going after Black Panthers and the Weather Underground, but I was also rather proud. The most recent event in this line is a hack of my computer by hacktool:328keygen. All my emails disappeared, together with my accounting software and bank accounts. I suspect the NSA or FBI, as I place a great deal of critical material on the internet. My point here is not to expound on my subversive credentials but to say to movement activists of today—make them waste their resources in futile efforts to keep track of millions of you. They can't do that effectively, even with the sophistication of the National Security Agency, Homeland Security, and the FBI. Let them have their lists, that there be many with millions of names.

2. The great Iranian writer Salmon Rushdie lived in America for a time. In his book *The Ground Beneath Her Feet*, he notes "America the Beautiful,...that never existed but needs to exist—with that, like everyone else, I was thoroughly in love. But ask the rest of the world what American meant and with one voice the rest of the world answered back, Might, it means Might. A power so great that it shapes our daily lives even though it barely knows we exist, it couldn't point out us on a map. America is no finger-snapping bopster. It's a fist."

3. Tom Engelhardt "Escalation by the Numbers," www.truthout. org/docs_2006/081307E.shtml a truly astounding documentation of war consequences.

4. Michael Schwartz, *War Without End*, Haymarket Books, 2008. Jessica Stern, *Terror in the Name of God: Why Religious Militants Kill*, Ecco, 2003. See also Arundhati Roy, "War Is Peace", www.zmag.org/roywarpeace.htm On the Iraqi resistance to the occupation and the coopted puppets in government posts, see Michael Reagan, *Against all Odds: Raising Iraqi Voices of Grassroots Resistance*, Tadween Publishing, 2015.

5. Aijaz Ahmad, "Islam, Islamisms and the West," *Socialist Register*, Monthly Review Press, 2008. Aijaz Ahmad, *In Theory: Nations, Classes, Literatures*, Verso Press, 2008. Aijaz Ahmad, "Class, Nation, and State: Intermediate Classes in Peripheral Societies," in Dale L. Johnson (ed.), *Middle Classes in Dependent Countries*, Sage Publications, 1985.

6. Samir Amin, *The Reawakening of the Arab World: Challenge and Change in the Aftermath of the Arab Spring*, Monthly Review Press, 2015. On Libya, outstanding is Horace Campbell, *Global NATO and the Catastrophic Failure in Libya*, Monthly Review Press, 2013. Noam Chomsky's most recent book is an excellent overview of the American imperial thrust worldwide, *Who Rules The World?* Metropolitan Books, 2016.

7. Mark Pilisuk and Jennifer Rountree, *The Hidden Structure of Violence: Who Benefits from Global Violence and War*, ebook, 2013.

8. Campbell, pp. 224–225.

9. www.truth-out.org/hail-true-victors-revolution/115501888

10. A good capsule summary of the features of fascism is Aijaz Ahmad, "Colonialism, Fascism and 'Uncle Shylock'," *Frontline*, vol. 17, August 19, 2000.

11. Eduardo Galeano, "The Theatre of Good and Evil," *La Jornada*, September 21, 2001.

CHAPTER 9

The Globalization of Capital and Its Ideologically Framed Policies

SKIMMING RECENT HISTORY

Emerging victorious from war in 1945, the Americans went to cold war against the Soviets and hot wars against revolutionary forces in Korea and, later, Vietnam. By the 1960s in Latin America, efforts from mercenary invasion to terrorism and embargo crippled but failed to destroy the Cuban revolution; however, they were successful in efforts to instill reactionary military regimes in South America and turn back insurgent forces in Central America.

Lest we forget, the new world order sought by America Inc. was enforced by dictatorship. In Latin America during the 1960s, 1970s, and 1980s, neo-liberal policies of the new scheme of globalization were ruthlessly implemented by military regimes, as in Brazil, Chile, Argentina, Ecuador, Peru, Bolivia, and Uruguay, and by right-wing Central American governments, supported by the United States, employing death squads and military massacres in counter-insurgency operations.

In short, world history since 1945 has been written by attempts to hold back threats to American supremacy by war and subversion, and the instigation of military interventions. From the 1980s onward, with the new strategy of globalization, neo-liberal policies (to be detailed shortly) were imposed by international institutions such as the World Bank and International Monetary Fund, with "conditionality" attached to all lending. A number of nations, especially in Latin America, experienced debt crisis,

© The Author(s) 2017

D.L. Johnson, *Social Inequality, Economic Decline, and Plutocracy,*

DOI 10.1007/978-3-319-49043-4_9

rather similar to Greece today. "Structural adjustments" were required to move these countries into a proper mode of globalization. Economic difficulties, growing social inequalities and social injustice, and disgust with military rule and foreign impositions in Latin America had political consequences by the 2000s. Left-of-center governments were elected in Argentina, Brazil, Uruguay, Nicaragua, El Salvador, even Honduras and Paraguay, until the progressive presidents were removed from office by right-wing coups. Elections had more radical results in Venezuela, Bolivia, and Ecuador. The civilian socialist governments that ruled Chile since the fall of General Pinochet largely maintained the neo-liberal policies imposed by the heeled boot of the dictatorship, with some programs of social amelioration, but most of the rest of the region has been moving decidedly away from these foreign prescriptions, save in Colombia, Panama, Mexico, Guatemala, and Costa Rica, and now Honduras and Paraguay, with these countries safely back in the globalization mold.

In brief, then, the aftermath of World War II involved an end to competing center nations dividing up the world into colonial domains. European colonies in Africa, the Middle East, and Asia achieved their formal independence. Power wielded at the international level shifted from competing imperialisms to the imposition of U.S. economic and military hegemony on a world scale. The post-World War II period witnessed not only a great shift away from nations competing for empire, but also the changing nature of a new imperialism. In the last decades of the twentieth century, world empire became consolidated under the rule of capital, backed by force of the dominant power as necessary. The rule of capital by the 1980s became consolidated through the imposition of policies, identified as "neo-liberalism", and a strategy for expansion and consolidation: "globalization."

NEO-LIBERALISM AND GLOBALIZATION

The ruling ideology of capital, as described in Chap. 5, has clearly enunciated policy guidelines. The economic and social policies that flow from this ideology and the power configurations of capital are often termed "neo-liberalism," closely associated with the notion of "globalization." Neo-liberalism's essential principles are worldwide in reach and are daily repeated in the American political scene and in the countries of Europe forced into austerity by the European Commission, the European Central Bank, the IMF and the German, French, and Swiss bankers that control these institutions. In many other countries of the global South, the policies that flow from neo-liberal ideology have been forcibly pursued by dictatorship, some of them the worst since European fascism. With the war on Libya, the last of modernizing Arab nationalism was eliminated. The "Arab Spring" is now a dark winter of suppression. Retrograde Islamic forces filled the breach, resulting in violent and wide resistance to the interventions and imposition of foreign dogma and Western secular culture among Muslim peoples.

The clichés propounded worldwide center around free market fundamentalism—financial deregulation; elimination of economic controls and subsidies to promote national development, with broadened opening to foreign capital; dismantling of state-sponsored development programs leaving all to private enterprise; labor flexibility; monetary orthodoxy of central bank policies, divorced from fiscal development policy; free trade in commodities and services; no restrictions on global capital movement but no freedom in international labor mobility; privatization of state enterprises and many government services (in the U.S., including prisons and mercenary forces); roll-back or dismantling of programs of social amelioration; commodification of useful services to bring all cultural, social, and economic activity into the sphere of capital. Neo-liberal policies have the end of subordinating nation states to pro-market changes that further the globalization of center corporate interests and controls, especially those associated with finance capital.

Neo-liberal policies are imposed on a world scale by the International Monetary Fund (IMF), the World Trade Organization (WTO), the World Bank, the European Central Bank (ECB), the Inter-American Development Bank, U.S. government agencies—the Agency for International Development (AID), the Treasury, the Federal Reserve (Fed)—and others such as non-governmental organizations (NGOs), and the big investment banks of Wall Street and Europe. Fiscal policies that foment economic development are left aside in favor of monetarism that favors finance. Strict monetarism does not necessarily apply to the U.S. Federal Reserve or the Treasury Department, the controlling agencies of global finance, which do whatever is necessary—such as bail-out investment banks with hundreds of billions of dollars, or lower interests rates to near zero to facilitate the activities of speculative capital that searches the world for opportunities for short-term profit-taking. The American investment banks, freed of U.S. regulations under Presidents Clinton and Bush, were successful in extending controls to predominate in global finance. The banksters in this period had a double chance to win big, no regulation and guarantee on the no loss side by bail-out backup. Neither does strict monetarism apply to the ECB, which bails out German banks that over-extended themselves in loans to the countries of southern Europe by forcing repayment by way of austerity requirements and privatization of public enterprise in order to repay loans that should be defaulted.

The tenants of neo-liberalism predate the Reaganism/Thatcherism of the 1980s and Clinton's promotion of the "Washington Consensus" on the virtues of globalization but, from that period onward, became the religion of all sectors of capital, most centrally transnational corporations and within the finance capitals of the United States and Europe. NAFTA enshrined these tenants for "free trade" between the United States, Canada, and Mexico, with Mexico the principal victim. (The horrendous consequences of NAFTA and neo-liberal policy impositions, on the one hand, and the war on drugs, on the other, will be explored later. Essentially, Mexico is now a "narco-state" that imposes neo-liberal policies with extreme repression.)

The religion of neo-liberalism found resonance in the militarized and oligarchic states and dominant classes of the South, particularly in the 1970s and 1980s in Latin America. While it would be an exaggeration to say that, by the 1990s, there was a consolidated international ruling class of global capital (the nation-state and its class formations retain meaning), it is reasonable to identify a congruence of class interest among dominant capitalist classes in many nations, north and south, west and east. The congruence of interests between the dominant transnational and financial classes of the center and the dominant classes of the periphery became ever more salient. Loosening protectionist tariffs and opening free trade in goods and services left the traditional primary goods export economies of the South room for expansion of export economies, and opened up more internal markets for the penetration of transnational corporate activity and financial services from the center. The worldwide thrust for flexible labor policies benefited national business and undermined local unions. The curtailment of social services everywhere (until recently in parts of Latin America, where there are efforts to construct a "socialism for the 21st century") hurt workers and poor people, and benefited local business as state funds passed to activities complementing their interests. Privatization, usually taking the form of sale of state enterprises to private capital, national and foreign, at bargain prices, also meant that public goods and services became commodified and sold at higher prices to the consuming public. The anti-state interventionist rhetoric actually covered a shift from intervention in the public interest to expanded state intervention in promotion of private interest.

Globalization did succeed in a considerable restructuring of the world economy; from the 1980s there was an extensive expansion of the market everywhere and an intensive deepening of the penetration of international capital. Transnational corporations transferred much activity from industrial enterprise in the United States and Europe to low-waged countries, especially in China and East and Southeast Asia. Extractive industries in Latin America also boomed for a time as a result of international demand for primary products caused by increased manufacturing in Asia. The big American banks facilitated global expansionism on behalf of transnational corporations and themselves became the principal extension and enforcer of globalization. This was much facilitated by the development of new technologies in communication that eased the movement of information and virtual capital. But technology is only a convenient and efficient tool; globalization is an integrated system of economic, financial, political, military, ideological, and geopolitical elements.

"Labor arbitrage" and "outsourcing" became key instruments in restructuring the world economy, especially during the 1990s and 2000s. One example illustrative of how this works for transnational corporations is the case of manufacture of the Apple iPad marketed in 2010–2011. Apple sold over 100 million iPads during those years. Apple outsources all its fabrication of devices to low-waged areas. A study by Lausen and Cope found that Apple integrated 748 mainly Asian suppliers of materials and components into a production chain for assembly in China. The factory price in China was $275, the market price in the United States $499. Of the factory price, only $33 went to wages of workers in the Asian production chain, around 10% of the wage bill if the iPad were produced in the United States. Of Apple's gross profit, $150 went to Apple's corporate center for design, marketing, and administrative salaries. Another advantage of outsourcing is that Apple does not have to cover any externality costs for pollution, environmental degradation, and resource depletion. An iPad is a small portable devise but apparently requires an enormous input of raw materials to produce. Lausen and Cope amazed me by the statement: "Each iPad uses thirty-three pounds of minerals…seventy-nine gallons of water, and enough fossil fuel-based electricity to generate sixty-six pounds of carbon dioxide…105 kilograms of greenhouse gas emissions…These factors never appear in the accounting of production costs: they are invisible 'gifts' to capitalists and to buyers."[1]

In America and Europe, globalization led to the decline of entire regions, depression of wage levels, chronic underemployment and unemployment, slow growth, and growing inequality. Financialization and degenerative development in the center countries resulted in financial crisis. Europe has still to experience a recovery from this crisis—in 2015, the Eurozone economy was still smaller than it was in 2008, only Germany and France experienced a very small increase in GDP (3% and 1%, respectively), between 2008 and 2014. Italy lost 9% of it GDP and Spain 6%. Greece and other countries of southern and eastern Europe are in depression without end in sight.

While China boomed in this new phase of development with its state-directed capitalism (persistent growth rates of 10% annually, declining a bit in recent years), in most countries incorporated globalized production and neo-liberal consolidation led to slow economic growth, massive inequality and environmental unsustainability. Even the IMF, in a rare moment of thoughtfulness, issued a study on global inequality which concluded "the decline in unionization is strongly associated with the rise of income shares at the top."[2] From the 1980s, economic growth proceeded in traditional export spheres of primary goods and, to some degree, resulting from the influx of foreign investment in the domestic economy. Annual per capita economic growth of "third world" economies from 1960 to 1980 was 3.2%. This was a period of import-substitution strategy and state-directed development projects. From 1980 to 2000, during the ascendance of globalization, per capita growth fell to 0.7%. (These figures exclude China which, in the later period, experienced very high economic growth under its decidedly non-neo-liberal, state-directed capitalism.)

At writing I don't have the growth data from 2000 to 2015 but, in Latin America, many of the countries are eschewing pure neo-liberalism in favor of ameliorative social programs and more state direction in attempting to move out of the clutches of neo-liberal hegemony. Countries such Ecuador and Bolivia, with Venezuela in the lead, are striving to break the bonds of dependency in favor of socially just development. Political developments in Latin America do not set well with the challenged imperial state and local business elements, and there are de-stabilization efforts, intensifying since 2014 in all these countries and decisively in Venezuela and Ecuador; these efforts will be analyzed in more depth shortly. Argentina and Brazil are back in the neo-liberal mode. The darkest side of neo-liberalism is the resort to interventionism. This can take the form of economic coercion, as in Greece; stiff sanctions, as in Iran and Cuba; regime change, as in the Ukraine; subversion with regime change as the end, as in Venezuela and Uruguay; or regime change by military force, as in Libya and Syria.

Big banks were very much part of globalization of activity in the South, both directly in terms of penetration of banking, and through facilitation and coordination of activity in manufacturing and extractive industries by transnational corporations. Since the crisis of 2008, finance capital has shifted the better part of its capital flows toward speculative activity, facilitated by the U.S. Treasury Department and, especially, the Federal Reserve.

Very much part of globalization has been the implementation of financial orthodoxy of central bank policies worldwide that are, by international convention, confined to inflation control, money supply, exchange rates, and interest rate adjustments, with no attention to fitting monetary measures to government fiscal and development policy. Dating from the 1980s, these policies became globalized.

The tentacles of American finance capital are worldwide and have extremely adverse consequences for the economies and peoples of other nations. Among the major consequences of the international financial crisis of 2008, and continuing to the present day, is a considerable investment of speculative capital from the United States to the more vibrant economies of Latin America and Asia that are trying to edge away from neo-liberalism. In Latin America in 2010, net private foreign investment reached $203.4 billion, up from $57.5 billion in 2003. In a number of countries in the region, especially Brazil, Chile, Colombia, and Costa Rica, this influx of dollars has had the effect of rapid and substantial appreciation of local currencies. This has serious implications for these economies. Monetary orthodoxy has it that exchange rates are determined by the ratio of foreign currency to local currency in the economy, while capital controls over currency transfers are outside the orthodoxy of neo-liberalism. To the extent that dollar investments emanating from the United States find their outlet in foreign stock markets, local investment funds and financial instruments, real estate, commodity futures, government bonds, credits to local banks, short-term currency speculations, and other mainly non-productive investments, the currency appreciates, local assets become overpriced, and bubbles of the kind that brought on the U.S. crisis of 2007–2009 can come about. Currency appreciation is a serious problem for Latin American economies that are highly dependent on primary exports in minerals and food products. An overvalued currency exchanges export earned dollars for fewer reales, pesos, or colons required by export businesses to cover operating expenses in the local currency,[3] reducing profitability and limiting the export-led development strategy that these countries have adopted—or, more accurately stated, strategies that have been forced upon them by their dependent position in the global economy. Conversely, imports become relatively cheaper, harming local industry that serves the domestic market, while deepening balance of payments deficits. Over-valuation of local currencies invites speculative investment, especially short-term activity with easy conversion to liquidity, but not to long-term productive investment, as these investors must convert dollars or euros to local currency at artificially inflated rates.

The main problem since the great crash of 2008 is that recessionary stagnation, and the investment climate in the United States in particular, is not inviting to those with liquid assets or access to cheap credit. So, capital flows around the world, in manufacturing disproportionately to China; to some extent in extractive industries in Latin America; in commodity futures driving up the price of raw materials, grains, and oil—prices which began to decline in 2014–2015, dramatically with oil; in buying and selling stock in markets that do not serve the needs of corporations for investment capital but reflect a system of casino capitalism; and billions into economies that show signs of vitality that the U.S. economy entirely lacks, or where interest rates and bond returns are higher. As analyzed in Chaps. 2 and 3, the crisis is rooted in stagnation of the center industrial economy and financial speculation, and a power grab by banksters as a response to the crisis.

It seems clear that degenerative development is now extending globally. Most of the capital escaping the United States is investment, borrowed at low interest, speculative in nature, and not destined for production of useful goods and services. Trillions of U.S. dollars are stashed in offshore accounts to avoid U.S. and other countries' taxes. With the U.S. real estate market in slow recovery since 2008 and the bursting of the various bubbles that, until 2007–2008, sustained financial speculation by the big banks, investment firms, and plutocrats, idle money flows into foreign currencies, foreign stocks, and government and private bonds, short-term loans to foreign banks to relend at higher interest, and financial instruments and entities around the world where sources of funds can be concealed and made liquid, and shifted to other activities at the convenience of short-term profit.

A proximate cause of the international flow of speculative capital is the policy of quantitative easing (QE) by the U.S. Federal Reserve. QE1 was designed as a complement to the Department of Treasury's bail-out program and as stimulus to move the economy out of the collapse of 2008–2009. (The QE program is formally large-scale asset purchases—LSAP). The Fed bought $3 trillion of financial assets with the aim of raising the prices of assets, lowering interest, and providing liquidity and credit to the economy. This has not made extensive low-interest credit available to business and consumers, but does inject some liquidity into the financial system and works to relieve the banks of holding dubious assets and allows them to use their reserves to borrow at low interest for speculative investments. QE2 was, in part, a scheme to fund federal borrowing interest free. In essence, the Fed simply declared $600 billion available to banks from non-existent real money (that is to say, "prints money" on its computers) that is backed by the inflow of funds from foreigners buying Treasury Bonds. There has been no substantial increase in "real money" in the form of credit circulating widely in the productive economy, just "printed money" the Fed created so that banks have cleaner balance sheets. But there are billions in low-interest monies to engage in speculative activity.[4]

In January 2015, the ECB announced its own version of quantitative easing for the Eurozone. The ECB is buying €60 billion monthly of various forms of debt destined to expand the ECB balance sheet by €1 trillion by 2016. The problem of recessionary stagnation is just as serious in Europe as in the United States, perhaps more so. But the QE of the ECB is likely to have the same effect as QE by the Fed: relieving banks of dubious assets and replacement with cash from bond sales; pushing down interest rates to near zero; funneling capital into assets like stocks and speculative investment in the Eurozone and around the world. The purchase of bank assets and sovereign debt will have the effect of making banks even less interested in loaning money to businesses as they can't profit from low interest rates, so the QE euro funds will go to stocks, commodity futures, and speculative investments around the world. Nor is QE going to help sovereign debt issues in troubled southern Europe.

THE EUROPEAN UNION AND THE MODERN ODYSSEY
OF GREECE

A real test case of resistance to neo-liberal controls is Greece. Events there have spread to Spain. Italy and Portugal are next in the resistance line. Even the administrative center of European neo-liberalism, Germany, now has its left-wing, Die Linke, and there is greater union militancy throughout Europe. French grass roots socialist and trade union militants are up in arms, especially about the neo-liberal labor reform of the Socialist government. The left-wing of the British Labor Party consolidated control after the 2015 Conservative electoral victory and the Scottish left controls their parliament. The British popular vote to exit the European Union will no doubt have a significant impact on the future of the EU. Europe in general should experience increasing discontent with austerity and the rule of plutocracy there, with greater assertions by unions that, while weakened, are stronger than in the U.S. The Greek situation has some bearing for questions of strategy for the U.S. Movement. The relevance of the European experience for the American movement is stated in an interesting article "Six Lessons for the U.S. From Spain's Democratic Revolution."[5] The situation in the Ukraine is more of the same nefarious American and Western European interventionism.

The original idea promoted to forge a unity of European countries was a worthy one. The programs and virtues of the social democracies of northern Europe would be extended throughout the continent, first south and later east. What emerged was a travesty of that vision. Neo-liberal policy of European business and banks became the policy of the social democratic parties in center nations, Germany, France, Italy, and Spain. Germany became the major exporter of industrial goods to the poorer south and east, importing cheap labor and undermining formerly strong unions. German and French banks designed the architecture of centralized financial controls and over time created in the peripheral countries debt servitude. The debt was used as leverage for rollbacks, rather than enhancement, of the social state. The peoples of Ireland, Greece, Spain, Portugal, Cyprus, and Eastern Europe became the victims of the bankers imposing neo-liberal policies of social services cuts, privatization, and labor flexibility. Iceland so far has been the only country to more or less successfully resist and reorganize a workable banking system and an economy with a modicum of social justice.

By the decade of the 2000s the EU became consolidated and administered by the "Troika," the administrative board of the European Community, the ECB, and the IMF, all controlled by finance capital, mainly German and French, but with Wall Street very much part of the scene. The IMF is a particularly nefarious institution, with a history of being led by financial criminals. The current Executive Director, Christine Lagarde, lent $30 billion to the Ukrainian oligarchs, even though it was this class that precipitated economic crisis that led to a neo-Nazi coup. Lagarde then changed the rules allowing the Ukraine to default on its payment of sovereign debt to Russia. Lagarde faced trial in France for misappropriation of $400 million for a payoff to a private tycoon when she was Finance Minister in the government of Sarkozy. The previous director, Dominique Strauss-Kahn, had to resign after being charged with rape of a maid in a New York hotel and arrested for pimping in France. The predecessor to Strauss-Kahn, Rodrigo Rato (2004–2007), a Spanish banker, was arrested for tax evasion and concealing €27 million in 70 banks that had been swindled from small investors in a Spanish bank scandal. The IMF appears to be governed by criminals, persons with no scruples about applying the screws to entire countries and regions.

Policy options by member countries, especially those within the Eurozone, became increasing crimped by policies of the Troika, crafted largely by German bankers and finance ministers. European governments, by EU rules, have their sovereignty to legislate fiscal and monetary policy greatly constrained, and the formal democracy of the European Parliament has no real power in relation to that of the Troika. The policy choices of how to deal with economic stagnation, which affected the EU economy as well as that of the United States, shifted from the social democratic alternatives of extending social programs and Keynesian fiscal policy to stimulate growth in favor of the imposition of austerity on the public sector, with the citizenry the victim. The older conception of imperial center/colonized periphery became real in a new historical context. The epi-center, Germany, in coordination with the Northern European countries and France, administered the southern and eastern periphery, and also Ireland. Private German banks loaned Greece huge sums to finance German imports. Then, with the spread of the great crisis of 2008 from America to Europe, came the opportunity to tighten the grip. As in the United States, the banks were bailed out in the Eurozone. Then the IMF, the ECB, and private banks issued emergency loans to the peripheral countries. The sovereign debt increased enormously.

The private bank loans were transferred to the ECB and IMF, institutions that insisted on conditionality—austerity; public services sold to private interests to make loan payments; tax increases on consumers; pension cuts; public employment reductions to reduce the ability of government to combat depression while making public funds available for loan payments; substitution of union bargaining on wages by government decree.... In Greece and Spain, unemployment among youth reached 50% and the GDP plunged. Germany has certainly recovered from the ashes of war. Germany is now the economic center of all Europe. Today, Germany extends control over the rest of Europe, not by force of arms, but by economic and financial controls. In Greece, German occupation of the World War II period has been replaced by the subordination of Greece by economic coercion. The German bankers and industrialists are not Nazis pursuing conquest by force; they are a class that pursues hegemony throughout the continent by control of EU institutions, with support of American capital that pursues an even broader global strategy than that of their German partners.

Greece is an economic and social disaster, suffering conditions every bit as deep as those of the Great Depression. The bulk of the population has experienced a 50% drop in living standards, unemployment of 25%, and youth unemployment pushes 50%. Young people have to leave the country in search of work or move back in with their parents. One-third of the population has lost health care. The rate of absolute poverty has tripled; the suicide rate doubled.... The Greek debt of €240 billion is 175% of GDP. Still, the EU presses on with austerity prescriptions, no serious debt relief, no development programs to revive the economy.

Greece was not always a weak link in the European Community (EC). Greece became the first associate member of the European Economic Community (EEC) in 1962. It has been a member of the EU since 1981 and adopted the euro as its currency in 2001. In the 2000s, the World Bank classified Greece as a high-income economy. In 2005, it had the 22nd highest human development and quality of life index in the world—higher, in fact, than Germany, France, and the UK. Greece's productivity was also higher than that of France, Germany and the United States. At the time the Great Recession hit in 2008, Greece had the 24th highest per capita GDP. So, what caused the disastrous turn of events?

Not sufficiently informed of Greek history and political economy, I can't answer the question as to what happened and why in any depth. But, in my view, there is the obvious loss of sovereignty by being a subordinate dependency in a Union that is controlled by a powerful center. Entering the EU meant that there was free movement of goods and services from other EU members, no protective tariffs, no export subsidies, no import quotas. With the adoption of the euro, Greece lost any control of its financial system; the ECB, not the Greek Central Bank, sets monetary policy. Greece cannot increase money supply, lower interest rates, or change its exchange rate to spur national development; neither can it impose capital controls to keep euros circulating within the economy. A Eurozone member cannot control its trade policy, or its monetary policy, and its fiscal policy is circumscribed by EU stipulations on deficit spending and debt ceiling. The euro is a dark tunnel with the end the crushing of any democratic control that can prevent a designed crisis that realigns power to the financiers and German plutocracy, and crushes what little remains of the social state. The Greek debt is unpayable and should be defaulted. It is an "odious debt" under international standards, in that it is result of loan-sharking, fraud, and usury imposed under duress.

But there are other underlying factors that seem to me have to be part of a more detailed historical study. Greece evolved a social democracy of sorts that, for a time, had some success, as noted in the previous paragraph, but state bureaucrats, party hacks, and local businessmen evolved into a class the Greek critics call "kleptocrats." This class made its deals with the European financial oligarchs, resulting in enrichment of the few and gross deprivation of the Greek people. The election of Syriza in January 2015 meant that the era of kleptocracy was put to rest, but the consequences of past deals with the devil remain. The Greek tragedy, written in Brussels and Berlin by banksters, has pushed the Greek people deep into the fires of Hades. And the choices presented to Syriza are to leave the euro and the EC—with certain great economic disruption, social disarray, and political crisis, or to stay with the euro and accept EU austerity. Either way, Greeks will suffer the fires of the damned. In August 2015, Syriza opted to accept the EU imposed austerity impositions and, in 2016, enacted some of the neo-liberal reforms demanded by the Troika. My position, shared by many within Syriza and those that split off, is that staying is not a viable alternative, leaving the Eurozone at least offers the longer-term prospect of escaping the fires of Hades scorched but not entirely consumed by fire and brimstone.

The Greek debt burden is a fiscal crisis that is qualitatively different than the banking collapse of Iceland, Ireland, Portugal, Spain, and Cyprus subsequent to the great crash of 2008. The Greek debt is mainly a public sector debt of astronomical heights that can never be repaid. The best that the Troika can do is "extend and pretend"—extend more loans, push back the deadlines, accept partial payment, and pretend that eventually there will be repayment. How was this debt incurred? By European bankers, in the context of stagnation and financialization, searching for outlets for their monies in the dependent periphery.

In the first chapters of this work, the direct link between financialization and economic stagnation was linked to the proclivity for unproductive, wasteful, and unsustainable activity, and speculative investment that promotes the capture of surplus by finance capital. While this analysis was mainly oriented to the United States, in the first sections of this chapter it was argued that stagnation in the center economies, the United States and Europe, led to globalization on a world scale. This, too, had its limits as far as genuine, sustainable development was left by the wayside in favor of an ever larger share of the limited surplus generated being appropriated by financial elites, shared to some extent between the oligarchs of the center and those in other countries. This cross-national collaboration of elites is one root of the Greek crisis.

In joining the Eurozone, Greece's political and economic elite, the kleptocrats, took advantage of the relative low borrowing costs willingly advanced by European banks and financiers. With these funds, there was a great deal of personal enrichment and reckless spending pushing debt and deficits to ever higher levels—and with nothing to show for the borrowing in terms of improved infrastructure, much less sustainable economic development. As a peripheral dependency, Greece (as did Spain, Portugal, Italy, and Cyprus as well) imported manufactures, loans from the center, and pale-skinned northern tourists needing a suntan. There was no movement away from the reliance on tourism and agricultural exports. The economic model became entrenched as dependent underdevelopment and kleptocracy superseded social democracy. With the total collapse of the economy during the great crash, the Greeks begged for bail-out. After the 2008 collapse, German and French banks made large loans to Greek firms. Recognizing the risk involved, the banks took bail-out by transferring the debt to the ECB and IMF. The EU, on the one hand, extended emergency loans to Greece in 2010 and 2012 with the intent of protecting European banks against default and, on the other hand, imposed austerity measures to keep the Greeks in line, to transfer Greek wealth to the center, and to set-up Greece as an example to all of Europe of what can happen to wayward dependencies. Little of this money stayed in Greece, it went to private EU banks.

Money yields privilege and the power to protect privilege. Privilege forms a class of corrupt plutocrats. A prime example is the Soviet Union. The evolution of Soviet socialism to bureaucratic centralism developed a class of highly privileged party and enterprise elite, and the eventual collapse of the system. A similar process of accruing privilege came about not just in Greece, but also in all the European countries where socialist parties came to administer the state apparatus, enamored of their coveted positions, and with their eyes open and ears attentive to where power really resides—not with people, social justice, and democracy, but with plutocracy ready to reward the lesser privileged with their just rewards. In the United States, plutocracy bribes politicians. Throughout the entire world, the American and European plutocrats extend attractive deals to local businessmen and politicians as means of further buttressing their hegemony.

Europe's once powerful socialist parties are now in eclipse, replaced by elected conservative parties, as in Germany, Spain, and the UK (social democrats are even declining to some degree in the Scandinavian countries, but in the UK have brought about Labour Party militancy), and held in disdain by popular revolt and increasingly losing their grip on labor unions. The Greek and European experiences have a range of lessons for the American movement, not least of which is to build organizations that do not permit the accrual of privilege to leaders. Socialists, too, can be corrupted by public office and the rewards it attracts.

The negotiating position of Syriza since January 2015 was partial debt relief, reversal of imposed austerity measures, and public investments to stimulate employment and the economy—measures that are Keynesian in character, hardly socialist. In a very real sense, Syriza, with socialist horizons, now tries, valiantly, to administer a capitalist state that will not go anywhere but downhill. The negotiating position of the EU Troika cannot be reasonably considered negotiation; it is a take-it or leave-it imposition. The EU, cognizant of the threat of challenges to the rule of finance in the EU, aim for putting Syriza in a situation where it must fail, resulting in regime change. The Greek debt, which amounts to 175% of GDP, must be repaid.

But, at this juncture, the point is not so much for bankers to be repaid forthwith and to profit from the interest; the loan terms will be extended, but to keep the debtor in permanent dependency and subordination.

Conditionality requires that the labor market must be even more flexibilized—an end to collective bargaining, reduction of minimum wages. Pensions must be further reduced, even though half the pensions deliver sums below the poverty line (passed in a legislative act in April 2016). The deal is extensive privatization of remaining state enterprises, airports, seaports, electric utilities, and others, with the revenue to be used for repayment of at least the interest on the debt. The Troika wants an increase in the value-added (sales) tax, at the high rate of 23%—again, to free up funds to pay down the foreign debt. Wage and pension cuts, tax increases cutting consumption, and the fire sale of assets are all means that EU financial elite expects to eventually collect debt and interest, in no way reform that would stimulate the failed economy. The alternative to these impositions is leaving the Eurozone and adopting a new currency (or reverting to the pre-euro drachma), defaulting on debt, placing capital controls on the financial system, and finding sources of funding of development of the national economy (tax reform and better tax collection, seeking support from Russia and China, and mobilization of the people to support a "war economy" of sacrifice and resistance).

In July 2015, the Syriza government initiated a popular referendum whether these impositions should be accepted. The vote was an overwhelming NO. At the same time, though, public opinion was strongly in favor of staying in the EU and keeping the euro. Back to the Brussels bargaining table. Syriza came home with no significant concessions on the EU austerity conditions. Caught between contradictory public pressures rejecting austerity while staying with the euro, Syriza went to the parliament and pushed acceptance of the EU austerity package. The parliament went along, but Syriza suffered a serious split, the finance minister negotiating resigned Syriza, the prime minister felt constrained to resign, and new elections maintained a much weakened Syriza in office. Whether Syriza can survive as a political party is an open question. The fall of Syriza is exactly what the EU administrators are after. The Greeks invented democracy, which terrifies the oligarchs who now script a Greek tragedy. Regardless of the eventual fate of Syriza as a party, the ideals of a twenty-first-century renovation of democracy and human development will persist and spread. Popular disenchantment with European capitalism under the sway of finance capital, and the economic and social conditions imposed, will only engender more and more protest throughout Europe and a more widely shared vision of genuine equality, justice, and democracy.[6]

THE UKRANIAN TRAVESTY

The Ukraine presents a different scene. As a consequence of the Ukrainian situation, in 2015 the Bulletin of Atomic Scientists moved their Doomsday clock one minute closer to midnight, 11:47 pm Trump's election moved doomsday even closer. Although I think a hot war with nuclear weapons is not too likely, this is an escalation by the United States and NATO against Russia, as well as an extension of strict neo-liberalism to the east of the EU. In late 2015, the Pentagon provocatively announced a vast increase in the positioning of U.S.–NATO weapons and troops near Russia's eastern border. Russia will logically react by increasing its own forces and the escalation makes cooperation with Russia to resolve issues in the Ukraine and Syria more difficult. It is convenient to pursue the imperial vision by demonizing Putin and the Russians. The cold war situation has a new face; we are not, today, dealing with two irreconcilable social systems, but with one super power extending its hegemony and a rival capitalist country, Russia, striving to find its place in the global order, in de facto alliance with China but, to some extent, also with the other Brics countries, India and South Africa, but Brazil has fallen more into the U.S. orbit with the downfall of Dilma Rouseff. This is more in line with the pre-World War I and World War II situations of bristling inter-imperial rivalries with potential disastrous consequences. American generals announce that Russia is the "greatest enemy" of the United States and the media stirs a frenzy of indignation over "Russian aggression" in the Ukraine. The world's population can only hope that nuclear arms on both sides will function now, as during the cold war, to be a deterrent to nuclear holocaust. It is yet uncertain whether Trump's supposed friendship with Putin will calm the situation.

Russia is not an aggressor in this situation; in fact, it is more a victim. The coup which overthrew the elected government of Yanukovych on February 22, 2014, was engineered by the United States and carried out by neo-Nazi militias of extremist nationalist ideology, together with Ukrainian businessmen who saw their interests more aligned with the West than Russia. (The neo-Nazi label is not exaggerated. The Ukraine harbored a large collaboration force that worked with the German occupation in World War II to slaughter more than one million Jews and communists. This legacy remains these many years after and today's militias still carry the emblems of the Nazis). These are the forces that are attacking and killing thousands of ethnic Russians on the eastern frontier. In August 2015, the Ukraine parliament was debating a plan for decentralization and some degree of regional autonomy that might help to pacify the Eastern region. In response, thousands of the nationalist elements massed in front of the parliament and lobbed grenades at the police guarding it.

The coup was a case of planned regime change, as with Libya, with the cooperation of NATO. The U.S. Assistant Secretary for European Affairs, Victoria Nuland, played the key role in solidifying the establishment of a client state in the Ukraine. Nuland was a former security advisor to the New American Century and Iraq War architect, Vice-President Dick Cheney. In the State Department, she was promoted by Secretary Clinton and Secretary John Kerry approved her moves in the Ukraine. Nuland is not alone among the warmongers. Nuland's husband, Robert Kagan, a founder of the Project for the New American Century that masterminded the Iraq War, said that Obama had invited Putin's "aggression" by being "weak" on the Ukraine. Obama's nominee for Secretary of Defense, Ashton Carter, assured senators at his confirmation hearing that he favors lethal arms for Ukraine and would push Obama for more aggressive military action in the Ukraine and elsewhere. Secretary Kerry has been demonizing Russia and placing sanctions. James Clapper, Director of National Intelligence, views Russia as the greatest threat to the United States. The chair of the Joint Chiefs of Staff, General Martin Dempsey, early on called for arming the Ukraine regime. NATO's top commander, General Philip Breedlove, grossly exaggerates the extent of Russian support for the ethnic Russians under attack by the neo-Nazi militias, much to the consternation of the German chancellery, which called Breedlove's comments "dangerous propaganda," as well as other NATO country political leaders who prefer a negotiated settlement of the conflict. President Obama said he, too, favored a truce and negotiations leading to a settlement, but by his own appointment of the war hawks in the military and intelligence agencies, and conspiracists such as Nuland to the Department of State, one has to question his sincerity. There is good reason too to be skeptical of Trump's reproachmont with Russia.

There are two main reasons for the instigation of forceful regime change in the Ukraine: first, strategic military considerations and, second, the expansion of American and European capital into an under-exploited area, an extension of the reach of globalization. The policy of the United States and NATO since the breakup of the Soviet Union has been to convert former Russian satellites in Eastern Europe to Western dependencies, to build up a perimeter around Russia with countries that are brought into the sphere of European neo-liberal capitalism and, with that, the extension of NATO forces to the borders of Russia. The Ukraine is the last of these dependencies to fall into line, and that country is now going all the way.

The Ukraine is a bonanza for Western energy, extractive, and agri-business corporations. The Ukraine possesses an abundance of natural resources that are only partially developed. Natural gas, oil, uranium and other minerals, and vast expanses of extraordinarily rich farm land. The Ukraine went more or less in the fashion of Russia after the disintegration of the Soviet Union. Party and enterprise heads became what came to be called "capitalist oligarchs." These oligarchs came to the view that their wealth and privilege could be more enhanced by commercial alignment with Western business than with the Russians. So, they plotted with the likes of Victoria Numan, the U.S. National Endowment for Democracy, U.S. AID, and the right-wing armed militias to effect regime change.

The Ukrainian government has been unsuccessful in creating an effective national army, civilians actively resist the draft. American military advisors were sent to train the militias of extremist ideology, including the CIA-backed Organization of Ukrainian Nationalists (fascists), and to integrate them into a National Guard to better carry on the war on the Eastern frontier. To the storm trooper forces anxious to kill Ruskies in 2015 were added three battalions of Islamic extremists out of Chechnya. This is a familiar pattern of the United States working with the most reactionary forces to attempt to achieve its ends, as in Afghanistan, Libya, Syria, and Egypt. Given that one-third of the population of Ukraine speaks Russian, this is an invitation to continuing violent civil strife, if not ethnic cleansing as in the former Yugoslavia. Soon after the coup, the new regime signed a Ukraine–European Union agreement, which the prior elected government had rejected. The agreement reorients Ukraine's economic, political and military policies and activities toward the West and away from long-standing commercial ties with Russia. Nevertheless, in the period since the coup, the economy has steadily declined—a 7.5% fall in GDP forecast for 2015, exports down by 40%, and a currency value decline of 50%, causing grave hardship for the population. The IMF obligingly extended a $17.5 billion loan. Of course, the loan comes with the usual neo-liberal conditionality. The Ukraine is to become a free market, dependent state of the Eastern periphery. The conditions are similar to austerity demands on Greece—public employment reductions, pension benefits cut and a higher retirement age, increased work requirements, government subsidies slashed.... The loan and its conditions are to be administered by the new finance minister, Natalie Jaresko. Jaresko is a U.S. diplomat who became an overnight Ukrainian citizen and who is said to have enriched herself at the expense of a $150 million U.S. investment fund for the

Ukraine. In July and August 2015, the IMF again offered more money with still more strings attached. For a $40 billion emergency finance package, Ukraine must accept a $15 billion loan restructuring agreement.

The Ukraine is a client state of America Inc. that is an economic basket case domestically administrated by kleptocratic oligarchs engaging a war of repression with openly neo-Nazi brigades against ethnic Russians with legitimate grievances. As in Iraq, Libya, and Venezuela, the media propound not just obfuscation, but outright lies. This time around the lie is that the Ukraine is a victim of Russian aggression. So, what should be the demands of the American movement? Minimally, withdrawal of all U.S. forces and military aid to the Ukrainian puppet regime, demand for peaceful settlement of the legitimate claims for regional autonomy of the ethnic Russian eastern areas of the country, recognition of the legitimacy of Crimea to secede from Ukraine and be Russian, and renunciation of NATO encirclement of Russia, which reinvigorates the cold war and potentially could lead to nuclear war should Republican war-mongers come to power.

Under the more or less authoritarian rule of Putin and the big Russian capitalists, one cannot view Russia, at least for now, as an ally for a better future (that depends on social movements and political developments in Russia). However, it is safer for the people everywhere to live in a bi-bolar world of competing capitalist powers, Russia, China, the other Brics countries versus America and Europe, than the very insecure uni-polar world of unrestrained U.S. economic and military domination backed by NATO. That gives much more latitude for other countries seeking to emerge out of global capitalism.

Free Trade Has a Big Price Tag

In March 2015, as Obama was announcing that Venezuela was a "threat to the national security of the United States", I received an email from barackobama.com on pending trade agreements. The Obama administration has had trade representatives meeting with CEOs of transnational corporations and trade negotiators from other countries for several years to draft new "free trade" treaties, the Trans-Pacific Partnership (TPP, involving 12 Pacific Rim countries) and the Trans-Atlantic Trade and Investment Partnership (TTIP, Europe). As might be expected, the U.S. negotiating team is headed by a banker, Michael Froman, from Citibank.

Five hundred U.S. corporations and banks sit on advisory committees that have access to chapters of the Agreement, but Congress people had to make a special trip to the White House to view the document prior to fast-track consideration.

These new deals follow NAFTA and the World Trade Organization of the 1990s. (The WTO sets strict rules on international trade that favor only corporate interests, but has lost much of its effectiveness due to worldwide resistance. Free trade agreements are meant to compensate for WTO failures.) In 2007, the CAFTS-DR treaty with Central American countries and the Dominican Republic was fast-track ratified. Similar agreements have been reached or are pending with individual countries, notably Colombia, which has a long history of 50 years of brutal civil war, death squads, labor repression, and gross violations of human rights.

In the email, Obama claims that TPP "will be guided by one simple principle: putting American workers first...The Trans-Pacific Partnership we're working on would be the most progressive trade agreement in American history—with the strongest labor, environmental, and intellectual property standards yet. It's designed to protect jobs and help grow the economy by focusing on working and middle-class families."

Well, NAFTA and CAFTA have provisions that other countries are supposed to respect, labor and environmental standards—there are, to my knowledge, no cases of enforcement and Central American countries, especially Honduras, stand in flagrant violation. (While the United States condemns Venezuela for human rights violations when there are none, but says not a word about repression and murders in Honduras since the coup that the United States applauded.) Then, of course, there is the narco-state of Mexico (created by NAFTA and the war on drugs) with its border maquilas polluting the environment and extremely low-waged women workers, who are made desperate by the displacement and unemployment effects of NAFTA, and who are regularly subject to femicide. Fifty-five million Mexicans live in poverty, 46.2% of the population. The import of cheap American corn and agricultural products has decimated Mexican agriculture. The peasants who protest are repressed, sometimes murdered, along with massacres of youthful supporters.[7]

The critics are quite correct in pointing to the profound effect of trade agreements on American industry and workers. After President Clinton fast-tracked NAFTA in 1994 and the WTO in 1995, U.S. trade deficits with free trade countries have soared by 430% ($8 trillion since 2000 alone), as American corporations shifted investments and jobs to these countries. Five million U.S. manufacturing jobs, one in four, have been lost to NAFTA and post-NAFTA expansion deals, and displaced workers who found a job are earning less pay. But trade agreements go well beyond American economic decline and jobs. The agreements have affected. and will affect, if these agreements are enacted, everything that everybody worldwide experiences, the food to eat, the jobs available, the health of the planet, the fate of peoples everywhere in front of the subordination of well-being and democracy to the rule of capital. Obama also managed to get through the fast-tracked deals TPP and with Europe a "Trade in Services Agreement" (TISA), which Wikileaks disclosures reveal as a deal to enhance the ongoing process of financialization on a global scale, but goes well beyond that. TISA involves 51 countries. The deal would liberalize global trade in all services, financial, health care, education, engineering, telecommunications.... It would restrict how government can legislate in these areas, for example, by setting-up a public service as a "monopoly", be it in water, electric, banking, or health care, and could privatize still more public services. Governments could not favor local companies over foreign corporations, or limit the size of the market position of foreign firms. Also inserted into the agreements is a provision undermining the boycott, divestment, and sanctions (BDS) movement against Israeli oppression of Palestinians, and this could have wider impact as BDS is applied against American corporations.

When fast tracked, it was hard to say if the rest of Obama's statement contained any truth; the TPP was classified secret. The "working and middle-class families" it is supposed to benefit only know what was leaked. Obama consulted the CEOs of transnational corporations and their Wall Street partners, but certainly not the American Federation of Labor and Congress of Industrial Organizations (AFL-CIO), which strongly opposes such agreements. With its publication, finally, in November 2015, it became clear that the statement was a gross lie with the purpose of secretly extending the rule of capital to yet other nations, to the detriment of the American working population, and even more so to populations in other countries subject to increased subordination, while the local politicians and businessmen and international capital achieve a closer partnership. The special interests get special consideration. Wall Street gets rules making the flow of money very fluid; the pharmaceuticals get protection against generic drugs, and Hollywood their intellectual property rights; Agri-business gets protection of GMO foodstuffs. The opposition to fast track in Congress, labor groupings, and movement militants has been almost entirely couched in terms of the effect in the United States of continuing job losses, although there is some concern about undermining of U.S. democracy by heightened corporate powers. While serious effects on the U.S. economy and society are real enough, the big problem resides in the further extension of capital's power and privilege in global society.

These two agreements and TISA, and all those to follow in years to come in this legislation, were "fast tracked" through the Congress in June 2015. When they come back to Congress, there is no debate, no public commentary, no amendments, only an up or down vote by the Congress. Pushed by Bernie Sanders, Hillary Clinton opposed the treaties. Trump states that he will dismantle current trade agreements such as NAFTA. Yet, as Republicans and corporate-friendly Democrats continue their large presence in Congress in 2017, if the trade agreements are brought to a vote, the corporate noose will be even tighter, the rule of plutocracy even stronger.[8] The content of the numerous chapters of TPP give the lie to Obama's outrageous claim.

TPP and TTIP contain provisions for "Investor-State Dispute Settlement." Corporations can enter complaints and claims of lost future profits if they make a case of government interference with their investment prospects. A corporation can lodge a complaint that its rights and profits are violated by environmental or other laws, or government subsidies or policies. Punitive damages can be assessed and governments forced to change tariff or subsidy programs that have national development ends, dismantle environmental protection measures, and force flexibility in labor laws. This would apply also to the United States. An example could be that countries promoting alternative energy policies might be subject to complaint by big oil, or pharmaceuticals could claim violations of intellectual property rights for production of generic drugs. There are current disputes that foreign mining companies have filed under Dispute Settlement in CAFTA against several countries for punitive damages and against local environmental laws. The Dispute Settlement is presided over by a body of corporate lawyers and is invested with more power than the governments affected. Their decisions are superior to national laws and final, no appeal. Under NAFTA, CAFTA, and other trade agreements, there have been more than 600 cases of corporate challenges. Most likely this mechanism will be used to reduce environmental, labor, health, and safety measures everywhere to the lowest level, with national development policies confined to the dictates of neo-liberalism.

Under provisions in NAFTA Canada is now demanding $15 billion in compensation for the cancellation by the United States of the Keystone XL pipeline for oil from Canadian tar sands across the United States to Texas, while U.S. corporations have demands under CAFTA upon Central American countries for lost profits from cancelled investments.

These treaties are part of a coup against established governments by American plutocracy and their class-privileged counterparts in Canada, the Asia/Pacific, and Europe. Given the privatization emphasis of neo-liberal doctrines that underlie such agreements, public assets in utilities, water systems, roads, and social services could be forced to be sold to private interests. Good-bye to GMO labeling, hello to high-priced drugs, pipe-lines and fracking, still more sweatshops, further degradation of labor, toxic plants and factory farms and sludge fields next to homes, a curbing of zoning laws, and end to even a semblance of democracy. A planned *golpe de estado* is on the horizon with these treaties, but I don't think, or at least hope, that these worst scenario events will not happen—free trade, the further extension of neo-liberal policy, and the consolidation of plutocratic rule internationally will be strenuously opposed by world-wide social forces. In July 2015, negotiations of TTIP in Brussels, the European Commission responding to widespread concern proposed that private tribunals be replaced with panels of publicly appointed professional judges. Whether that will be a crimp in corporate action to protect their profits against governments that pursue sovereignty remains to be seen. The July 2015 meeting of the TPP Pacific Rim countries and the United States in Hawaii broke up without any agreement. Canada, Australia, New Zealand, and Japan objected to the provisions extending protection of prescription drug patents, and the threat that this and other provisions regarding privatization in health care poses to their systems of universal health care. As in the European community, the provisions for investor-state dispute settlement provisions were questioned. In an October 2015 meeting in Atlanta, the TPP was finally negotiated, and the most notori-ous provisions, such as the dispute settlement provisions, are still there.

We have to consider that treaties to date have had a devastating impact on the world economy and society, and the TPP and other agreements in process will be even more devastating. Corporate dominance of the bulk of the world economy will be greatly furthered and all forms of people's democratic controls will be circumscribed.

When the TPP was finally published in November 2015, I went to the website of the Office of the United States Trade Representative and read as many chapters as I had the patience to review. (If the reader has a great deal of patience, see www.ustr.gov/trade-agreements/) The numerous chapters are tedious, filled with jargon, convoluted technical legalese, ambiguous phrasing…. But the essence is a program for a rigorous corporate power grab on a global scale. The analysis published on U.S. alternative websites is mainly geared to the effects on the United States, but I think that the international codification of corporate dominance is much more serious.

- This is an agreement that enshrines corporate rights, regulates the internet, limits national health care systems and provides for hospital privatization, regulates financial services, circumscribes labor and environmental laws enacted by governments, makes it illegal for governments (including local and state governments in the United States) to enact legislation favoring local businesses, and in general advances a new form of colonization on a global scale.
- In general, TPP forces equal rules on unequal partners, foreign corporations must be treated equally with national business; no government procurement to assist local firms; there can be no capital controls over the import or expatriation of funds or to deter speculation; trade policy such as tariffs to protect national industry are not allowed….
- With NAFTA, CAFTA, and other Free Trade Agreements, and under mainly American pressures, preexisting development-oriented states have been weakened or dismantled and external dependency increased. This will be extended to all the participating countries.
- Austerity programs will be imposed that reduce social spending while limited economic growth comes at the expense of exclusionary patterns of social and political development that pauperize sectors of the population, increase social inequalities, weaken civil society and the democratic order, and degrade the environment.
- Essential public services will be extensively privatized, leading to increased costs to the public for electric and telephone service, even water, education and health care, as well as to graft among the politicians responsible for the giveaway of public resources.
- With globalization to date, where workers' unions have not been smashed by military and police forces, they have been weakened by programs of "labor flexibility." Labor in general is degraded as

investment is channeled into sectors where labor is cheapened and molded as servile. This will now be extended to all participating countries.

- Where instituted (Mexico being a graphic example) food sovereignty is undermined. Previous programs of rural development undone, tariff protection of domestic agriculture dropped, subsidies to stimulate national food production eliminated (while USDA-subsidized agriculture may still stay in place to export its cheapened products). With TPP, even food safety import regulations are circumscribed.

Free trade is the commercial side of global corporate dominance. As I have repeatedly pointed out, the other side is coercive and military force applied by the United States.

Given that these treaties and the neo-liberal doctrines that underlie them are central to the consolidation of plutocratic power, wide resistance has been mobilized and even become central to Trump's campaign. As with so many other issues, this is fundamentally a class war question— broadly speaking, a 90% versus the 1% issue. Defeating free trade treaties strikes at the heart of plutocratic power and, for now, it appears that such agreements are at least slowed. Trump says the TPP is dead and that NAFTA will be renegotiated. However, this anti-free trade stance is totally inconsistent with his appointments of precisely those bankers and other officials that are the very ones that have been pushing free trade.

We have explored fairly thoroughly the several facets of how capital rules through imposition of its class-based ideology in the homeland and abroad, and have critically evaluated the policies that flow from that thought. That the plutocracy rules by transforming politics through bribery was explored in Chap. 6, and by a divide and conquer strategy in Chap. 7. The most savage means by which capital imposes its will is by terror and war abroad and repression at home, discussed in Chap. 8 and here.

What can be said about the prospects of resistance? There appears to be increasing resistance to the rule of capital in Southern Europe, the EU exit by Great Britain, and protest against neo-liberal reforms in France. From adversity springs opportunity. The depressive economic conditions, the social disaster of gross unemployment, and the imposition of austerity measures have resulted in a multitude of vibrant social movements. Syriza in Greece; Unidos Podemos (Yes We Can) in Spain; in Italy Movimento 5 Stella (M5S, 5 Star Movement); in Portugal in November 2015 a coalition of the Left Block, Socialists, and Communist won a critical election; even in Germany Die Linke ("The Left") is doing well, and the Greens and labor movements everywhere in Europe are gaining strength. All of these movements view with contempt the complicity of the social democratic parties in bringing about the current situation. The base of social democracy, the trade unions, is drifting away from the party. Unlike the United States, some social movements are evolving into successful political parties. Syriza, after growing out of social protest in the last few years, won national elections in January 2015. In Spain, Podemos and associated movements gather citizens in assemblies to discuss issues and the assemblies elect a national citizens' council. Podemos citizens' councils formed as a political party in 2015 and won control of several key cities, and in 2016 had the possibility of forming a coalition government of the left. (Links to European Movement websites in English, Spanish, Italian, German, and other languages are in the Appendix). But there is also a response to EU conditions, and especially to the refugee crisis affecting Europe, in the form of nativist and right-wing nationalist assertions, resulting in the British withdrawal from the EU.

The struggle in Latin America is ongoing but suffering some recent setbacks.

Socialism for the Twenty-first Century

In moving out of underdevelopment as a de facto U.S. colony, Cuba is still surviving after more than a half century of U.S. interventions bent on destroying the revolution. In confronting neo-liberal subservience, Venezuela has taken the lead in constructing a new society that serves the needs of its people. Bolivia and Ecuador are marching in step, and other countries in the region are making an effort to construct a more just society and working economy.

In 1999, Hugo Chavez became President of Venezuela. Between that date and his death from cancer in March 2013, Venezuela had 16 elections and Chavez won 15 by wide margins, including a recall election promoted by the right-wing opposition. Venezuela has an extraordinarily effective and honest electoral system. An analysis by Salim Lamrani[9] analyzes a wide range of accomplishments of Venezuelan socialism that benefits the people of that previously underdeveloped country and set an example for Latin America and the world. Lamrani's main points (52 accomplishments) are here summarized.

Among the first steps in the years spanning the 2000s were advances in education, health, nutrition, and housing, areas that in Venezuela, as in much of Latin America, were grossly deficient. A literacy campaign reached 1.7 million persons who now read and write. The number of children attending primary school increased from 6 million in 1998 to 13 million in 2013. Primary school enrollment is nearly universal and secondary school enrollment reached 73.3% in 2011. Thirteen new universities were created and enrollment in higher education is 2.7 million. Venezuela has a universal health care system with no fees to the public. Between 2005 and 2012, 787 new medical centers were created. The number of doctors increased by 400% in ten years. Infant mortality was reduced by 49% and life expectancy increased from 72.2 years in 1999 to 74.3 in 2011. With the assistance of Cuban specialists, 1.5 million persons had cataracts or other eye problems resolved. The housing goal is three million new homes especially benefiting the poorest sectors and with subsidized home loans.

Venezuela now has, after Cuba, the lowest rate of inequality in Latin America and, on the UN Human Development Index, moved from 83 on the country list in 2000 to 73 in 2011. On the World Happiness Index, Venezuela is second in Latin America (after Costa Rica; Cuba is not surveyed). Elderly people now have pensions. Women and disabled persons without income receive support. Basic foods are subsidized and available in 22,000 stores. Average calorie intake has increased by 50%. Children get free meals at schools. Venezuela spearheaded a movement away from U.S. dominance in the region with the creation of the Bolivarian Alliance for the Peoples of Our America (ALBA).

Venezuela is socialist in the economic sphere to only a limited degree. The oil industry was placed under government control in 2003 after a management shutdown in an effort to unseat Chavez. The electrical and telecommunications industries were nationalized. There are 1200 radio and TV stations run cooperatively by community groups. A major land reform was carried out. Fifty thousand cooperatives in all sectors were created. However, much of the economy is in the sphere of private capital, which is now creating a major problem for advancing the socialist project.

The high oil prices up to 2014 allowed the financing of these accomplishments, as well as high rates of economic growth. The collapse of oil prices and a concerted right-wing and U.S. effort to destabilize the government has created a major economic and political crisis in Venezuela.

Challenges to Venezuelan strivings will be discussed later. For now, a look at Cuba, its revolutionary example, and its future.

VIVA CUBA

Cuba, harassed by endless years of terrorist attacks, has survived the willful determination of the American empire to destroy the revolution. Its economic development has been checked by 56 years of embargo, but nevertheless Cuba is No. 1 in Latin America on indices of human development. Cuba has health and educational achievements comparable with the most advanced wealthy countries, is ahead of the United States in measures of health and education, and way ahead in energy consumption with CO_2 emissions 10% of those of the U.S. Cuba invests 10.3% of its GDP in education, the highest in the world, compared with 5.4% for the U.S. Propagandized as being a communist dictatorship, Cuba's participatory democracy looks pretty good in comparison with the alienation and atomization of American citizenry, where a vote can only be for a perceived lesser of two evils. Cuba's substantive democracy of opportunity and equality is unparalleled anywhere, limited only by the debilitating effects of the embargo, while the United States closes opportunity and widens inequality. Cuba's participatory mass organizations, and its elected local and regional councils, look good compared with the rigged elections of the United States, to the rule of plutocracy, to the totalitarianism of the National State of Insecurity.

For decades, Cuba has suffered the hardest economic sanctions ever imposed on any country, plus terrorist attacks and extremes of aggression—and survived. Cuba suffered mercenary invasion (Bay of Pigs, CIA-organized, in 1961), bombings, burnings of agricultural crops, assassinations, and, in the 1962 Cuban missile crisis, the CIA and the Kennedy administration brought the world to the edge of nuclear destruction. Subject to tens of thousands of terrorist attacks by agents of the CIA and Defense Department, the U.S. Department of State had the audacity to place Cuba on the list of countries that engage in "state sponsored terrorism!" Finally, in late 2014, sectors of the establishment recognized that the embargo and terrorist measures against Cuba did as much to isolate America as Cuba (there were annual UN General Assembly resolutions condemning the embargo, voted against only by the United States and its staunch allay Israel).

The Obama administration, frustrated at the failure of attempts at regime change, moved to establish diplomatic relations with Cuba. In September 2015, Pope Francis visited Cuba. Prior to that he had been instrumental in getting Obama to move to open diplomatic relations and

Cuba to accept the opening. Because of his efforts, the Pope was greeted in Havana by one million Cubans. In a mass, the Pope dedicated his commitment to "the fragile:" "To be Christian implies fighting and living for the dignity of Brothers." This is just what has marked the Cuban revolution since 1959. He admonished, in apparent reference to the United States: "Leave aside the search and desire for omnipotence." In his next stop, Pope Francis visited the United States, where his focus was on an economy that leaves no one behind. He spoke to the House of Representatives and the UN. In New York, he spoke to car-washers, day-laborers, and immigrant mothers, and, in Philadelphia, at a prison. Very different audiences in these two countries; similar messages, in Cuba a pat on the shoulder, in the United States a kick in the posterior.

President Raúl Castro gave a welcoming speech at the Havana airport in which he said, in part: "They have made blockades, slanders, aggressions with a high cost in human lives and grave economic damages. We have founded a society with equality and social justice, with wide access to culture and in keeping with the most advanced traditions and ideas from Cuba, Latin America and the Caribbean, and of the world." Raúl went on to cite Cuba's internationalist programs in health and education that have benefited 158 countries and hundreds of thousands of people (in sharp contrast to U.S. aid programs aimed at subversion). Raúl continued, saying "We will resolutely advance in the actualization of our economic and social model to construct a prosperous and sustainable socialism centered on the human being, the family, and free democratic, conscious, and creative participation of the entire society, especially of youth…. To preserve socialism is to guarantee independence, sovereignty, development and the wellbeing of the Nation." (This author's translation).

The opening of diplomatic relations has resulted in prisoner exchanges, the loosening of travel restrictions and monetary remissions, removal from the "state-sponsored terrorism" list, but little in the way of ending the embargo, or in vacating Guantanamo and reverting the U.S. military base and prison there to Cuban sovereignty. The essential idea of the Obama *et al.* visionaries is to accomplish by other means what could not be accomplished by 56 years of attempts of regime change (now mainly by nurturing an island capitalist class). Let us expect that Cuba can stay the exemplary socialist course in a better situation than before the opening.

Obama has continued long-enduring policies that were designed to bring down the revolution. In 1966, Congress passed the Cuban Adjustment Act, which allowed any Cuban who arrived in the United

States the status of permanent resident with benefits for work, housing, medical, and other benefits. Quite a comparison to how refugees from other countries are welcomed! Of course, the embargo had gross effects on the economy and there were many immigrants. As part of its emphasis on human development, Cuba fashioned a highly effective domestic and foreign aid program in the medical field. To counter this, in 2006 the Bush administration adopted the Cuban medical Professional Parole Program to encourage the emigration of Cuban medical professionals to the United States. These policies must go.

Now the idea is to bring Cuba back into the sphere of globalization by supporting "civil society," that is, forming a business class that will have growing political clout. To a certain extent this strategy fits with decisions already made by the Cubans to decentralize Cuba's system of state planning and to permit foreign investments and small-scale private business. European capital has invested substantial amounts in the tourism industry, under contract with Cuban authorities or in partnership with the Cuban government. Recent changes in organization of the Cuban economy focus on development of cooperatives (formerly confined to agriculture; there are now more than 500 urban co-ops) and allowing self-employment and small business in a number of sectors. This sector will be receiving remittances from the Miami exile community along with material aid, training, and marketing assistance for the nascent business class. Assistant Secretary of State Jacobson said of the policy: "We would hope to bring about change in the regime....to empower the Cuban people to be able to make that change....Our hope is that we can empower the small entrepreneurs." It is likely that the expectation is that Cuba will go the way of the Soviet Union, or at least evolve to a state capitalism similar to that of China and Vietnam.

Apparently the CIA, the principle actor in attempts to bring down the revolution, will now take a back-seat to the U.S. Agency for International Development. In September 2015, AID placed an employment ad seeking managers to run its Washington-based Cuba programs. Salaries range up to $139,523 per year. "Experience in the areas of democracy promotion, human rights, civil society development...is preferred....Expert knowledge and experience in the development of civil society, social capital... especially in closed society, is highly desired....Successful candidates must obtain a "secret security clearance."

The U.S. plan for regime change is not likely to get very far. On June 15, 2016, *Granma*, the official newspaper of the Cuban Communist

Party, reported that the concluding documents of the Party Congress, after lengthy debates, would be submitted to a process of democratic consultation to all elective bodies and people's organizations for critique and reactions. This goes well beyond what the British did by submitting the Stay or Leave the EU to popular vote. The documents are the "Social Model" and the "National Economic and Social Development Plan through 2030" that define the future of Cuban economy and society well into the future. The documents stipulate a very advanced concept of democratic socialism. "The National Development Plan through 2030 defines the strategic concepts (effective socialist government, social integration, productive transformation and international integration, infrastructure, human potential, science, technology and innovation, natural resources and the environment, and human development, justice and equality)"[10] Imagine if the Democratic Party Platform of August 2016 were submitted for popular consultation to every state government and city council, unions, and people's organization in the United States for their input!!

Let's expect that Cuba can hold onto and further develop its substantive democracy of mass participation, an economy that serves human need, and a social structure of opportunity and equality. Revolutionary support and euphoria persist in Cuba. *"Hasta la Victoria Siempre"* ("Ever onward to Victory") is not an empty slogan. For Americans, *"Solidaridad Siempre"* ("Solidarity Always") should be practiced.

End the Embargo, Issue Reparations. No to Normalization Just to Engage in Subversion. Get Out of Guantanamo.

CLASS RELATIONS AND GLOBALIZATION, LATIN AMERICA

The prelude to full-scale globalization transpired in the 1960s and 1970s. The fierce military dictatorships in Latin America in this period were imposed in a transitional conjuncture ending in the establishment of all the principles of neo-liberalism. The dictatorships became the most salient international phenomena since the fascisms of the 1930s and 1940s. Before going into the period of military dictatorship in Latin America, it is well to state the global context and the method for understanding these events.

Focusing on events in any given country or region requires a theoretical posturing of the articulation of economic/political thrusts from the center and the territorially based classes and their conflicts in the periphery. In the period prior to and since the globalization of the 1970s and

1980s, the predominant class and economic forces thrusting from the center have been the transnational corporations and international, especially American, finance capital. The process of capital extension from the center, today termed "globalization," can be conceptualized as a "general determinant" of the workings of the economy and the transformation of the social structure in which class forces are always in conflict and struggle within territorial states. The political economy of world system globalization exercises a general causality insofar as territorial classes are structured by external impulses and these classes are locked into relationships of subordinated dependency that extend beyond national frontiers. At the same time, such class relations find expression within territorial states and, in good part, determine the form that states assume, from the populist states of the 1960s, to the military dictatorships of the 1970s and 1980s and, subsequently, the assumption of formally democratic forms in the 1990s to the more democratic and reformist states in parts of Latin America since the 2000s. This conflict within nations can be posed as the "proximate determinant" of events in different territories subordinated with global capitalism and in a general condition of dependency—dependency being a condition in which economic and political options are structurally and politically limited by insertion with the global system. The relationship of general to proximate determinants is asymmetrical, but should be conceived dialectically, not as a one-way determinism. In brief, while territorial class struggles are the proximate causes of events, the forces forming classes and providing a context for their clashes are international in scope. "The external/internal nexus is unraveled if it viewed as a dialectic of asymmetrical process. The structuring impulses are international in scope, but the actual outcomes are the result of localized conditions and struggles. The method is historical-structural, involving analysis of political economy and class relations under conditions of dependency, where dependency itself is a class relationship among parties of unequal power."[11] This perspective is critical in appreciating the possibilities and limits to the region successfully moving out of the current neo-liberal dependency and into self-determination of a democratic state moving beyond capitalism in the pursuit of social justice. Shortly, we will look at what is happening in the most advanced democratic countries, Venezuela, Ecuador, and Bolivia, and the precarious current situation of important countries such as Brazil, Uruguay, and Argentina.

GOOSESTEPPING TOWARD HEGEMONY

The first military dictatorship was established in Brazil in 1964 with the military overthrow of the populist government of President Goulart. The military intervention was preceded by strong opposition to the reformist and nationalist policies of the government and large mobilizations of workers, peasants, and slum-dwellers. During this epoch of President's Kennedy's Alliance for Progress, the CIA unleased its version of progress in military liaisons and training programs. In the context of economic difficulties and high inflation, strong pressures from the United States and transnational corporations, and the exhaustion of national development depending on import-substitution and state intervention, the capitalist class as a whole, backed by mobilizations of sizeable segments of the middle class, gave clear indications that it was time for the military to move. By 1968, a fierce dictatorship was consolidated. Argentina's first military intervention was in 1968, then even more fiercely in 1976. Chile and Uruguay succumbed to the heeled boots of reaction in 1973.

The emergence phase of military dictatorship is characterized by the increasing extension of transnational corporate entry and U.S. political pressures. On the domestic front, features of the national class structures consolidated in the stage of national development began to break apart and become more conflictive. There was the formation of a substantial salaried middle class; classes associated with preceding social developments, landlords and peasants and independent businessmen, suffered a relative demise; most saliently there came about a growing polarization between modern monopoly capital, foreign and domestic, and a modern working class and vast underclass of immiserated peoples. Intervening in the growing level of class conflict were social and institutional forces—students, intellectuals, and religious groups became politically mobilized. This emergence of a new form of the state can be conceptualized as a dialectic of external determination, the general situation of dependency, and the proximate determinant of national class struggles in the context of a crisis of transition from one stage of capitalist development to another. In this case, a transition from national development to dependent development (explanation would require too lengthy a narrative here). Internationally induced shifts in the extension of capital coincide with sharpened local class conflicts.

The dictatorships of the Southern Cone evidenced a number of commonalities. First, the repressive apparatus subsumed or overshadowed all other facets of state activity. For this reason, the term "fascist" was frequently applied to these military dictatorships, although these regimes responded to a different set of historical circumstances than Europe in the 1930s. A military institutionality replaced civilian forms of state administration to such a degree that it touched all the interstices of daily life: states of siege, secret police, total censorship of media, military tribunals—the subordination of the whole of civil society to bureaucratic management and military discipline. Military dictatorship was not of a man, Chile's General Pinochet was not a Hitler, but of the Armed Forces as an institution, the Junta of Generals commanding.

Second, state activity was guided by the military that relentlessly applied policies narrowly serving the interests of the predominant sectors of international and national capitals. These policies bear little resemblance to the corporativism, nationalism, and statism of classic fascism. In this crucial respect, they were the opposite: the regimes aimed toward disorganizing interest groups and dividing classes; economic policies were geared to exterior markets, investment sources, and credits; the regimes imposed what was, in this epoch, referred to as neo-classical liberalism, which by the 1980s evolved into what is today known as "neo-liberalism" and openness to globalization.

Third, the regimes resorted to legitimation by way of pronouncements of threatened national security. While the torture, death squads, censorship, busting of unions, and killing of dissidents was routine, there was no Nazi or Falangist party, no great hordes of marching brown shirts to carry the message to the initial support groups of the dictatorship—the salaried middle class, small businessmen, sectors of the class of lesser capitalists. In fact, these groupings were demobilized, denied political voice, and increasingly repressed. South American bankers, industrialists, transnational corporate interests, the juntas, and their American patrons shared a perspective that became an overriding obsession—economic growth is imperative for the long-term stability of free enterprise and the values of Western civilization as manifested at the level of the nation. The concept of development was ideologically paired with the notion of national security, corresponding also to the U.S. promulgation of "hemispheric security" and its militaristic interventions from the 1960s onward. More development means greater security, and greater security is a prerequisite for development. The juntas became political directorates of the dominant class forces. The chaos of social struggles and democracy was brought to an end. Technocratic efficiency by persons trained in policy orthodoxy to man the state bureaucracy was combined with a notion of nationalism not directed toward mobilization of popular support, but toward defining the "unpatriotic."

TRANSITION TO DEMOCRACY OF THE 1990s AND BREAKING OUT IN THE 2000s

The demobilization and repression of social forces that made the dictatorships possible in the first instance was, in part, responsible for their eventual collapse. Fortunately, even the fiercest of class dictatorships engender their own contradictions that eventually lead to a transition to less authoritarian states and a greater level of formal democracy. In the nearly two decades of dictatorship, former supporters of the dictatorships were given the cold shoulder, clandestine opposition increased, citizens became horrified by the gross violations of human rights, consternation was worldwide, even the Catholic Church, generally a conservative force in the region, criticized and offered shelter to the persecuted.[12]

A historical-structural method proceeds on the basis of understanding existing reality as a historical construction on what was and what is in the making. What was in the 1980s rested on a consolidated class of local top businessmen in alignment with international capital and U.S. support, with military juntas that constituted a political directorship promoting and securing their interests. Appended to the dominant class were a managerial cadre and technocratic staff. The industrial working class, while on the defensive, nevertheless matured and seethed in their oppressive class situation. A salaried middle class had a critical location in the social structure and the political order, with many elements that mobilized initial support for military intervention beginning to question military rule. Diverse rural and urban groupings of dispossessed and immiserated people exploded in numbers and volatility. Institutional sectors, such as the Church, intellectuals, and students, acted out in the local scene with considerable force. The highly repressive nature of the dictatorship gave rise to increasing resistance and juntas were eventually forced to call elections and retreat from direct control of the state. What became in the making was a qualitatively changed constellation of local class forces exercising proximate causality to a change in the form of the state, from dictatorship to formal democracy. This transition was also partly attributable to the fact that neo-liberal policies were not only disruptive to the social order, but also failed to bring about economic growth. From 1980 to 2000, real per capita income grew by only 5.7%. What continued with democratization, however, was the general situation of dependency imposed from the U.S. center and the peripheral close relationship of local and foreign capital.

In the pivotal country of Chile, 1990 elections were won by the *Concertación*, a coalition of Christian Democrats and socialists of various tendencies. The new government curbed repression but maintained the country's links to the growing pressure and sophistication of globalization. Succeeding socialist governments, down to the present government of President Micelle Bachelet, instituted some social policies of amelioration and respect for democratic rights and procedures, but maintained Chile's firm integration in the international system. (Bachelet's father, a military officer opposed to the intervention, was murdered by the junta and she was arrested and tortured). Chile negotiated incorporation in the Trans-Pacific Pact that represents the ultimate in subordination to global capitalism. Chile has a sophisticated political culture and militant forces on the left, so all is not hopeless.

In Argentina, the elected civilian governments culminated in the late 1980s in a government that privatized public institutions and imposed other neo-liberal policies, while instituting the U.S. dollar as the currency and negotiating billions in loans from the IMF, World Bank, and private foreign creditors. As with the euro in Southern Europe today, Argentina lost control of its national currency that allowed shifts in exchange rates and control of monetary and fiscal policy. By the 1990s, Argentina was in a complete state of financial collapse and deep depression. A left-of-center government, led by President Kirchner, defaulted then successfully renegotiated the foreign debt, reinstituted the peso as the currency, and adopted monetary stimulus and fiscal policies that brought about a rapid recovery. Although the circumstances are different, the Argentine experience has some relevance to a possible Greek euro exit.

Brazil, with the largest economy in the region followed the neo-liberal policy path of Argentina in the 1980s and 1990s, but with less severe measures. Rich in natural resources, Brazil in this period became a power house in the export of primary commodities, grains from the rich farm lands of the south and interior, minerals, coffee, oil, tropical products from the Amazon, and to some degree manufactures. This development, not shared with workers, peasants, and the vast underclass of immiserated slum dwellers, had the effect of greatly increasing the strength of social movements of peasants and poor people, but especially the working class.

In 2002, Lula da Silva, the leader of Sao Paulo unions and the Workers Party, won the election. The policies of Lula and his successor, Dilma Rousseff, began to make breaks in the bonds of dependency by diversifying Brazil's trade relations with China and the rest of the world, and by pursuing a more independent foreign policy not tied to U.S. constraints. The state oil company Petrobras and a well-financed Brazilian Development Bank brought about a considerable development of national industry. In 2015–2016, Petrobras and the Bank came under fire for alleged corruption of politicians. Shortly to be discussed are the limits to further progress in these key countries, along with other Latin American left-of-center governments. These limits are increasingly bearing down in the entire region. Venezuela is now taking the brunt of subversion with the end of regime change. Dilma Rousseff of the Workers Party in Brazil was impeached in a right-wing, neo-liberal coup.

Latin America, Local Oligarchs and U.S. Interventionism

The local privileged class interests and the United States have been futilely trying to do-in Hugo Chavez and Venezuelan socialism for more than a decade, carrying out a failed military coup in 2002, an oil sector shut-down in 2003, recall elections for President Chavez, and right-wing mobilizations and economic sabotage to destabilize and reverse socialist advances. United States agencies, such as the AID and CIA, have been funneling large sums of money to the neo-liberal opposition within the privileged classes set on regime change by any means feasible—engaging in all manner of subversion, economic sabotage, and violent actions, down to the present day. They are joined by State Department front organizations such as the National Endowment for Democracy and NGOs such as CANVAS and Freedom House.[13] Human Rights Watch (HRW) joins the chorus of denunciation of Venezuela (HRW watches out for imperial interests, not human rights). While not yet fully documented in a Venezuelan Court of Law, in February 2015 the government denounced a plot to bomb strategic targets and the Presidential Building, kill President Maduro, mobilize opposition forces, and install regime change by force and violence. According to the evidence gathered by the government (the veracity of which is unknown as of this date), a plane disguised as belonging to the Venezuelan Air Force, contracted to an American mercenary contractor,

Academi (successor to Blackwater that slaughtered civilians in Iraq), was to do the bombing. The coup attempt also had backing, and prior conspiratorial subversion from some military officers and the right-wing Mayor of Caracas (one of the few cities electing opposition candidates), who has been arrested along with some military personnel.

This was followed in March 2015 by President Obama's declaration of emergency powers to invoke additional sanctions against Venezuela on the basis of "a national emergency with respect to the unusual and extraordinary threat to the national security and foreign policy of the United States posed by the situation in Venezuela." Never a more upside down situation! Venezuela is considered a threat because it has honest elections that have led to a transition to socialism, sits on huge reserves of oil, uses oil revenue to combat poverty and forge alliances in Latin America, pursues a foreign policy of independence that opens to a plural world, and sets a forward-looking example for the region and the world.

Hugo Chavez was an extraordinarily leader, much lauded by the majority of Venezuelans and respected abroad.[14] Since the first election of Hugo Chavez in 1998 (subsequent elections were won by large majorities on numerous occasions and a Chavez opposition-sponsored recall vote was roundly rejected) the United States has been pouring in millions of dollars in funding to right-wing opposition groupings. U.S. AID and its Office for Transition Initiatives has funded more than $50 million, and the official U.S. National Endowment for Democracy has been very generous with distributing dollars. The Chavez government had refused to accept the appointment of a U.S. ambassador for interference in Venezuela's internal affairs, and the United States reciprocated by ousting the Venezuelan ambassador in Washington. The respective embassies were, in effect, reduced to interest sections. Nevertheless, the illicit money continued to flow and, in March 2015, President Maduro tried to end this illegal activity by ordering a reduction in the size of the U.S. interest section staff. In 2014, opposition groups led violent street actions that ended with many persons being killed, most of them police and government supporters. These events then lead to a concerted international media campaign that the government was violating human rights and holding "political prisoners" (persons arrested for violent actions), followed by sanctions imposed by President Obama and the U.S. Congress. In May 2015, the international press circulated an exposé that the President of the Congress, a major United Socialist Party of Venezuela (PSUV) figure, was a drug trafficker. There appears to be no end to the smear campaign, the media never mention the killings that happen daily in Honduras to regimen opponents nor the Egyptian military overthrowing elected governments, condemning the elected President to death, and shooting people on the streets.

Again more upsidedownness! The privileged vested interests engage in sabotage of the economy by hoarding, exporting scarce goods to Colombia, creating a black market in goods and currency…in an attempt to win over and mobilize the middle class (greatly expanded with the social gains since the turn of the millennium) for reaction and to demoralize the population and undermine the revolution. This was a strategy that worked to undermine the Sandinista revolution in Nicaragua in the 1980s, and led to military dictatorship in Chile and other Latin American countries in the 1970s. It appears to be beginning to work in Venezuela, the December 2015 legislative elections were decisively won by the right-wing opposition. In the face of shortages of consumer goods essentials, President Maduro has ordered a state of emergency and is asking workers at closed factories to start up production that the bosses have closed down.

The right-wing opposition is traveling all roads for regime change. In May 2016, they collected signatures for a recall election of President Maduro. In a review by the electoral bureau, they found 190,000 names of deceased people and the Venezuelan court did not recognize the legitimacy of the recall petition. The head of the Organization of American States, Luis Almagro, has been denouncing Venezuela. In May 2016, he met in Washington with top State Department officials and General John Kelly of the Southern Command. (The Southern Command has bases for intervention in Latin America, in Colombia, and elsewhere in the region). President Maduro denounced violations of Venezuelan airspace by U.S. reconnaissance planes. In May 2016, Henrique Capriles of the opposition group Mesa de la Unidad Democrática (MUD) made an explicit call to the country's military to rebel against the government.

Given the achievements for "Socialism of the 21st Century" in Venezuela, why did President Obama declare that Venezuela is a threat to U.S. national security and impose sanctions? (What, Venezuelan agents were going secretly to fund a renewed Occupy Movement? Retaliate for the attempted assassination of President Maduro by putting a hit on Obama?) Why is there a clear intent to reverse all these accomplishments and revert to the class rule of the privileged by instigating regime change by subversion, force, and violence? Precisely because these are worthy achievements, examples for the region and the world; and because Venezuela sits on vast oil reserves; because oil revenue serves social development instead of private enrichment; because Venezuela pursues policies that challenge U.S. regional dominance; because Obama and all servants of power, Republican and Democrat, cannot abide challenge to the rule of capital. Obama did back off his inflammatory statement on the threat posed by Venezuela at the April 2015 Summit of the Americas in Panama, but later reaffirmed the sanctions. The policy of fomenting regime change in favor of the privileged classes subservient to the United States remains in place, and is being stepped up in Ecuador and throughout the region. In December 2015, it was revealed by *The Intercept* and *Telesur* that Edward Snowden had provided documentation that Obama ordered the NSA and CIA to spy on Venezuela. This included the NSA hacker device "Tailored Access Operations" to penetrate the Venezuelan National Oil Company's computer files, monitor executive files, and infect computers with malware.

Personally, I really grow weary of "liberal" Democrats, Obama, former Secretary Clinton, current Secretary of State Kerry, who feign as defenders of democracy, human rights, justice and progress while imposing violence, violations of human rights, injustice, and concerted attempts at regime change, and move to roll back progress. Truman and the Democrats started the cold war and a half century of anti-communist hysteria. Kennedy and his cohorts poured fire and brimstone on Cuba, then promoted an Alliance for Progress in Latin America that provided a cover for fomenting military dictatorship. Kennedy, the greatest of all cold warriors, started the Vietnam War. Johnson carried on that war to, fortunately, ultimate defeat. Carter was less fearsome, but did mess up the Iranian situation that continues until today. Clinton lied about weapons of mass destruction and spearheaded sanctions against Iraq that caused the death of hundreds of thousands of Iraqi children and led to Bush's war. One rather expects the worst from Republicans, as in the Chilean military coup of 1973 under Nixon and Kissinger.[15] But save us from Democrats!

CHALLENGES TO DEVELOPMENT AND ACHIEVING A JUST SOCIETY

The problems facing twenty-first-century socialism in the region go well beyond the coalition of local privileged interests conspiring with American interventionism to revert to savage, authoritarian, neo-liberal capitalism. The entire region is plagued with the legacy of underdevelopment and the continuing limitations of peripheral dependency and the globalization of capital, which are very difficult to overcome. The very substantial Venezuelan accomplishments have been made possible by its vast oil deposits. The Chavez government gained full control over the oil business in 2002 and 2003 after the unsuccessful military coup and the management shut down of oil exports. The high price of petroleum exports until 2014 allowed a huge investment in social development. The drastic fall in oil prices from 2014 has created a major crisis in Venezuela. The legacy of oil dependence also meant that the domestic economy was slow in development to provide all the essentials to the population. Venezuela imports too much of its food and consumer goods. The problem of sustainable development of a diversified national economy producing the goods and services needed by the population was not fully confronted. The increasing income in the pockets of a prospering working and growing middle class could not be satisfied by local production. This gave the business interests that traffic in consumption goods opportunity to create black markets and artificial shortages that are then used to discredit the government and make electoral gains, especially in the December 2015 legislative elections when the opposition, bent on regime change, gained a majority.

The problem of excessive dependence on primary goods exports to the detriment of diversified industrial development is not unique to Venezuela. This is a condition inherited from the periods of classic underdevelopment and subsequent dependent development. Every country in the region suffers the same problem. Ecuador, valiantly trying to duplicate the successes of Venezuela, has turned to oil, natural gas, and mineral exploitation for export in order to finance social development. This has met with considerable success in raising the level of living of the great majority through redistributive social programs. But it has also meant a neglect of putting resources into a more balanced development that produces the goods and services necessary for supplying the needs of the population. It has also created a huge conflict with a sector of the indigenous population and environmentalists who are otherwise in sympathy with the aims of the Correa government. In August 2015, a faction of the main indigenous organization staged a major demonstration in Quito and Guayaquil against extractivism, which the right-wing opposition, bent on bringing down the government, took advantage of. As in Venezuela, the United States assists the local right-wing business elements working for regime change by, among other means, creating local NGOs that insert themselves in local meddling. One such effort was closed down by President Correa in September 2015 by applying laws against activities of foreign subversion. A media NGO "Fundamedios" was funded by the U.S. Agency for International Development, the National Endowment for Democracy, and Freedom House to engage in diffusing anti-regime propaganda. The United States responded to government closure with dire pronouncements about media restrictions in Ecuador.

A similar situation prevails in Bolivia, paralleling Venezuela in its progress toward a more just society. Evo Morales, of indigenous origin and leader of the party Movimiento al Socialismo (MAS), was first elected President in 2005, and has since been reelected twice with MAS parliamentary majorities. Strident opposition in the provinces where economic elites predominated was largely overcome. But extractivism became the government's economic policy. While embracing "Mother of Earth" pronouncements, Morales promoted building roads and opening mining operations in nature preserves. The traditional export reliance on tin became dwarfed with new projects in oil, natural gas, and metals. The proceeds were used to improve the situation of the indigenous population, workers, and nurtured a new middle class. The result has been twofold. First, a decline in export revenues with the fall of demand and prices for primary commodities in the last few years has meant crimping of development and social expenditures. Second, a growing conservatism and opposition among the new privileged elements associated with the extractive industry, middle classes, and government bureaucrats has emerged to place limits on the MAS socialist aspirations. The United States has been largely frustrated in subverting Bolivian socialism as, early on, Morales expelled AID and other American agencies. In 2008, the Drug Enforcement Agency was accused of bribing police officers, violating human rights, and destroying the environment with chemical sprays and demolishing infrastructure. Morales expelled the U.S. ambassador and the DEA, and set up a program to diversify crops away from coca and promote alternative crops. The program was successful in reducing coca production, as certified by the UN. The U.S. response was to decertify Bolivia as cooperating with efforts to suppress the drug trade, thereby cutting off access to international assistance programs. In 2015, it was reported that the DEA was secretly targeting Morales with a drug sting "Operation Naked King." Venezuela is also decertified, even though stringent anti-trafficking programs are in place. Making unfounded drug trafficking charges was a smear tactic used by the United States against an important Venezuelan politician, as well. Both countries are subject to bullying in measures to undermine the governments, while the drug war, along with NAFTA, has made Mexico into a failed state.

Venezuela, Uruguay, and Bolivia have, indeed, formed more just societies, and has largely done so by breaking some of the bonds of international dependency and charting a more independent course. Yet, the three principal sites of Socialism for the twenty first century are limited in a twofold way: first, and most importantly, by the continuing presence of integration into the world economy and by policies that rely upon the openings for primary exports to build the economy. This makes possible redistributive measures to uplift working and poor people from abject poverty, but leads also to the strengthening of the more privileged classes that resist change while inhibiting a more sustainable development that offers a better future for all. Second, change is met by concerted attempts by the local conservative class forces, aided by U.S. pressures and interventions, to roll back social and democratic progress to revert to a savage capitalism pursuing degenerative development.

This difficult situation is even more pronounced in Brazil, Uruguay, and Argentina. The Brazilian reformist government of Dilma Rousseff has been deposed in a kind of palace coup. In May 2016, the opposition managed to force her resignation and be subject to impeachment (on charges that are absurd), which was then confirmed by a Senate vote in September, 2016. This is compounded by a major corruption scandal caused by the state oil company, Petrobras, issuing bribes to politicians and business contractors. In Uruguay, governed in two successive electoral victories by presidents that were former Tupamaro fighters against military dictatorship, the reformist regime is becoming more and more neo-liberal in its policies. In Argentina, the government of Christina Fernandez came under pressure and the November 2015 presidential election was lost to a right-wing neo-liberal.

In brief, a principal weakness of Latin America's progressive governments has been continuing reliance, even deepening, of extractive, export-oriented development. In the boom years from the early 2000s to 2013, great advances were made by implementing socially oriented redistributive programs. Then, by 2014–15, with the world economy stagnating, the booming Chinese market for raw materials becoming constricted, and across the board price declines in oil and almost all primary exports, revenue for social amelioration fell, social discontent grew, and the right-wing offensive became ever stronger. The problem in the United States and Europe is degenerative development under the guidance of finance capital with its policies of globalization and neo-liberalism. Even the most progressive countries have complemented degenerative development by producing cheap primary products, instead of goods and services needed by their populations. What other countries need to do is to break the hold of international capital and develop programs of sustainable development. In the United States and Europe, movement demands must move these countries from degenerative to sustainable development that responds to the needs of the population for social justice, economic well-being, and political democracy.

The international and domestic forces of reaction are definitely gaining ground in Latin America. However, the right-wing forces gaining ascendance face the same situation of unfavorable circumstances for extractive/primary development as the preceding governments. The coming reimposition of extremes of neo-liberal policies will curtail economic growth and only exacerbate the situation for the popular forces, now with more experience, and we can expect a growing class struggle and political instability.

The increase in popular revolt is now quite evident in Mexico against the regime of neo-liberal policy. With NAFTA and the war on drugs, Mexico became a narcostate, with politicians and police and military forces integrated into the drug business. The corrupt security forces are unleashed against those who resist the imposition of neo-liberal measures. The latest wave of fierce repression is against school teachers who went on strike in June 2016 against the privatization of education. Many teachers have been killed and wounded, this following the prior police and narco agents murder of 43 students of education. The education reform is part of a "Structured Adjustment Program" (IDB) created by the World Bank, IMF, and the Inter-American Development Bank. The Mexican government sells bonds for educational projects and then forms a private for-profit company that sells stock and manages the project. The plan is to privatize education and introduce reforms that emphasize testing and remove any critical component from curricula. The IMF promotes 11 structural reforms that the Mexican conservative government has agreed to: education, labor, monetary policy and the Treasury Department, energy (the large and successful Mexican oil company, PEMEX, is already well on the road to privatization), the electoral system, telecommunications and broadcasting, criminal procedures, promoting economic competition, and others. In general, the "reforms" go beyond even the provisions of NAFTA to require the government to sell public institutions to private investors, to end capital controls over currencies and raise interest rates, to introduce market pricing of basic commodities, and to remove all barriers to foreign imports that protect local producers and industries. It remains to be seen how Trump's demand that Mexico pay for the Great Wall of Trump on the border, placing a 20% duty on Mexican imports if they don't, and abrogating NAFTA will be received in Mexico, even by the conservative Narco-State government. Trump's policies toward immigration and Mexico might very well bring to a head the long-simmering anti-Americanism in Mexico, turning a compliant friend into a serious enemy.

The American movement needs to do everything possible in a hands-off Venezuela and Latin America campaign. Solidarity organizations for Venezuela and other Latin American countries are listed in the Appendix. Beyond solidarity campaigns, it is clear that the greater the advances made in America against U.S. interventionism and militarism, the greater becomes the opportunity for Latin America to move forward to a more vibrant Socialism for the twenty first century. And that progress, in turn, will make for more space for progress in America Inc. There is a decided polarization of the class-interest alliance of the dominant classes of the center and periphery against the dominated classes of the same global arena. The international alliance of dominant classes is well-established; the alliance of subordinate classes, while difficult to achieve, is critical to establish and the American movement has a task to accomplish just that. Loosening the bonds of dependence is the only way out for Latin America and other peripheral regions, and this requires international coordination and effort. The situation of even the most advanced countries, Cuba, Venezuela, Bolivia, and Ecuador, which have succeeded in gaining some space in the international sphere is that they remain subject to the encompassing scope of dependence. The progressive governments of Brazil, Uruguay, and Argentina are increasingly pressed by domestic opposition from right and left, while Mexico under NAFTA and the war on drugs has essentially become a murderous narco-state. The more progressive governments of El Salvador and Nicaragua are fairly well hemmed in by internationally-imposed limits.

!Solidaridad! Todos unidos venceremos (Solidarity! United we will win).

Notes

1. Torkil Lausen and Zak Cope, "Imperialism and the Transformation of Values into Prices," *Monthly Review*, vol. 67, July–August, 2015, p. 65. This analysis is included in a special issue of *Monthly Review* on "The New Imperialism—Globalized Monopoly-finance Capital." An early study of globalization is Aijaz Ahmad,

"Globalisation: A Society of Aliens?" *Frontline*, vol. 17, September 30, 2000. An interesting study by William L. Robinson poses the idea that more classic versions of imperialism in the age of globalization have been surpassed by the solidification of power in the hands of a transnational capitalist class, *Global Capitalism and the Crisis of Humanity*, Cambridge University Press, 2014. See also the recent book by John Smith, *Imperialism in the Twenty-first Century*, Monthly Review Press, 2016.

2. The IMF study on rising inequality and declining unionism was reported in the *Huffington Post*, March 5, 2015. See also Terry Gibbs and Garry Leech, *The Failure of Global Capitalism*, Cape Breton University Press, 2009.

3. For a more detailed analysis of the international impact of speculative capital flowing from the United States to Latin America, see Dale Johnson, "Emerging Economies and Exchange Rate Appreciation," www.zcommunications.org/zspace/DaleJohnson In some cases, such as Brazil, increased prices for primary commodities, minerals, grains, and oil have partially compensated for high production costs in local currency. Primary commodities had generally increased in price, even with international recession, due to speculative investment in commodity futures in the U.S. and Europe. However, by 2014–2015 excessive speculative activity and slow economic growth led to instability and a decline in prices for most commodities, especially oil. Brazil invoked more effective measures of capital controls than other countries in the region, but over-valuation of the local currency remains a problem in much of Latin America.

4. I have chosen to deal with the role of the Fed in a somewhat limited way, focusing mainly on its place in purchasing bank assets to free up liquidity to continue financialization and engage in worldwide speculation. An in-depth and historical analysis of the Fed is Leo Panitch and Martijen Konings, *American Empire and the Political Economy of Global Finance*, Monthly Review Press, 2009. I have not analyzed the critical role of the U.S. Treasury Department in maintaining the reign of the dollar as international currency, U.S. dominance in the international economy, and facilitating financialization and globalization. The Panitch and Konings book contains an excellent analysis of the Treasury by David Sarai, "U.S. Structural Power and the Internationalization of the U.S. Treasury."

5. Erica Sagrans, "6 Lessons for the U.S. from Spain's Democratic Revolution," *In These Times*, May 29, 2015.

6. Two articles from 2013 analyze the rise of Syriza. Michalis Spourdalakis, "Left Strategy in the Greek Cauldron: Explaining Syriza's success" and Aristides Baltas, "The Rise of Syriza: An Interview," both in *Socialist Register*, Monthly Review Press, 2013. It is important to follow events in Greece as they unfold. Likely sources of sound analysis of current events are www.portside.org and www.truth-dig.com

7. In 2013, the police stopped 3 buses in Iguala, Mexico, carrying students to a demonstration in Mexico City. The police opened fire on the students; 24 were wounded and 6 killed. Forty-three students were taken captive by the police and turned over to the local narcos, with the green light from the local mayor. The bodies of the 43 were said to have been burned and the ashes dumped into a river. In the search for the missing students, 60 clandestine graves with 129 bodies, not including the students, were found. In parts of Mexico, the police, local government officials, and narcos constitute powerful gangs (www.rsn.org/news-section2/318-66/29989). That Mexico has become a violent narco-state is, in good part, a consequence of the dual impact of NAFTA and the war on drugs. While in Mexico learning Spanish so many years ago, I picked up the saying "Pobre México, tan lejos de dios, tan cerca a los Estados Unidos" ("Poor Mexico, so far from God, so close to the United States").

8. Stiglitz is good on the issue of trade agreements (http://readersupportednews.org/news-sction2/318-66/29072-joseph-stiglize-on-the-trans-pacific-partnership). For effects of neo-liberalism and trade agreements on African countries and elsewhere, see Yash Tandon, *Trade is War: The West's War Against the World*, OR Books, 2015.

9. From a March 9, 2013, analysis by Salim Lamrani—<u>Opera Mundi</u> (http://venezuelanalysis.com/analysis/8133)

10. Article in Granma, June 15, 2016. In English, Granma can be read at www.en.granma.cu, o, en Español, a www.granma.cu

11. Dale L. Johnson, "Class Analysis and Dependency," in *Theories of Development: Mode of Production or Dependency?*, Sage Publications, 1983, p. 252.

12. The present Pope espouses an encouraging line of social justice, environmental sanity, and reform of the more backward aspects of Church organization. However, there was criticism of the original

ordination by Catholic elements because of his reputedly surrendering radical priests active in Argentina to the military regime during the dictatorship of the late 1970s. If this was so, he is apparently in a process of personal redemption.

13. The absurdly mis-named National Endowment for Democracy (NED) originated in the 1980s when the CIA delegated some of its functions to this front organization. Its activities have since been controlled by extremist hawks.

14. A general analysis of the Venezuelan experience by a participant is Marta Harnecker, *A World to Build*, Monthly Review Press, 2013. See also the Marta Harnecker article "Venezuela: Economic War or Government Errors?," *Journal of Socialist Renewal*, November 19, 2016 (also at http://portside.org-Venezuela-economic-war-or-government-errors). Hugo Chavez was first elected in 1998 and won all subsequent elections and an attempted recall by large majorities. Similarly, President Correa in Ecuador has consistent high approval in surveys, 76% in March 2015. The Venezuela experience has considerable relevance for revolutionary strategy worldwide. A good summary of Venezuelan efforts to build a socialism of the sttwenty-first century and the central place of popular communes is John Bellamy Foster, "Chavez and the Communal State: On the Transition to Socialism in Venezuela", *Monthly Review*, vol. 66, April 2015. Communes are a system of dual power that aims to displace the institutions of capitalism. After the death of Chavez, the presidential vote for Maduro was by a narrower margin, but most mayoral and provincial elections were won by the majority party. The other regional most progressive governments in Ecuador and Bolivia have very solid political support, but that in Ecuador is coming under increasing pressure. Evo Morales won a third term in the 2015 election.

15. I had a personal experience (fortunately not of being tortured or shot) that brought home to me the direct correlation between global power, the unrestrained defense of class privilege, and violent repression. In August of 1972, with the socialist government of elected socialist President Allende under increasing attack with consumer goods shortages, rich ladies banging pots on the street, and all kinds of techniques today applied to Venezuela, I went to a theatre in an upper-class district of Santiago, Chile. Before the feature, a propaganda film was presented showing the Chilean military

mobilized to protect the nation. My Argentine wife and I were shocked at the implication, the overt threat of forcible overthrow of the elected socialist government. We brazenly shouted "ABAJO LOS MILITARES" ("DOWN WITH THE MILITARY"). The privileged people seated around us took grave offense and we felt it prudent to depart before being assaulted. One year later, on the first memorable September 11, on that fateful date in 1973, the military attacked the Presidential Palace in which President Allende died, rounded up tens of thousands of socialists, communists, and union activists, and crowded them into the National Stadium for torture and murder. Many years of extreme repression followed; labor unions and civic associations smashed, universities intervened, 3000 people were "disappeared," and economic policies of neo-liberalism were forcibly imposed. The heralded route of the peaceful, democratic Chilean road to socialism was smashed. The Chilean military regime, with its support by Henry Kissinger and Nixon, the CIA, and the University of Chicago neo-liberal economists, became the symbol of crushed hope, of violent repressive dictatorship, the rule of the privileged few by force and violence backed by foreign power. In those same years, the fiercest of dictatorship was imposed in Argentina and Uruguay. Today, Venezuela is the target. For analyses of the prelude to the military coup, see Dale L. Johnson, *The Chilean Road to Socialism*, Doubleday Anchor Books, 1972. (I was on General Pinochet's black list and so could not return to Chile for many years.)

CHAPTER 10

A Summary of Strategic Considerations

A substantial part of the analysis so far has been devoted to examination of the structural forces that create worldwide conditions of gross inequality and injustice that force a path of degenerative development with adverse consequences for people and the environment. These forces work to shrink wrap minds with the ideology invented by the privileged. They shift democracy to plutocracy and create perpetual war. No plutocracy can be enduring; no structural force is exempt from meeting resistance. Victims are also subjects, potentially agents of change.

Consciousness: The Dialectic of What Is and What Ought to Be

Over time, the movement will construct a project of counter-hegemony in opposition to the ideological, political, and forceful reign of capital and its servants. In ever changing circumstances, people's assertions create by their actions new visions of what *ought to be* in opposition to *what is*. To paraphrase Karl Marx, people make their own history but only in given historical circumstances. But given historical circumstances are created in relation to contradictory structural factors that give rise to class struggle and can be modified, or created, by what Paulo Freire termed the "pedagogy of the oppressed."

In previous analysis, I identified and explored four means by which capital dominates economy and society, and its diverse population divided

D.L. Johnson, *Social Inequality, Economic Decline, and Plutocracy,*
DOI 10.1007/978-3-319-49043-4_10

into identities and classes. First, by instilling their class-privileged ideology in the populace; second, by subjugating agencies of state to their agenda; third, by divide and conquer, by stratifying the population in competitive strata; and fourth, by force, repression, and war.

This is true as far as it goes. Capital does impose its hegemony in these ways and the class struggle has long been a one-sided war, in the latest phase of capitalism even more than in the past. The problem with this analysis is that critical, denunciatory discourse mainly only inveighs against one-dimensional domination. Similarly, in the analysis of political economy and class relations, as in the initial chapters of this work, the exposition is primarily structural analysis and oriented to exposing how power operates. We have to be careful that the form of denouncing hegemony does not simply extend it by fostering feelings of hopelessness. What is needed is a sense of the immanence of change, of the constantly shifting forms of struggle against systems of exploitation and domination, of the structurally rooted contradictions of the system that are exposed as they unravel.

In trying to find a method for understanding historical transformation of human society, in this worthy endeavor of history and social science, the gap between structure and consciousness, being and thought, too often goes unbridged. People as active subjects can disappear. But people's beings are constituted by the social relations that comprise their natural and social existence. People bring to the social relations that shape their life situations a capacity for thought, imagination, creativity, purpose, and will. In social relations that are oppressive, the predominant mode of being may limit thought, stultify imagination, and inhibit creativity. Yet, it is also the oppressed who quietly think the unthinkable and scheme their freedom And it is in the nature of the mental capacities of humans to bring purpose and will not only to the mastery of nature, but also to their relation to the social world—and stubbornly to seek to transform this relation.

These social relations are, first and foremost, class relations. Social classes are not abstract entities but groupings of concretely situated people engaging in the rigors of daily activities. The experiences of being born to die at birth or have longevity; living with destitution or privilege, and dying poor or comfortably of old age; of making a living and eating well or going hungry; of being white or black, or brown, yellow or red, male or female, young or old; of being extended privilege or denied justice; of having one's feelings of self-worth overblown or put down; of acquiescing or rebelling; of being socially rewarded or arrested and tortured—

all are set within fundamental patterned social relations of domination and exploitation, power and struggle. The subjective experience that is imposed by and constituent to these relations shapes and guides much of human activity. The day-to-day experience of living forces people to think their social being and to act in relation to their class situation, and this thought/activity shapes, guides, and transforms the structure of the defining relations.

Class struggle is not something that only dominant classes engage in, or at least are successful at; neither is it strictly something that the working class, after seizing class consciousness, promotes as it becomes a class for itself and a historical agent. Class struggle is a chronicle of events forming history because it is endemic to the ensemble of social relations of class societies. A social relation of exploitation and domination is inherently antagonistic; it is an institutionalized, permanent struggle that waxes and wanes with changing circumstances. This being so, a coterie of secondary relations, such as those of race, ethnicity, sex, and social stratifications, necessarily surround the fundamental class relation, as do the political, ideological, and legal relations that guide, sanction, and legitimate the system. These secondary relations can be considered the "superstructure", the underlying class relations the "base." Class struggle is the dialectic between base and superstructure.

The methodological problems are unraveling the determinism of structured class relations from the indeterminism of human purpose and volition, of differentiating the determinants of the formation of classes from the variant course of class and emancipatory struggles, of understanding how subjects confront and transform seemingly imperious structures, of analyzing ruling ideas imposed on consciousness from the consciousness of active subjects.

People are "assigned" their places in the class order by the workings of the political economy of capital. People live the conditions of their class existence. They develop a self-consciousness from this experience, and that consciousness finds expression within class relations. People of similar position suffer or enjoy similar social conditions, develop common social bonds and interests, think and value in class ways, and, as thinking and valuing subjects, live out the relations as best they can and, sometimes, as subjects with collective interest and will, effectively struggle together to transform the social relations that form their consciousness and make up their lives. Facilitating this struggle is the task of the movement, its intellectuals to clarify, it militants to lead.

There is a centuries-long intellectual history examining the question of consciousness in an historical or essential sense: In philosophy, Hegel, Kant, Marx, Gramsci, Marcuse, and Sartre; in psychology, Sigmund Freud, Eric Fromm, and others. I see no need to make theoretical exploration here of the variants in conceptions of consciousness. Of these currents though, the Marxist tradition shapes the thinking of most serious analysts. For those who want to explore this in more depth, a recent erudite, although dense, exposition in the Marxist tradition is István Mészáros.[1]

In the Marxist view, consciousness is not just what is in people's heads, but the collective ideas of what guides history. Previous chapters explored what I generally termed the "ruling ideology" in some depth. In Chap. 5, the "power of myth" was examined, with an emphasis on American history as guided by ideologies such as that of "exceptionalism." In the broad sweep of history conception, one of the most persistent notions is the idea of civilization (Western, of course) and barbarism (these days, Muslim), again as analyzed in Chap. 5. Social Darwinism, the cult of individualism, and the other dogmas analyzed are all part of the "modal ideology" that guides and buttresses the system of capitalism through its historical contortions, while also obfuscating the perceptions of realities, and twisting and distorting the consciousness of people.

The concept of "modal ideology" is a better term than "ruling ideology." The concept, having only a limited history in Marxist theory, was explored by me in a 1982 analysis of "Dialectics and Determination in the Theory of Social Classes."[2] Modal ideology represents the point of connection between the mode of production and the deepest layer of the ideological region. Social Darwinism, for example, can be considered a key element of the modal ideology. Modal ideology originates as an intrinsic aspect of the relations of exploitation and domination, and becomes generalized to all institutions and social relations. It involves a cognitive style, such as instrumental rationality and formal freedom, and a conceptual field, such as the virtues of individualism, acquisitiveness, and competition. Modal ideology functions to limit ideological discourse to ideas compatible with the prevailing order and to select out from the wide range of thought those ideas that have a good fit with the underlying social relations. People internalize in their consciousness a mental relation to what are perceived as objective realities independent of one's will, constructing thus their own subjectivity. But the dynamic of history embodies a dialectic. The thinking of capital's think-tanks and in corporate board rooms can change as new conditions of furthering accumulation come about. A new power bloc within the dominant class may pursue variations on their pursuit of hegemony. Or, as in the present circumstances in the United States, the dominant class is divided by competing conceptions, in this case Trumpism vs. traditional Republican conservatism. In short, a fluid situation of Republican reactionary thought and policy vs. neo-fascism. Moreover, changing economic and social realities contradict peoples' internalized relation to their social positioning and allow people to think, and to act, a critical relation to their conditions of existence. We can expect more protest and rebellion in the fluid situation in the United States from 2017 on.

Thought hegemony is always precarious, challenged by changing circumstances that reveal contradictions and force rethinking. Class forces evolve strategies to deal with challenges. These can be referred to as "hegemonic projects." Hegemonic projects are particular forms of class ideological and political struggle. Such projects are often in response to crisis, especially in a situation of transition from one stage or phase of capitalist development to another. In this crisis, a particular class, or fraction of a class (in our era, the financial oligarchy leads a power bloc of capital), attempts to carry through the logic of the transition and realize its predominance throughout the economic, social, cultural, and political order. The objective is dominance in all the mediating institutions of the "superstructure" that instill the modal ideology—schools, media, churches, the military, the family, political parties, trade unions, government....

These institutions are not simply instruments of a dominant class, they have a history and dynamic of their own, and antagonistic class relations are expressed within them; but the aspiring class attempts to reconfigure them to more sharply reflect its policies and interests. That is why plutocracy today is restructuring education; monopolizes the media; tries to put women in their place as mothers, wives, and sex objects; funds political parties and bribes politicians; moves against unions; and makes government subservient to the interests of capital. In these days, the project is especially spearheaded by the leading sector, finance capital. The project aims at subordinating rival projects and the class interests behind them, at changing the balance of power in society. To accomplish this, it is necessary to secure a new alliance of classes and social forces, to form a new "power bloc," and to engage in concerted ideological and political struggle. Were Hillary Clinton elected in 2016, one could have expected finance capital to remain the controlling oligarchy pursuing degenerative development and similar social movements to the past to continue. Trump's appointment to the Treasury, a Goldman Sachs financial oligarch, suggests we can expect more of the same. Indeed, there are no less than six Goldman Sachs bankers that now surround Trump. This can be interpreted as a consolidation of rule by the financial oligarchy. However, the 2016 elections expressed a great upsurge in popular discontent that took the form of support for Trump. The course of the struggle is therefore less predictable, given that Trump is likely to pursue some outrageous policies that may antagonize parts of this social base and bring dissention within the plutocracy.

Today, in the context of economic and political crises to be resolved, we can view the financial sector of the dominant class as forging a highly ambitious project for the absolute rule of capital worldwide through neo-liberal policy and globalization, and the subversion of any form of democracy to establish plutocracy. To a certain degree this is being challenged—or perhaps better said, complemented—by a more or less overtly fascist groundswell of extremist grassroots mobilization by the Republican Party in the United States and ultra-nationalist elements in various European countries. There is, at the very least, division and dissension within the capitalist class and a decided tension over the direction of the hegemony of capital.

On the other side of social struggle, Gramsci has instructed us that the working class and its allies can fight to achieve hegemony in a revolutionary process. So, what would be the main elements of a project of counter-hegemony? I would pose a project that is the antithesis of everything promulgated or practiced by the ruling class. To the political rule of plutocracy the rule of real democracy; to social Darwinism and competition the molding of social cooperation; to hierarchy and inequality working toward equality; to individual acquisitiveness and privilege achieving the common good; to war the demand for peace; to the fascist complement to capital's project, strenuous resistance. Working toward establishing a counter-hegemony will be analyzed in more depth later. One of Gramsci's many insights was the idea of "interregnum"—a historical period when a discredited regime is collapsing but a new order is not there to take its place. Perhaps America Inc. is entering its interregnum. It is up to the movement to build a New America.

Capital's project is devoid of history, absent of cause and effect, couched in a climate of generated fear, such that there is only a black hole of imposed consciousness shrinking and misplaced attribution to phantom perpetrators. But ideologues of capital in their pronouncements ignore or grossly distort indisputable facts and have no ability to frame their discourse in ethics. This is a major point of vulnerability for those who challenge *what is*. The downtrodden experience the facts of subordination and know this is wrong. The question is, then, how to build social movements that challenge lies and speak moral truths. The ruling ethos victimizes, so the task is to turn victimhood to transformative struggles.

The contradiction of the imposition of perverted, commodified culture and misinformation is that people in movement create their own cultural milieu, dissident from the impositions. Theoretically this was stated exceptionally well in the classic text, *Prison Notebooks*, by the Italian Marxist Antonio Gramsci. Gramsci posed the questions of the state/civil society nexus and hegemony/counter-hegemony with extraordinary clarity.[3] But we don't have to go to Italy in the period of the rise of fascism to understand the manner in which people in movement create their own counter-culture. This was very much part of the movements of the 1960s in America and worldwide, and before that in the great historical struggles of labor. In our time, plutocracy controls the mainstream media, but technology has opened social media, alternative news sites, blogs…diverse means of and ease of communication are already there and will be further developed as the movement grows. (See the lengthy list of communication media and sites in the Appendix.)

The imposition of culture goes well beyond that perpetrated by the media. The founding myth and centerpiece of the modal ideology of capitalism is social Darwinism, and this is based on the labor/capital social relation in which labor is a commodity sold to the lowest bidder for the purpose of extracting profit, labor being atomized in a competitive struggle for survival. From this basis of exploitation and founding myth other dogmas arise, analyzed here in discourses on social Darwinism, neo-liberalism, globalization, and limiting state activity to austerity programs. In capitalist society (and pre-capitalist, too, in different forms), dogmas of racism, ethnocentrism, sexism, intra-class hierarchies of real or supposed privilege, and competitive ethics that divide an atomized and alienated people are passed on from generation to generation. Yet, there is another side to this imposition. Decency is also a cultural inheritance and human decency and morality are in absolute contradiction to the wretchedly failed sociality of American society, to the war of all against all imposed by capital in its phase of degenerative development. Decency absolutely contradicts indecency, and the resolution in favor of humanity is in the struggles to make decency prevail in all the manifestations of culture and the travails of daily life, as manifested in people as active subjects of their own liberation.

Central to the struggles for decency are emancipatory strivings for freedom from oppressive conditions. It is in the realm of suppression of freedom from oppression by agencies of state subordinated to the interests of capital that lies the most obvious ingredient of the present American scene. Plutocracy is not democracy, almost everyone recognizes that. The "superstructure" resting on the base of labor/capital relations is composed, in good part, of the system of law, the bedrock of the capitalist state, and branches of government, executive, legislative and judicial branches. Public opinion surveys reveal that the legislative branch is viewed by almost all as ineffective and retrograde; the president's favorable or unfavorable evaluations go up and down, but the public is rightly concerned about the actions of other executive controlled institutions, especially the security agencies that spy on people and a CIA that practices torture. The Supreme Court, as the guardian of the rule of law, interprets the law consistently in favor of the interests of capital and, these days, rules against the rights of subordinated groups and individuals. If Trump is able to get extreme conservatives appointed to the Supreme Court, the progressive gains in the legal sphere over many years could be wiped out. Again, we have a dialectical relation between government favoring privileged interests, and the justice and real democracy that is sought after but denied. Recall the theoretical statements earlier: the "state is an expression of class relations," and politics transpires in a situation of "multiclass struggles in a bi-polarizing structure." The 1% and their hangers-on, on the one pole, and the 90%, on the other, are indeed polarized. Yet, as argued in the section on rulers strategy of divide and conquer, the 90% are fragmented in diverse racial and ethnic segregations, by artificial divisions flowing from the legacy of race, sexual division of labor, and sexism, and by hierarches of stratifications within the working and middle classes. To the degree that diverse struggles celebrate diversity, fight disunity, and unite in common effort, social gains for dignity and freedom can become reflected in the state that is now more and more an instrument of the ruling class of capital.

The psychology of consciousness is a reflection of placement in the class hierarchy of privilege/subjugation. The privileged elements, the dominant class of capital and their staff and line, the 10% and those below who cling to threatened privilege, love rules, be they ordained by God's commandments or by the secular wisdom of law-makers. They think that hierarchy is natural to the social world. They love the authority of those rightly in charge and know that rule-breaking must be punished. They have a hard time seeing class divisions, the world is made up of individuals who are responsible only to themselves; if a person does not do well, only he is responsible (she don't count for much). The top dogs of the hierarchy take their privileges very seriously; when threatened they will resort to what is necessary for containment.

The subjugated naturally don't think like zombies, but their minds often get muddled by the mind-shrink of the system. When thoughtful, they views rules as created to oppress them. They don't like hierarchy. They are oriented toward their own needs and those of people in general; they have a sense of justice and injustice. They recognize that individuals are divided into classes; that there are rulers and ruled. Consciousness-raising, be it through popular assemblies that promote pedagogy of the oppressed, or simply through experience, can be advanced in struggles for decency, by elevating individual consciousness of oppression to class consciousness of struggle.

"Truth" is an aged search of philosophers—few of whom, Marx excepted, recognized that the search for truth has to be, first, a search for the class-conditioned life situations of different social groupings and classes. Truth is relative to class positioning. I have tried in this book to reduce fundamental truths to radical pronouncements of the lies that further class subjugation to the norms of capital's reproduction. Truth is embedded in a system of class and power relations, the powerful impose their perverted version of truth, the downtrodden have their own truth and a "politics of truth" is much needed in America Inc. *The truths of the oppressors are but lies, they can't face facts, facts belie their interests; or make moral judgments, for there are none they can make. The truths of the oppressed are based on the reality of* what is, *and therefore at least approximate genuine truth.* A worker thinks, "My job sucks, the boss exploits me, the corporation oppresses me, the police threaten me"— he thinks truth. Truth is always relative to value judgment, the worker thinks this is wrong, immoral. His and her truth is also an ethical statement to be struggled for in the company of others of his or her class.

If the state is an expression of class relations, then to the degree to which social movements worldwide make gains, as the struggles for just causes are articulated for the public mind, as progress is made and ideas take root, these gains will be reflected in the nature and activities of local, state, and federal government. If the movement gains a mile with strident demands, the state may give an inch of reform, with the expectation of preserving thus the system. Reforms are, from time to time, extended when pushed by popular demand. Reforms can be good, but this is not the same as liberation from oppression. People's ability to control their lives and to develop their full human capacities, to live in harmony with each other and with the natural environment they depend upon—that is not possible within the limits of capitalism. Reform may ameliorate some social conditions but system imperatives insure that gross inequality, alienation, exploitation, and immiseration will continue. *Eventually, through persistent struggle over a long period of time, the movement will evolve strategies to neutralize the police and military forces of repression, and to forge a counter-hegemonic project, the doing-away with the present system and its replacement with one based on principles of liberty, justice, equality, human decency, and democratic control of our mutual destiny.*

This is not a vision of revolution such as those held by the traditional socialist and communist left, the seizure of power and the dismantling of the state to transform, by political and forceful means, the nature of the economy and society. Revolution will be gradual with strengthening local communities and the institutions of civil society, by defeating the ideologies that subvert consciousness, and with dissemination of a counter-hegemony throughout the population based on principles of common welfare. *Occupy minds first, then institutions, then the state!*

Class Forces to Work Toward a Counter-Hegemony

We turn to examining the class and social forces that can forge a counter-hegemony.

The Working Class and Trade Unions

To trade unions, we owe most of the social gains that made our world during the last century a better and more civilized place for all peoples. In Europe, union support for Socialist and Communist parties, and the Labour Party in Great Britain, made possible the advance of Europe toward an effective social democracy from the ashes of World War II. Today, the West European Communist parties are dead and Socialist and Labor parties became the administrators of neo-liberal capitalism and turned upon the unions to discipline them into roll-backs and austerity. (This may be changing with grassroots pressures in the current European situation.) In Latin America, union struggles and articulations to progressive political parties and movements have been, and remain, critical to the most important countries of the region being able to gain some independence within the American Empire. In the United States, the state of the unions is much worse than in Europe, they have been greatly weakened as effective forces to protect members' most vital interests. As organizations to promote class solidarity of working people and as promoters of the broader social interests, they have been for decades largely ineffective. Only one in ten American workers is in a union. As a matter of urgency, the movement—as a matter of its own success or failure—needs to find ways to support efforts to revitalize unions.

Union struggles in America were once the examples for the world to emulate. A reminder of this is that Mayday, celebrated throughout the world, except in the United States, as a manifestation of workers" rights gained and to be yet fought for, originated in the killing of anarchists organizing workers in late nineteenth-century America. The anarchist Industrial Workers of the World (IWW) in the first decades of the twentieth century, the emergence of industrial unionism, the merger of craft and industrial unions in a broad class organization, the AFL-CIO, the militancy of mine workers in the United Mine Workers (UMW) and the dock workers of the International Longshore and Warehouse Union (ILWU), the broad organizing strategy of the International Brotherhood of Teamsters, the sit-down strikes of the 1930s, the forward-looking strategy of the United Auto Workers, labor's role in forcing the New Deal of the Great Depression—all made American trade unions strong and effective as a class force shaping a better future for America. *The classic labor principle of Solidarity Forever—mutual aid and support—can be resurrected to broaden contemporary struggles.*

All that progress went into decline in the late 1940s and early 1950s with McCarthyism and the purge of communist, socialist, and progressive and visionary leadership from the unions. The surviving union leadership shifted strategy away from workers as promoters of broader social demands toward what came to be called "bread-and-butter unionism." This, by and large, worked for several decades—until the 1970s with stagflation and the 1980s with the advent of neo-liberalism and globalization—to keep real wages advancing for organized workers. The cost was doing nothing about the broader class interests of working people. The efforts to organize the unorganized were few and mostly futile. Division within the working class between organized workers and racial and ethnic minorities widened. The influx of women into the waged labor force initially found little response in union organizing.[4] It took the civil rights movement and the women's movement to advance in these areas, with only hesitant support from unions.

The AFL-CIO vigorously supported U.S. cold war activities abroad by aiding anti-communist unions in many countries. Unions failed to follow the direction of the economy away from manufacturing into the service sector and concentrate organizing efforts there. The leadership of the unions subordinated itself to an increasingly conservative, corporate responsive Democratic Party, and failed entirely to press for the broader interests of workers and the population as a whole in the programs of the Party. Change comes about through demands and pressures from below, not being co-opted into a ruling party. In some communities, there are now demands that reach out to the unorganized, minorities, and undocumented immigrants. The movement can broaden this struggle so that unions get fully in step with a class perspective based on solidarity. In the pre-election contest for 2016, more unions moved toward support for Bernie Sanders and his social justice perspective, but most supported Clinton. The support of environmental organizations was helpful to the United Steelworkers 2015 strike against Shell Oil. The AFL-CIO is now cooperating with black, immigrant, and environmental groups, and making efforts to support unionization of low-waged workers. The Communication Workers of America is spearheading the formation of a political party, the Working Families Party, across the country.[5]

In developing a class perspective, the movement and workers themselves will not get anywhere with the Democratic Party, given that Bernie Sanders will not be the candidate and the unlikely turn of the Party in a more progressive direction. We had a president for eight years that spoke to the presumed privileged interests of a middle class, a class that no longer exists as such. Some of the elements elevated to be corporate handymen, the bulk propelled into the abyss, clutching fearfully at lost privilege. And the most progressive among the Democrats are so head-shrunk by the ruling ideology that they cannot vocalize the term "working class," much less think in class terms. When a mainstream Democrat says something about workers, it is to the effect that the white working class is racist and therefore supportive of the Republicans. Democrats, in general, fail to recognize that their policy of serving plutocracy rather than workers is the reason that there are many with unfavorable views of Democrats. Nevertheless, most union leadership supports Hillary Clinton. In January 2015, the darling of progressive Democrats, Elizabeth Warren, spoke at an AFL-CIO National Summit on Raising Wages. After lauding President Obama for the economic recovery, citing "5% GDP growth in the third quarter of 2014, unemployment under 6%, and a new all-time high for the Dow, low inflation." Then, *in speaking to union reps of the working class*, goes on to say "I've spend most of my career studying what's happening to America's middle class, and I know that these four widely-cited statistics give an important snapshot of the success of the overall economy. But the overall picture doesn't tell us much about what's happening at ground level to tens of millions of Americans. Despite these cheery numbers, America's middle class is in deep trouble." I don't really know if not recognizing the certainty of continuing recessionary stagnation is economic ignorance on Ms. Warren's part, or if she is perpetuating the myth that America is a middle-class society that needs a little amelioration. Most likely both. This middle-class theme is taken up by even our sole socialist in Congress and presidential candidate, Senator Bernie Sanders, although in a less blatant way than others. Candidate Sanders raised serious issues, and in his campaign did have a political impact, but in general save us from those Democrats who pose as progressives but reiterate the myth of middle-class society.

The relative decline of unions can be reversed as the class situation of the working class continues to deteriorate, and as the public sector employees become deprofesionalized and their unions attacked, as in recent years in Wisconsin and in Chicago, the unions fight back and attempt, with some success, to broaden the struggle. Broad Movement support is essential. The working class is the bulk of the suffering population. And unions can be revitalized as more women are incorporated into low waged sectors and the downgraded of chains like Walmart and fast food workers revolt and push unionization and the $15 an hour minimum wage.

The Underclass and Minorities, Protest and Rebellion

From time to time, sectors of the underclass say "Enough!" and break out into open rebellion, taking the form of riot, or actions that law enforcement, parroted by the media, label "riot" or "terrorism." More often, the demands of underclasses have been for the provision of rudimentary social services, for equitable access to the institutions of the larger society that other classes enjoy, and against the routine police repression in communities. By 2015, the movement Black Lives Matter had achieved a considerable momentum. All sectors of the movement need to mobilize in opposition to racism and in support of ending police murder, and, more generally, a complete overhaul of the system of criminal justice (outlined in Chap. 11).

The social demands of underclass protests are often reformist in character but have strategic implication in the present context because, within the limits of the system, it is impossible to incorporate significant numbers of new aspirants into the mainstream of society. During the 1950s and 1960s, the Civil Rights Movement made significant gains for African-Americans for legal equality and more opportunity. Some of the ameliorative programs of the war on poverty, such as Head Start, still persist in the face of roll-backs in programs of amelioration. In general, when groups of the powerless succeed in organizing themselves to provoke the power structure, the response, as in the 1960s war on poverty, is to co-opt the moderate leaders into official structures extending some privilege and isolating them from their base, to repress the militant leaders, and to yield to the mass something of what they want, work opportunities, city services, measured relief from police or administrative oppression.... These benefits are often transitory; the struggle is continual and the positive response reluctant. Then, from time to time, militant protests break out.

Incorporation of sectors of the underclass can be accomplished through extension of civil rights and political representation, by expanding job opportunities for unskilled or semi-skilled labor, or by programs of qualifying unskilled labor, such as extending educational opportunities or using the military or other institutions as agencies of socialization into what are considered appropriate skills, motivations, and attitudes. These are policies that act upon the situation of the underclass without necessarily implying basic changes in the institutions or social structures of society. These programs were state policy in America and Europe for a time beginning in the 1960s but, by the 1990s, were rolled back or killed. Welfare stipends to poor mothers with children were replaced under President Clinton with workfare programs forcing people into menial labor for survival. In general, ameliorative programs have been replaced by police containment of communities and imprisonment of poor people, particularly black and brown youth. In the depressed conditions of contemporary capitalism, the political climate of neo-liberal austerity, the culture of survival that is imposed upon the underclass, and the shift from ameliorative programs to police repression, reformist solutions are not on any legislative agenda, with the hopeful exception of police violence and reform of the criminal justice system. But Trump trumpets law and order. We can expect more acts of rebellion from oppressed sectors of the underclass. The movement needs to analyze how to relate to rebellion, insurrection, and riots.

The main economic opportunity that poor youth now have is entering the military. The U.S. military found during the Vietnam War that the draft of young people from the general population resulted in an army that did not take on the enemy effectively; in fact, draft resistance was widespread among civilian youth, and many soldiers turned against war and became an important part of the anti-war movement. So, the military now depends upon volunteer military forces. And who volunteers? Mostly youth with few alternatives in life. Military recruiters visit schools in poor and minority neighborhoods, set up Junior Reserve Officer Training Corps in high schools, offer cash bonuses, a choice of jobs in the military, and educational benefits for recruits. To meet the manpower needs in Iraq and Afghanistan, the military waived requirements of no criminal record, high school diplomas, no extremist views, good physical health.... The U.S. military forces are disproportionately composed of underclass youth, some of them street kids cultured in brutality, violence, and criminality. This may account for some of the atrocities committed by American soldiers in Iraq and Afghanistan. On the other hand, a volunteer army composed of poor kids is not a dependable force to make war on protestors on the home front.

The difficult situation of underclasses creates conditions of volatility. I recall returning to California in 1965 from getting training as a sociologist and my political education in a two-year experience in Chile. I watched the insurrection in Los Angeles on TV, the Watts Riots, and thought "Wow! This is a big change from my experience in the early 1960s Civil Rights Movement." Over the next several years, ghetto rebellions occurred in larger U.S. cities and in many smaller communities. (In fact, I owe my job offer in 1970 at Rutgers University in Sociology to the Newark riots of 1967. A new undergraduate college with an admissions policy for "disadvantaged youth" was created and encharged to create "change agents.")

The Civil Rights Movement went into relative decline in favor of the Black Power Movement. The movement rejected notions of the poor and downtrodden forming an underclass in favor of the conception of African-Americans as an "internal colony." In the international context of the time, the Catholics of Northern Ireland carried out an armed national liberation struggle against British rule and their Protestant colonial administrators, the French Canadians were in nationalist revolt against English Canadian oppressors, and there were indigenous uprisings in Central and South America against the essentially colonial domination of national power structures. The Black Panther Party became the vanguard of nationalist struggle for emancipation from racist colonial rule by the white power structure. The Black Panthers were done in by jailing and police force assassination. Malcom X was assassinated. And prominent civil rights leaders who moved beyond the boundaries of civil rights into human rights, union organizing, and anti-Vietnam War activity, such as Martin Luther King, were also murdered. Revolt by the most downtrodden is a serious threat to the powers-that-be. In Chap. 11, racism and the reform of the criminal justice system will be analyzed.

It will be very difficult to achieve a measure of unity within the underclass; they are divided into populations of African-Americans; Latinos; "illegal immigrants" from all over the world; former white workers in depressed industrial cities and communities where mining is now defunct; the mentally ill, either from genetics or living the hell of marginality; ex-convicts who are denied employment; casual laborers in agriculture and construction; locked-out youth; "gangbangers;" drug addicts; drug dealers; criminals; elderly people and the infirm whose pensions or assistance don't reach to provide a living—it is a long list. But these groupings in American history have organized and formed protest groups, and engaged in actions that the broader movement for change within the mainstream class society can work with and learn from in broad coalitions demanding social justice for all—and they will do so again. Given the desperate situations of the underclass, there will also be elements—veterans with consciousness brutalized by war and training as killers, white extremist groups armed with military weapons, those desperate for a hand-out and recognition, those driven to violent mental disturbance—ready to become the paid mercenaries and goons of those who would defend the system by whatever means necessary. Death squads unleashed against "subversives" in our era will not be confined to countries such as Colombia and Honduras, and they will likely be organized and funded, as they were in Central America in the 1980s, by corporations and government agencies.

The Ambiguous Role of the Middle Class

In previous analysis, it was established that the once expansive American middle class is subject to processes of de-qualification and de-professionalization of their labor. This has bi-furcated the class into sectors being pushed in the direction of, or into, the working class, now even to outright unemployment, and into an upper echelon moved into positions of line and staff servants of capital and operatives within the administrative apparatus of the state. One cannot expect employees on Wall Street, analysts at the CIA, many among the 400,000 employees of the Homeland Security Agency, to have any particular sympathy for change, although there are, and will be, "whistle-blowers." The place of middle-class functionaries, in general, is to subordinate workers in the labor process, and to administrate corporate hierarchies and the apparatuses of the state; but it is also the case that sectors of de-qualified and de-professionalized employees are potential allies. Many are losing their jobs and homes—poverty is now in the suburbs as well as inner-cities. Many of these people were Trump supporters but, if the movement can reach them, they can be on the right side of history. The main problems are to overcome anxieties produced in the culture of fear, to mitigate the consciousness of petty privilege by campaigns that identify that the real threats to their well-being are not terrorists, illegal immigrants, or other scapegoats but, instead, the forces that have depressed their class situation. Support for the struggles of public sector unions to defend their functions as professional groupings, and at the same time the public good, is essential.

Activities directed at winning over, or at least neutralizing, sectors of the middle class are strategically vital. In history, these fractions of the intermediate class have provided a militant and solid basis for right-wing reaction. The social bases of fascist regimes of Spain, Italy, and Germany, and the enthusiastic support of middle sectors for the military dictatorships of South America in the 1970s and 1980s, are examples that we cannot afford to have repeated in America. Exit polls of Trump voters indicate that most rally attendees were white and middle-class.

Division Among Capitalists

It is said that capital thrives on competition. This is not just the enshrined competition of individuals within the broader culture, but of businesses in ascending and declining sectors; of firms integrated or subordinated into conglomerates and those under threat of hostile takeover; of firms in monopolistic, oligopolistic, or competitive sectors; of large, medium-sized and smaller business. All these capitals are effected in different ways, many adversely, by what has become a "degenerative phase of development" guided by the financial oligarchy, the more successful transnational corporations, the energy interests, and the corporate-security complex. The crisis-induced bankruptcy of General Motors and Chrysler, and the extreme decline of the de-industrializing areas in America, is also a result of the globalization of capital bringing forth the decline of industrial capital in the heartland. In competitive sectors of the national economy of medium-sized and small business, advancing inequality restricts consumer markets and business prospects. This competition of capitals has some relevance for the role of the state. The consolidation of finance capital as the heart of plutocracy has implication not only for the deteriorating situation of the working and middle classes, but also disadvantaged sectors of capital.

The divisions in the Republican Party are a reflection of a substantial disagreement among those who think conservative. The Party has clearly changed from the years when it was a business-oriented grouping with middle-American Protestant beliefs. Large sectors of the Party now voice bigotry, misogyny, ignorance, intellectual dishonesty, dogmatism, ethnocentrism, intransigence, warmongering, and cruelty. The entire lineup of Republican candidates fell in line on these elements, but got trumped then dumped by the Donald. Trump voters and rally attendees are usually caste as middle- and working-class whites whose privileges are being threatened by the current economic situation or changing American demographics. I suspect that there are many proprietors of small and medium-sized business who are threatened by finance capital and larger corporations that join the Trump celebration, while other businessmen will shift financing and political support to Democrats. The power bloc in the hegemonic project of capital in general is in disarray.

Youth and Social Change

Exit polls and rally attendance indicate that young people were overwhelmingly in support of Bernie Sanders. This is quite understandable. Young men and women are the principle victims of degenerative capitalism. Young people are increasingly marginalized to zones of exclusion and despair. They have nothing to lose but the chains that hold them down from being a principal force of social transformation. This is by no means a U.S. question. Young people in Southern Europe have unemployment rates as high as 50% and, in Greece, I read that youth unemployment is even higher, as compared to 15% to 37% in the United States, depending upon race and ethnicity—the unemployment rate for African-American youth is 36%, and among Hispanic young people 37%. The general situation of American youth is closure of opportunity. Schools are being made over into custodial institutions, jobs in factories are nonexistent, technical jobs for educated youth are outsourced to countries with low wages. More and more, American youth give up an independent life to live with parents because they can't afford an apartment or room of their own; higher education is so expensive that young people who do enter a college or university are burdened to their graves with debt while finding that their degrees don't necessarily become the entry ticket into a middle class in decline. Some enlist to fight in foreign wars because the military offers bonuses and benefits for their future. Others succumb to being treated as inferior and disposable by becoming bitter, mean, criminal, and violent. Many seek solace in the comfort of drugs, and dealing becomes a way to support their dependence and make a living. Huge numbers of youth, especially black and brown young people, are locked up in prisons and, when released, have no future except to become permanent members of the marginalized underclass.

Public Education

Schools are now a frontline in the battle for preserving education as a public good. Schools mirror all the class and racial injustices of American society, and all the insidious stratifications of hierarchy that divide the social classes. More than half the students in kindergarten through grade 12 are now groomed in poverty, reflecting the growing inequality and degradation of work to jobs that perpetuate families in poverty. Poor kids are angry kids. Custodial discipline is now the norm in urban and many suburban schools. Schools become a pipeline to prisons. Teachers' performance and jobs depend upon their students' scores on tests that are standardized to reflect the kind of education that the corporate planners believe is most conducive to passive acceptance of subordination in the labor process and to the prevailing social order. The thrust of educational "reforms" being pushed by business and their political and religious allies are neo-liberal in form, reactionary in content—privatization of public education in the form of charter schools, test-geared rote teaching, removal of parent, community, and teacher control of schools, the breaking of teachers unions, curricula geared to narrow training for low-level jobs. Even the Federal Reserve provides materials for "financial literacy." History and social studies instruction is sanitized so that there is no sense of how we got to be where we are at, much less what might be done about the grave ills that affect our social order. Civics is taught as rote learning about institutions, not about a functioning civil society and democratic political order. Art and literature are let go, as they might foster creativity and intelligent thought. The educational "reforms" in vogue among prominent corporate Democrats, such as Mayor Rahm Emanuel of Chicago, the former Chief of Staff of President Obama, aim to confine literacy to what is behind standardized tests, that is to say, the purpose of reform is to embrace an illiteracy that defies logic or facts, abhors critical thinking, and disdains the idea that personal troubles and social problems can be subject to political solution. We owe a debt of gratitude to the Chicago Teachers Union in their strike of September 2012 for bringing these issues to public awareness. Teachers are now being downgraded, denied participation in school governance, reduced to clerks tracing corporate sovereignty, even subordinated to the authority of security guards.[6] Trump's appointment to head the Department of Education will attempt to transform all public schools into private, profit-making Charter Schools. Tax payers will pay tuitions with vouchers to the schools.

Teachers everywhere are the frontline combatants in the larger class war; they are being de-professionalized to the status of guard labor and subordinated to better serve the ends of the "reforms" being forced on the education of youth. Teachers and their unions deserve the movement's energetic support to transform education to a public service that goes beyond reproducing the existing social order to the challenge of understanding the history of how we got to be where we are, to imparting critical thinking in civics and social sciences, to promoting tolerance and respect for diversity and crimping the youth culture of bullying, to tapping creativity by exposure to the arts, by gearing athletics to cooperative team sports rather than to the ruthless competitiveness that permeates the larger culture.

Higher Education

As an aspiring social scientist in the better days of the early 1960s, I was paid as a graduate student to get a Ph.D. as much as the younger professors at Stanford University. I never had to borrow any money. Those were better days than now. Opportunity abounded for country kids like me and higher education was the vehicle. In the 1960s, we were an ungrateful lot; rejecting the conformity of middle-class lifestyle; sneering at the cold war and celebrating the Cuban revolution; "tuning in, turning on, and dropping out;" resisting the draft to fight and die in Vietnam; participating in the struggle for civil rights.... In 1968, French students nearly created a real social revolution. In April 1970, American students staged the first Earth Day, and then declared a general strike at all American colleges and universities in protest of the invasion of Cambodia and the killing of student anti-war protestors at Kent State and Jackson State. (I read now that teach-ins are coming back on the anniversary of these events.)

In those days we could afford to rebel; the system welcomed us back when we were ready, giving us a good job and a place in social order. Not today, since the recession half of all college graduates are unemployed—that's 400,000 every year. Now, they take unpaid internships or work at low-waged service jobs with overwhelming debt from student loans. The average student debt is $23,300, but the total for 36 million debtors is at $1 trillion, rivaling the credit card debt total, and a real threat of yet another bursting financial bubble as students and their families are not able to pay their debt. Between 1978 and 2012, the price of tuition at U.S. colleges and universities increased over 900%, resulting in debt peonage for youth and their parents. Government loan programs were privatized to banks, thus costing students more in interest. One in six debtors was in default in 2012, and this debt cannot be discharged through bankruptcy. To hunt them down, the Department of Education in 2012 spent $1.4 billion with collection agencies, and the agencies engage in extreme harassment. From 1987 to 2012, median net household worth of students and their parents decreased by 68% to $3,662.

With the generalized guidance of neo-liberal ideology, educational policies and practices became harnessed to the requirements of the dominant class and the needs of the Warfare State. This transformation of universities was generalized in American higher education from the 1980s down to the present day. Imparting of critical thinking is stymied, engagement with critical social and economic issues scoffed at, and what passes for conventional wisdom passed on to the next generation; teaching is done by part-time adjunct instructors (now 67% of the faculty) at poverty wages and by graduate student teaching assistants; elite senior professors administrate a system rampant with conventionality, elitism, cynical subservience to higher interests. To survive, professors must seek research grants, with a generous overhead payable to the university. The grants come from corporations and foundations established by corporations to further "knowledge" and scientific advance, as defined by the grantor. Of course, some of the ethical, intelligent professors and better programs have survived. A young person wanting to think and learn has to go to considerable lengths to hunt down the right niche.

In the main, entering an institution of higher education today means young people become trained to fill the dwindling niches in technical and professional careers. To get an education in any meaningful sense beyond rudimentary training for a credential is not easy. And students won't get the scholarships and other stipends that my generation was generously afforded. They borrow huge sums to get a degree that is of debatable value in today's job market. But students are young people with hope and vision, they can, again, return to demanding *Free Education, Real Education.* Colleges and universities, like other institutions and the state, are expressions of underlying class relations. That higher education is more and more a privatized commodity and, where still public, becomes more expensive and class exclusive, while being transformed to serve corporate ends more closely, is a result of the upper hand in class struggles that the dominant interests have waged since the 1980s. That can be reversed by student and movement struggles. *Education must not be a commodity paid for by young consumers for their self-advancement in the hierarchy of class, but a right of the entire population for the advancement of a democratic society.*

There is much more to say about the place of youth in the struggle for a just, democratic society. The very best analyses of the situation of young persons in our day are the writings of Henry Giroux.

"From Paris, Athens, and London to Montreal and New York City, young people are challenging the current repressive historical conjuncture by rejecting its dominant premises and practices. They are fighting to create a future inclusive of their dreams as the principles of justice and equality become key elements of a radicalized democratic and social project. At stake in their efforts is not only a protest against tuition hikes, austerity measures, joblessness, and deep cuts in public spending, but also the awakening of a revolutionary ideal in the service of a new society." [7] Giroux's writings on youth are truly impressive and highly recommended reading.[8]

NOTES

1. István Mészáros, *Social Structure and Forms of Consciousness, Volume 11, The Dialectic of Structure and History*, Monthly Review Press, 2011.
2. Dale L. Johnson, "Dialectics and Determination in the Theory of Social Classes," and Michael Heffren, "Ideology and Hegemonic Projects: The Alliance between Corporate Capital and the New Middle Class in Early Twentieth-Century United States," both in Dale L. Johnson (ed.), *Class and Social Development: A New Theory of the Middle Class*, Sage Publications, 1982.

3. Antonio Gramsci, *Prison Notebooks*, International Publishers, 1973.
4. On the strength and limitations of U.S. unions, see Stanley Aronowitz, *The Death and Life of American Labor*, Verso, 2014.
5. Chris Shelton, President of the CWA, "Why Workers Need the Working Families Party," *The American Prospect*, September 7, 2015.
6. See the special edition of *Monthly Review* on education and the Chicago teachers' revolt, vol. 65, June 2013.
7. Henry A. Giroux, "Days of Rage: The Quebec Student Protest Movement and the New Social Awakening," http://truth-out.org/opinion/item/11040
8. Henry A. Giroux, *America's Education Deficit and the War on Youth*, Monthly Review Press, 2013. Also, *Education and the Crisis of Public Values*, Peter Lang, 2012. Other pertinent writings are indicated at his website, www.henryagiroux.com

CHAPTER 11

Confronting *What Is* to Achieve Counter-Hegemony

Absolutely central to forging a counter-hegemony is combating the terror of war and taking on the repressive apparatus. American officials guilty of war crimes and crimes against humanity must no longer enjoy immunity from prosecution. The rape of the environment will be deepened with the energy policies now being pursued. The criminal justice system that imprisons millions must be totally reformed. The rule of plutocracy, with bankers at the helm, can no longer be sustained.

Fear, War, and Official Terrorism

Since the large anti-war protests in the United States and Europe against the invasion of Iraq, there has been very limited action against American militarism. The policies of official terrorism are recognized as such by too few people. Unless the United States militarily intervenes in Iran, places a ground army in Syria, or reinvades Iraq, there does not appear to be much current activity leading to campaigns of protest such as occurred during the Vietnam War, or even the worldwide mobilizations prior to the Iraq invasion. In part, this may be due to the more immediate oppressive class situations that bear down on the downtrodden's sense of priorities. But the incessant fear mongering of the war on terror has to be addressed. And Donald Trump recognizes no limits to his and America's power.

D.L. Johnson, *Social Inequality, Economic Decline, and Plutocracy,*
DOI 10.1007/978-3-319-49043-4_11

Official terror and war abroad, and the diversion of public funds to militarism, are a root cause of the measures that bear down on people's lives in the homeland. To become an effective movement against the culture of fear, war, and the terrorism of the powerful, the complex around the State of National Insecurity, the misappropriation of public funds from social well-being to creating world havoc, the movement needs to engage tactics that bring these issues to the fore and show the connection to people's lives at home. America Inc. needs a massive peace movement that rivals that of the Vietnam War era. Since militarism and the State of National Insecurity are the roots of domestic evil, this is a broad class and popular issue, a unifying issue for diverse causes, and should be brought to the top of the list of strategic concerns and mobilizations. The Sanders campaign has not been raising this issue with sufficient attention.

To mention, at this point, just one avenue of resistance—neglected are actions against military recruitment. The recruiters are taking advantage of the very disadvantaged situation of youth to entice them into the Armed Forces with the promises of all kinds of benefits not available in civilian life. Follow the recruiters and force them out of schools! Educate youth what they face in military service. Bring outside agitators to the outskirts of U.S. military bases! Work in every way to resist militarism, xenophobia, and irrational fears.

Demand amnesty for Edward Snowden, Chelsea Manning, Julian Assange, and all whistle-blowers. End amnesty for American war criminals.

More broadly, what is needed is the eventual dismantling of the State of National Insecurity by demanding an end to impunity for crimes against humanity. And demanding the "for now impossible." The CIA is a very convenient target.

CIA: Central Intelligence Assassins

The history of the CIA is long and very dirty. The Central Agency of Assassins, since the initiation of the cold war, has been the chief instrument of the blackest side of American policy.

- The engineering of the overthrow in 1953 of the nationalist government of Iran, responding to Iran's nationalization of their oil.
- Guatemala, 1954. Overthrow of a reformist government, followed by decades of dictatorship and death squads organized by local oligarchs and the CIA.
- El Salvador, 1930s, for decades following dictatorship; 1980s, death squads in the age of Ronnie Raygun.

- Nicaragua, 1930s to 1979, support for the Somoza dynasty dictatorship; 1980s, CIA organizes and finances with drug money the Contras to successfully turn back the Sandinista revolution.
- The CIA laid the groundwork for the Vietnam War. The CIA's Phoenix Program in Vietnam resulted in hundreds of thousands of dead Vietnamese. In Vietnam, the CIA program for "gooks" was "flying lessons" on "half a helicopter ride." Another measure was the "Bell Telephone Hour", a field telephone wire around a gook's testicles received a call.
- Chile 1973, the CIA giving a helping hand to fierce military dictatorship.
- Argentina, 1976. The military there adapted the "flying lessons" and "half a helicopter ride," and imprisonment with torture and "disappearance" of 30,000 souls.
- The Chilean, Argentine, Uruguayan, and Brazilian military torturers got their CIA training. The CIA wrote many of the torture manuals for the infamous School of the Americas, training future torturers and dictators to apply their skills in subverting social change in the Americas.
- The grossest example of the CIA and all the agencies of the State of National Insecurity—the policy of official terrorism—is Cuba. The sugar embargo of 1960; the 1961 CIA organized Bay of Pigs invasion; Defense Department preparation of an invasion in 1962; the world near brought to nuclear holocaust in the missile crisis; countless terrorist attacks of bombings and killings; hundreds of attempts to murder Fidel Castro; more than a half century of embargo....
- Sequestration of presumed "terrorists" to black sites for torture.

These are but a few examples of thousands of illicit interventions by this criminal organization.

Demand the Abolishing of the CIA

The foreign and domestic operations of the State of National Insecurity is the main root of almost all the other ills—and a number one priority for the movement to address. Demands to dismantle the CIA are central. Another avenue to address this might be the resurrection of a War Crimes Tribunal. During the Vietnam War, the British philosopher Bertrand Russell chaired the Tribunal with a panel of experts and notables that gave a decided boost to the Anti-War Movement. I nominate Noam Chomsky as chairperson; several jurists from the ACLU, the National Lawyers Guild, and a defense lawyer of a Guantanamo detainee; articulate veterans of the Iraq and Afghanistan Wars; dedicated investigative journalists such as Chris Hedges and Glen Greenwald; notable academics such as Henry Giroux; Middle Eastern experts such as Aijaz Ahmad; Edward Snowden, Chelsea Manning and Julian Assange of Wikileaks to submit evidence from their exile and prison locations…. If possible, a rented convention center in Washington D.C. would be ideal for the hearings.

The1946 Nuremberg war crimes trials set the legal and political precedent.

War Crimes, Historical Parallels

In 1946, American and Allied judges of the Nuremberg Trials condemned numerous Nazi officials to death by hanging and to long prison sentences. In retrospect, it could be argued that the Allies "substituted power for principle" as U.S. Supreme Court Justice William O. Douglas stated at the time. Yet, the Trials led to the UN Genocide Convention, Universal Declaration of Human Rights, Geneva Convention on Laws of War, Convention Against Torture, and eventually to the International Criminal Court.

Nazi. Alfred Jodl Chief of Operations for the German High Command. Directed invasions and occupations in Western Europe and Poland. Hanged in Nuremberg, 1946, for war crimes.

Nazi. Wilhelm Keitel Chief of Staff of the German High Command. Planned invasions in Eastern and Western Europe. Authorized killings of resisters in occupied countries and Germany. Sent by Hitler to give General Rommel a choice of court martial or suicide for attempted assassination of Fuhrer. Hanged in 1946.

American. David Petraeus Army officer for 37 years, rising to Commander of the International Security Assistance Force in the 2000s, where he oversaw military assistance to numerous countries throughout the world. Commander of the Multi-National Force in Iraq 2007–2008; Commander U.S. Central Command 2008–2010; Commander U.S. Forces Afghanistan 2010–2011; Director CIA 2011 until forced to resign in November 2012. As head of CIA directing the NATO war in Libya, he was also responsible, together with Secretary Clinton, for the oversight of the CIA complex in

Benghazi, Libya, the arming of Islamic insurgents in Libya, and sending militants into Syria. Identified as an extreme right-wing "Crusader" for intervention and war. Promoted evangelical fundamentalist Christianity in the Armed Forces. Directly responsible for war crimes and crimes against humanity in Iraq, Afghanistan, Libya, and Syria. Supportive of undermining the Arab Spring democratic gains and reestablishing military dictatorship in Egypt.

American. Colin Powell Generally thought to be a rehabilitated warrior, but has a long history of facilitating war crimes. Then Major Powell investigated the well-documented My Lai Massacre of a Vietnamese village in 1969. The report rejected any war crimes by U.S. soldiers in their attack. As General and National Security advisor to Ronald Reagan, he coordinated the invasion of Grenada and the bombing of Libya in an effort to assassinate President Qaddafi (it is a crime under American law to assassinate foreign leaders). As Reagan's advisor, he was privy to the American support for death squads in Central America. In 1989, he was appointed by President Bush to the chair of the Joint Chiefs of Staff. In that capacity, he directed Desert Shield and Desert Storm war against Iraq. Generalismo Colin Poder, as Secretary of State from 2000 to 2005, was instigator of the invasion of Afghanistan. Said to have doubts about the wisdom of the Iraq invasion, he nevertheless lied to the UN about Saddam Hussain harboring weapons of mass destruction.

Nazi. Hermann Goering Reichsmarschall and Luftwaffe Chief, President of Reichstag, Director of Four Year Plan directed at Jews. Committed suicide prior to sentence of hanging.

American. Donald Rumsfeld Secretary of Defense under George Bush. Directed wars in Afghanistan and Iraq, architect of war on terror, cooperated with CIA on sequestering and torturing persons. Should be charged with war crimes and crimes against humanity.

Nazi. Konstantin von Neurath Minister of Foreign Affairs to 1938, then Reich Protector. Sentenced to 15 years in prison.

American. Condoleezza Rice National Security Advisor to Bush 2001–2004; Secretary of State 2004–2008. Directly responsible for invasions of Afghanistan and Iraq, and the atrocities of the war on terror. No doubt Henry Kissinger and Hillary Clinton could be in the same category of criminals as von Neurath and Rice.

Nazi. Wilhelm Frick Minister of the Interior. Designed and administered Nazi dictatorship. Sentenced to death and hanged in 1946.

American. Michael Chertoff Head of the Criminal division of the Department of Justice 2001–2003—a critical period for incarcerating millions. Advisor to Bush on war on terror; Director of Homeland Security under Bush 2005–2009;a long history of anti-immigrant programs; co-author of Patriot Act. His business, the Chertoff Group, sells technology, such as body scanners, to Homeland Security.

American. Alberto Gonzalez White House consul to George Bush advising "legality" of torture; defended Bush's program of electronic monitoring, leading to massive surveillance program of the NSA; Attorney General 2005–2007, authorizing torture and other crimes. Senate Judiciary Committee questioned his veracity and competence, leading to his resignation in 2007.

Nazi. Ernest Kaltenbrunner SS leader. Chief of SD intelligence service, Gestapo, criminal police, and Einsatzgruppen. Hanged 1946.

American. George Tenet CIA Director 1997–2004. Responsible for falsified intelligence justifying Iraq invasion. Instigator of CIA sequestration and torture program.

American. Robert Gates CIA Director under Bush, directly responsible for torture program; Secretary of Defense for Bush. Reputed to be a "pragmatist" in contrast to former defense Secretary Rumsfeld. Obama reappointed Gates as Defense Secretary.

American. John Brennan Brennan's 25 years with the CIA included a post as station chief in Saudi Arabia and work as an analyst for the Near East and South Asia; directed National Counterterrorism Center. Links to private contractors (professional assassins, hackers, consultants on torture...) through his CIA affiliations and being CEO of the Analysis Corporation and chair of the Intelligence and National Security Alliance composed of intelligence professionals. Served as Obama's National Security Advisor for Homeland Security and Counterterrorism, meeting with the President daily. Concerns about his support for CIA torture caused Obama to delay his appointment as CIA Director in favor of a position as National Security

Advisor. In spite of his history, Obama appointed Brennan as Director of the CIA in 2013 and the Senate Committee on Intelligence approved his nomination. Brennan succeeded David Petraeus, another war criminal who headed the pacification programs in Iraq. He wrote his doctoral thesis on counter-insurgency strategy in Vietnam, extending his ideas to Central America and Afghanistan. Brennan's CIA hacked into the computers of U.S. Senate staff and the Senate Intelligence Committee report on torture. This appointment of a known criminal implicates President Obama in complicity in the war crimes and crimes against humanity. Brennan needs to be fired from office and prosecuted for countless crimes.

Nazi. Alfred Rosenberg Chief Nazi ideologue and Reichminster for Eastern Europe. Associated with the Holocaust. Hanged 1946.

Nazi. Heinrich Himmler Leader of the Nazi Party and ideologue, Administrator of the Third Reich. Dismissed by Hitler in 1945 and captured by British. Committed suicide in April 1945.

American. Karl Rove Republican political advisor and organizer, proponent of Republican extremist ideology. Senior Advisor and Deputy Chief of Staff to George Bush. Ideologue of reactionary thought and war on terror. As organizer and ideologue, bears similarity to Rosenberg and Himmler.

American. Richard Cheney Vice-President of America Inc. Ideologue of reactionary thought and activist in implementing war on terror and Bush administration wars. As Secretary of Defense under the first Bush, Cheney organized the invasion of Panama in 1989. Bush wanted President Noriega who, as CIA collaborator in Central American interventions, was playing a double game with drug trafficking. War was unprovoked and resulted in war crimes against civilian population, killing indiscriminately and destroying an entire poor neighborhood by bombing.

American. John Negroponte Ambassador to the military dictatorship in Honduras, 1980s; oversight of organizing counter-revolutionary forces in Nicaragua and death squads in Central America; Ambassador to Mexico 1989–1993, negotiated NAFTA and the war on drugs that has made Mexico a narco-state; UN Ambassador 2001–2004, justifying invasions of Afghanistan and Iraq; Ambassador to Iraq 2004, to manage the occupation;

224 D.L. JOHNSON

Director National Intelligence 2005–2007; Deputy Secretary of State 2007–2008. War criminal first-class.

Nazi. Adolf Hitler Reich's Fuhrer. Committed suicide in 1945. Responsible for overseeing all Nazi crimes.

American. George W. Bush President of America, Inc. Responsible for overseeing all American war crimes and crimes against humanity. Do we add Barack Obama to this list? Donald Trump?

While building an anti-war movement, the question of the destruction of the environment with degenerative development must be simultaneously addressed.

Degenerative Development and Environment

With the now uninhibited and unrestrained rule of capital, nature is treated in the same way as labor. Labor is crushed and the natural environment raped, both commodified and driven to the point of exhaustion. This commonality makes environmental issues class issues. As with war, the degradation of the environment is a problem that affects everyone worldwide, but only class mobilizations will begin to place some limits on what the system does to our future. Capitalism has, since its infancy, savaged the environment. With the present process of degenerative development, degradation of our natural habitat, upon which humanity depends for existence, is more deepening than ever. International bodies come up with all kinds of dire warnings and policy guidelines, and scientists warn of catastrophic global warming, but nothing genuinely effective can be done within the limits of the current system. Environmentalists declared that the December 2015 Paris meeting of many countries was a failure, as it could not reach a workable agreement on global warming. The kind of development that enhances labor, provides socially necessary goods and services, and respects the environment can be termed "sustainable development," the polar of degenerative development.[1]

The United States, as the world's leading polluter, is particularly responsible for likely catastrophe, but with entrenched interests and the rule of capital will not take appropriate actions. Oil fever continues to rage, leading to Middle East wars, lengthy pipelines across Middle East war zones and through the United States to transport petroleum from shale oils and natural gas from fracking, new off-shore and Arctic drilling leases, fracking for natural gas everywhere threatening underground water supplies, burning coal.... A slogan for Pope Francis might be "Thou Shalt Not Frack!" Trump's slogan would be more like how he views women as objects, "Fuck the environment."

Still, perhaps the environment is one area where some reform within the limits of the existing political framework might be feasible (the "might be feasible" is used hesitantly). The environmental movement is very vocal and strong in combating oil fever. Broader issues that affect the working class and the population in general need to be identified and pursued in coalition with diverse social forces. Denunciatory resistance needs to be more and more oriented to demanding alternatives that benefit everyone, such as loosening the reign of petroleum and moving toward clean energy, improving transportation systems, and energy saving technologies. Of course, this will only be possible with a state that is more responsive to popular demand, and open to use of fiscal policy and incentives to shift gears. Most saliently, private profit will still reign, the shift will only be possible if the incentives for alternatives steer corporate investment in new, profitable directions. (To some extent, this has been going on with investments geared toward U.S. energy independence). Reform and stimulus programs for clean energy may delay immanent catastrophe, but policy shaped by private interests will not change the end result of environmental decay and eventual destruction. The movement, then, has to promote new, sustainable development paths that appeal to broad sectors, and that merge to promote economic and social development for social ends that also curtails negative impact on the natural environment. The current path of degenerative development is totally contradictory to this end and sustainable development cannot be achieved without system transformation.

Combating Racism: Criminalization of Poverty and Reform of the Criminal Justice System

The underclass is viewed as dangerous elements to be contained in their communities, and individuals arrested and imprisoned, with the black population a special target. The ugly legacy of racism is now being resurrected in a virulent form, resulting in police murders and the making of black people the principle victims of economic duress, generalized oppression, and often violent repression. In the present era, racist rhetoric and practices are being extended to Hispanics, Muslims, and immigrants. The 2015–2016

Republican campaign eschewed any attempt at what came to be called "political correctness" and screamed overt racism. The cry is to "make America great again." A multi-cultural America is perceived as a threat to the privileges of white Americans. Step up war abroad, and repression and "laws and order" at home, translates to keep niggers, spics, and ragheads in their subordinate places; keep out Mexican drug dealers, rapists, and killers by building the Great Wall of Trump, deport the millions already here. Donald Trump's strident blasts command wide adherence among the Republican base and are very worrisome. It is apparent that those Michael Kimmel identifies as expressing "aggrieved entitlement" are very numerous (discussed in Chap. 7). Many of the advantaged feel that their privileges are being threatened. Millions being downgraded in the social order by the workings of the system are hoodwinked to believe that the sources of their loss of privileges are minorities, immigrants, and women. There are many angry white men. Whether these people can be considered "know-nothings" to be dismissed or a solid base for American style fascism remains to be seen. They flooded Trump rallies, along with sectors of the white, male middle class.

The police killings of black people since the Ferguson, Missouri, events of 2014 have aroused widespread indignation among many and diverse people. It was encouraging to see white people lying down in New York streets in a "die in" after a police murder of a black man was videotaped. An effective and new black organization, Black Lives Matter, has rapidly gained ground. A principle demand of Black Lives Matter is reform of the criminal justice system. This can be explored by examining (1) chronic use by police of excessive force, (2) the police strategy of community containment, (3) the use of police forces to generate municipal revenue, and (4) mass incarceration.

Murder From January to April 2015, a study published in *The Washington Post* found that 385 people were killed by police. A later publication by *The Post* indicated 1000 killed by police in 2015. Two-thirds of the 385 unarmed victims were black or Hispanic.[2] In March 2015 alone, over 100 people were killed by police. For the period January to June 2016, at least 532 people were killed by police, the majority unarmed or minorities. The Department of Justice, which does not keep an accurate account of police use of excessive force (said to now be in process), reported that Philadelphia police shot at least 400 people, 80% of them African-American, in the seven years to 2015. It was nearly as bad in Chicago, which heads the list of numbers of police killings among the larger U.S. cities. The killings were nearly all male, mostly black, half in South Side ghettos. The cover-up of a police murder clearly filmed on videotape for more than one year finally led to charges against the Chicago policeman, and pressures against the mayor and law enforcement officials. When cities are adjusted for population, Chicago ranked fourth in police killings behind Phoenix, Philadelphia, and Dallas. This is not a situation of a few city rogue departments; it is a nationwide problem. There are some variations in the level of police violence. In 2014, in predominantly black Newark, New Jersey, no one was killed, a rare non-event in larger cities. In St. Louis, Missouri, comparable in terms of population and crime level to Newark, 24 black people were killed. Police violence seems to be a general Missouri problem, not just in Ferguson. In the same year, only one person was killed by police in Canada and none by police in Great Britain. In international comparisons, U.S. police killings are by far at the top of the list. The same is true of non-police killings with fire-arms—the United States is the world leader in gun possession and death by shootings, with frequent mass killings, daily in 2015, which are a rare occurrence in other countries not located in Middle East or African war zones. *No sane society can permit that its police forces murder with impunity, nor permit the civilian population to arm themselves with military grade weapons.*

Containment The Injustice System charges police with maintaining "the public order." The public order, of course, is based on the maintenance of the inequalities of a class order and racial/ethnic divisions that embody gross injustice. The populations most disadvantaged are largely segregated in urban neighborhoods. So, the police job is to contain these communities. Patrol cars with armed police are everywhere. People are arbitrarily hassled, in petty ways such as arrested and fined for urinating on the street when people have no access to toilets, or given a traffic ticket for a minor or fictitious infraction. Police cruise neighborhoods and people are contained by arrest, trial, conviction, and jailing for possession of marijuana. With employment opportunities limited or non-existent, street vendors trying to make a living are stopped and frisked and are sent up for long prison terms. Social problems created by the workings of the system are criminalized. There is a war on the poor, not on poverty. Poor communities are war zones patrolled by mercenaries in the uniforms of police.

In some cities, such as Baltimore, the local administration is largely black. The Mayor, the Police Commissioner, the School Superintendent, the head of the Housing Commission, the majority of the City Council is African-American. This did not prevent the police from being involved, in 2015, with the death of an arrested black man. Nevertheless, it appears that four policemen, two of them black, are charged with crimes, but two were acquitted as of June 2016. The Baltimore police handled the protest demonstrations with reasonable restraint and the city agreed to a multi-million dollar settlement with the victim's family. The Head of the Police Union, however, has denounced the Police Chief and, especially, the Mayor for the settlement and the prosecuting attorney for the criminal charges. (There is a current campaign to get the AFL-CIO to disallow police unions from affiliating with the central organization due to consistent defense of the indefensible crimes of police officers.)

But the strategy of containment of ghettos and poor communities is not just a question of police activity. It is even more a result of policies implemented at national, state, and municipal levels that buttress structural inequality and institutionalized racism. In an age of austerity and social service curtailment, cities compete with each other to attract capital with incentives and tax cuts. They demolish blighted areas for gentrification and ignore the continual deteriorating situation of the poor in ever more constrained circumstances. In Baltimore ghettos, 62% do not have a job that earns a living wage; electric and water services are deficient or cut-off; in neighborhoods, there is a growing absence of parks, recreation centers, even schools. Publically funded projects, such as the tourist attraction Inner Harbor, provide only minimum-waged jobs. In this respect, the black administrators of Baltimore are not that much different in their approach to urban development than white bureaucrats in other cities. The black middle class did arise out of the gains of the civil rights movement that was largely supported by the black poor, black workers, and black professionals. Now it appears that the new black middle class is increasing divorced from black communities by deepening class and political divisions. The Congressional Black Caucus supports Hillary Clinton, not Bernie Sanders. Another side of the maintenance of order is suppression of protest organizations and demonstrations. Police in larger cities have their intelligence cadres keeping track, and the FBI and Homeland Security feed locals information. They appear in riot gear at demonstrations armed with tear gas and clubs, often used to provoke demonstrators to provide an excuse for the use of force. For serious manifestations of discontent, the arsenal of lethal weapons supplied by the Defense Department and Homeland Security can be brought to bear. In the Ferguson demonstrations, police appeared with armored vehicles mounted with heavy weaponry, supplied by the Defense Department. North Dakota, which is mainly rural, has a low crime rate is the first state to authorize police forces to use drone aircraft to strike with lasers, tear gas, pepper spray, sound cannons, and rubber bullets. In 2016, North Dakota police and the National Guard were using water spray in freezing temperatures, as well as pepper sprays and rubber bullets against native American demonstrators protesting yet another shale oil pipeline.

Under the Pentagon's 1033 Program, 460,000 pieces of military grade weaponry and equipment have been given to police departments since 1997. These include heavy duty arms, night vision devices, armored vehicles, tanks, and aircraft. In addition, the Department of Homeland Security (DHS) gives generous grants for equipment, from Bearcats to helicopters, to police department in "high-threat, high-density urban areas." The DHS Office of Intelligence and Analysis equates street activism to domestic terrorism and attributes "violent extremists" to the locals. It is not just the National Security Agency that monitors communications, the DHS and larger police forces with intelligence divisions monitor social networks.

Policing for Profit In the Justice Department investigation of the Ferguson events, it came out that the police are extensively used to giving tickets that end up in fines that provide a significant part of municipal revenue. Black people were twice as likely to be stopped and searched, receive a citation, or arrested. The Ferguson Police Department comprises 90% white officers, containing and repressing a black community that is two-thirds of the population. The Justice Department found "discriminatory intent," that is, racist practice aimed at generating municipal cash. In 2014, 23%, more than $3 million, of the municipal budget came from fines. One reported Ferguson case was a woman that had her car towed because it was parked missing a tire. She chose to pay the $1,200 fine rather than fight the case in court where she could not win.

Mass Incarceration The United States holds 25% of all persons in prison throughout the world, but represents only 5% of the world population. In 2015, 2.3 million adults were in prison, up from 500,000 in 1980. Spending on jails and prisons has zoomed from $6.9 billion in 1980 to

$80 billion in 2015, and increasing amounts are going to privatized prisons. This does not include the cost of internment centers for undocumented immigrants where entire families are held. The next country with the most prisoners, China, had 1.5 million incarcerated out of population five times greater than that of the United States. The rate of incarceration in the United States is by far the highest in the world, 750 persons per 100,000 population, compared with Germany with 93 per 100,000. Since the mid-1980s, more than 40 million people have been arrested on drug charges, four out of five arrests were for possession not trafficking, 80% for marijuana possession. Blacks are ten times more likely to be sent up for drug crimes than whites. African-Americans are 15% of drug users and they are 75% of those in prison on drug convictions. In Southern states, the proportion of the prison population that is black or other minority is up to 95%. One out of every 60 young white men is in prison, compared with one out of nine young black men. More black men are in prison in the United States today than were black South Africans imprisoned under apartheid. Conditions in prisons are inhumane, punishment oriented with no pretense of rehabilitation. The conditions prevailing in prisons were chronicled in depth by *Monthly Review* in 2001.[3]

The number of people spending time in local jails is 19 times greater than the number in prison. In 2013, there were 12 million jailed—again, disproportionately black and brown. The poor in general are doubly penalized by police harassment with repressive and pecuniary intent. First, by the workings of the economy that made them poor, subject to containment in their communities and repression on the streets; second, by being selected out for fines they cannot afford, pushing them into even more dire straits. Unpaid tickets can lead to suspension of public benefits, or even jail. In California, four million people are denied driver's licenses because they have unpaid fines for traffic tickets. Ex-prisoners are denied employment opportunities and many social services and, thus, are placed in perpetual underclass situations. The growing, permanently locked-out sector of the underclass is no longer even a "reserve army of labor." The criminal justice system is profoundly racist. Law enforcement personnel are largely white males. And not just police, 95% of state and local prosecutors in the United States in 2014 were white, 79% of those white men. A short but excellent run-down of the racist and class character of the justice system is Bill Quigley, "Forty Reasons Our Jails and Prisons are Full of Black, Brown, and Poor People."[4] The organization

Black Lives Matter is gaining strength and is deserving of support from all movement activists. The movement goes well beyond the single issue of police murders, and attempts to analyze and confront inequality, poverty, racism, social injustice, and all social ills. In August 2015, a manifesto with regard to the criminal justice system was issued. The document focuses on control of police use of deadly force, calls for the ending of procedures that obstruct investigations into police actions, an end to using fines to finance municipal budgets, training of police and recruitment of minority officers, decriminalization of substance offences, and other measures.

President Obama had some good words to say about the need for reform in an August 2015 speech to the convention of the National Association for the Advancement of Colored People (NAACP). "We keep more people behind bars than the top 35 European countries combined....Every year we spend $80 billion to keep folks incarcerated—$80 billion. Now, just to put that in perspective, for $80 billion, we could have universal preschool for every 3-year-old and 4-year old, in new roads and new bridges and new airports, job training programs, research and development.... But every dollar they have to spend keeping nonviolent drug offenders in prison is a dollar they can't spend going after drug kingpins, or tracking down terrorists, or hiring more police and giving them the resources that would allow them to do a more effective job community policing.... We have to restore trust between our police and some of the communities where they serve." Obama concluded with a personal note: "My heart breaks when I see families who are impacted. I spend time with those families and feel their grief. I see those young men on street corners and eventually in prisons, and I think to myself, they could be me; that the main difference between me and them is I had a more forgiving environment so that when I slipped up, when I made a mistake, I had a second chance. And they've got no margin for error." Well, Obama has not proposed any programs for preschool or infrastructure. But "going after drug kingpins" continues and "tracking down terrorists" escalates. It was hard to take the Obama seriously on reform; he was himself imprisoned as the formal head of the State of National Insecurity that he helped create in his years as Chief Executive.

Socialist candidate Bernie Sanders issued an impressive, and no doubt sincere, detailed agenda for confronting inequality, poverty, racism, and injustice (although his stance of war and intervention is toned down).[5] He organizes his agenda in ten-point statements around addressing police violence, addressing political violence, addressing legal violence, and addressing economic violence.

What we have always to keep in mind is that the State of National Insecurity means war abroad and containment of *what is* in the homeland, including the criminalization of dissent and the right to demonstrate grievance.

Confronting issues—such as repression and the racism inherent in police violence, and the reform of the criminal justice system—means taking on all the interrelated questions of inequality and injustice with broad class struggle. The calls for reform of the justice system, even the most profound, do not reach. What is needed is: (1) the purging—and I mean it flatly—of policemen that are implicated in use of excessive violence; (2) the conversion of police officers to, in effect, social workers—that change to be tied to an ambitious program of social services designed to meet the needs of the now contained populations; (3) the curtailment of the power of police unions and public prosecutors to impose a culture of impunity for criminal activity; (4) recruitment changes to make the police forces and prosecutors reflective of the community they "protect and serve"—50% female and proportional to community racial and ethnic populations.

Confronting Wall Street: Nationalization of Banks and Public Control of Bankrupt Firms

Together with actions against terror, war, and the State of National Insecurity as a critical movement target and demands for environmental enhancement by way of sustainable, rather than degenerativem development, the takeover of banking especially is a viable strategy for undermining of the economic basis and political power of the financial oligarchy. Real change is not possible until the power of the financial oligarchy is curtailed and big corporations brought under control.

During the 2008 financial crisis, the Bush and the Obama administrations quickly came up with programs to bail out the banks and bankrupt General Motors. This involved billions and billions of dollars, and resulted in the Federal Reserve and Treasury Department being in effective control of Wall Street investment firms and a large industrial enterprise. In effect, the investment banks and a key corporation were nationalized. The government owned majority stock of the failed big insurance company AIG and, by virtue of the funds extended, in de facto control of the banks. (Why not have turned AIG into a real insurance company that protects against the risks of natural disasters that private insurers try to avoid compensating?) The purpose of nationalization, however, was not to reorient investment banks to assume a role to facilitate economic development to produce socially useful goods and services, such as clean energy, or to improve a crumbling infrastructure. Neither was it to promote social development to reverse the terrible effects of financialization and neo-liberalism on the lives of people of people at home and abroad. The purpose was to provide the means for the financial oligarchy to regain control of their plutocratic power; this is what happened in short order, and the Wall Streeters rewarded themselves with bigger bonuses.

While the big banks were being lent a helping hand, nothing was done to rescue small banks serving local needs. In 1995, the large financial operations controlled 17% of banking assets. By 2011, the big guys controlled 59% of assets. The share of local banks fell from 27% to 11%. One idea that has emerged from the movement is to encharge a dying Post Office system (the Republicans want to do in the Post Office) with offering financial services to the public. Another is formation of state-level banks modeled on that of North Dakota. The Bank of North Dakota generates profits for the state because it has lower costs and takes fewer risks than commercial banks. There are no exorbitant salaries, commissions, or bonuses for executives. The Bank of North Dakota does not speculate in derivatives.

The Obama government held the controlling shares of General Motors and used that control to pressure management to further rationalize the labor process to reduce employment, force union concessions, and weaken the United Automobile Workers, not to convert General Motors to a broad transportation company, employing more people and revitalizing devastated communities, a public enterprise that could be converted away from production of private, gas-guzzling automobiles to mass transportation. (In World War II, the government was able, in short order, to reorient production by the automobile manufacturers of cars to tanks and jeeps). In 2014, General Motors gained record profit levels through its policies of reducing employment, bringing in new workers at reduced wages, and slashing pension funds.

The nationalization of major investment and commercial banks, and failed corporations, needs to be a central strategic goal of our movement for profound, democratic change. There will likely be another financial crisis and economic bust. In that situation, the Federal Deposit Insurance Corporation can force bankruptcy and receivership upon banks, the stockholders take the hit, and creditors are given some relief through negotiation. The Federal Reserve is not really a central bank controlled by the government. While created by an act of Congress, the Fed is actually a private corporation wholly owned by the banks and acting primarily in terms of the interests of the financial sector. The Fed should be the first to be nationalized so that monetary policy has public control and monetary measures can be made consistent with fiscal policy promoting sustainable development goals. Of course, there is not the slightest chance that nationalizations can be accomplished in a short, or perhaps even medium, timeframe. Rather, the demand will eventually forcefully emerge from an intensification of tactical actions that the movement is engaged in. There are campaigns for people to cancel accounts at the big banks to put their monies in credit unions and community banks; grassroots pressures for local and state governments to set-up development banks to finance public sector activities designed to provide essential services and boost employment; direct actions against home foreclosures.... A very interesting demand would be that communities use eminent domain to take over foreclosed properties and return them to their real owners. As local communities stop dealing with Wall Street and gain some measure of control over financing, the way may be open to make banking at all levels serve the real purpose of financial institutions: to provide credit for genuine, sustainable economic and social development.

An increasing number of cities are edging toward bankruptcy. Over the last decades, but especially from the 2000s, cities have faced tax revenues in relative decline and insufficient to fund infrastructure improvement and to meet public service obligations. So, they sold tax exempt municipal bonds to Wall Street and wealthy individuals to finance current expenditures. And what the bondholders now want from cities and states is austerity of the kind that afflicts Greece and European dependencies—roll-back of all public services from health care to education, elimination of public sector unions, the cutting back of pension funds, and other measures adverse to community well-being. They also want to privatize public services, pressuring city governments to sell off assets and turn formerly free services over to private capital as profit-making businesses. Chicago mayor Rahm Emanuel leased the Skyway for 99 years to toll-collectors and the city's parking meters for 75 years. Obama's former Chief of Staff failed in his efforts to defeat the teachers union and fully corporatize education, but he hired J.P.Morgan Asset Management to advise how to continue to privatize free public services in Chicago.

The intelligent response to city and state financial crises are default on bonds, the establishment of municipal banks to fund operations, and demands on the federal government for the bail-out and funding of infrastructure and services. Public ownership is being assaulted by privatization, but still remains in many communities. There are public hospitals, parks, utilities, hotels, wealth funds from oil and other leases, pension funds, even internet systems. The movement can play an important role in resisting the further extension of the neo-liberal program for cities and in creative responses to municipal crises. One measure is to institute accountability in funding allocations by "participatory budgeting," such as is developing in New York and a few other cities. Neighborhood meetings discuss their needs; voters decide how the budget is allocated.

In keeping with the grassroots communitarian and anarchist thrust of many segments of the movement, programs for local control of local institutions—schools, municipal governments, urban planning agencies, municipal fund management, transit systems...—makes a good deal of sense. Instead of privatization of public goods, we need the making public of private commodities that are essential to life—food, water, homes, health, education, transportation, and all manner of activities that promote solidarity and serve community need. In California, local efforts have succeeded in socializing the delivery of electric power from the private monopoly Pacific Gas and Electric in some areas by establishing non-profit public enterprises, with resultant lower electricity bills to consumers.

There are a number of practical steps at the local level: Establishment of funds from local institutions to help stabilize jobs, establish cooperatives, and improve the local economy; end contracting with large corporations in favor of local businesses and coops; establishing land trusts to capture profits for local use and to prevent gentrification.

As industrial companies, large and small, continue to fail as a result of globalization and crisis-prone recessionary stagnation, the movement and a revitalized banking system needs to be there to demand that employees and public and consumer representatives own and control the business in order to orient these public entities toward useful activity that revitalizes communities in decline, provides employment, and produces really useful goods and services. In the United States today, there are 11,000 companies that are employee-owned and employee-operated under a 1974 law on Employee Stock Ownership Plans (ESOP). Pension plans and employer health care plans, too, now used by Wall Street to further their speculative ends and by private insurers to further their profits from illness, need to be nationalized, that is, employer and employee contributions should go into a genuine, secure social security fund that provides a decent livelihood to persons who have worked hard all their lives and into the financing of universal health care. *Greatly expand social security, no privatizing and no cuts, universal health care!*

From the ashes of the de-construction of communities inherent to savage, degenerative capitalism, we need the gradual construction of a civil society based upon democratic control of our institutions and our lives. In the interim, what is happening with all the toxic and over-valued assets absorbed by the Federal Reserve in bail-outs and quantitative easing of the financial conglomerates? More bail-outs will be forthcoming in the next crisis. The taxpayers will eat the toxic waste of the financial system. Where is an even a minimal effort to fiscal stimulation of the economy that is not a giveaway to speculators or armaments contractors? New regulations of the financial system, if they happen at all, will be written by Wall Street tycoons. In the best of circumstances—or, better stated, in the worse circumstances, as recessionary stagnation continues or crisis deepens—a president and a Congress, under great pressures from the movement, that has a minimal vision for the future of America, will replace the staff of the Federal Reserve, the Treasury, and the President's Council of Economic Advisors with some intelligent Keynesian economists. This will not happen under Trump, but his is four year term if not forced from office prior to that. In circumstances yet to unfold, this might be a tactical demand consistent with the strategy of nationalization of all finance to build a sustainable economy and a just society. However, the movement has always to keep in mind that Keynesian solutions aim, as did the New Deal of the Great Depression, to make capitalism more viable. The reforms advocated by the best of them, such as Joseph Stiglitz and Thomas Piketty, are meant to rescue the system, not change it.

Class Organization to Extend Social Programs

After concerted resistance to terror, war, and the repressive apparatus, extending the environmental movement, and taking on the financial oligarchy, the remaining major strategic consideration is the extension of social programs to make the United States and the world a decent place for humankind. Change the war on the poor to a war on the causes of poverty!

It is unlikely that unions can again, in the short run, become greatly effective class organizations that promote the welfare of members while forcing changes at the level of the state for advances in social programs. But that does not mean at this time that sectors cannot organize and that coalitions of workers' unions, public sector employees, communities, progressive political groups, and movements of popular organizations cannot articulate programs to press broader social demands—from defending Social Security and Medicare to improving public pension plans for all, universal health care, and all manner of social programs. Social programs that are alternatives to ghetto containment and incarceration are critical. The key is to transform defensive protest toward demands to make the country a just place for all to live decently and to prosper. Jobs for the unemployed, homes for the homeless, food for the hungry.... Beyond these elementary decencies, demand effective measures to reduce inequality, end military and security related spending, and stop all bail-outs and Federal Reserve and Treasury giveaways to the financiers and corporations. The proceeds of such reduction and curtailed destructive spending need to be diverted to funding high minimum wages, adequate income for children and women engaged in reproductive work, food and housing security for all, social amelioration rather than incarceration, cheap and efficient public transportation to reduce dependence on cars and petroleum, programs of free and quality education at all levels, sustainable development to protect the natural environment and economic development geared entirely to meeting human need and the collective good. Call this movement whatever will combat division and unite diverse social forces—"Democratic Socialism for the 21st Century," or "Communitarism" (given the strength of anarchist thinking in the movement), or simply "New America."

Universal Health Care as a Central Demand "Obamacare" is a modest improvement over the prior totally privatized system, but is a giveaway for private insurers and inadequate as a medical system that provides programs for public health and the well-being of the population. And Trump's priority is to do in Obamacare. Universal health care is supported by large majorities in public opinion surveys. A worthy program can be funded with taxes at much less cost than the present system, in which private profit and bureaucratic organization of private insurers boost costs substantially. The United States spends 17.9% of the gross domestic product on health care, a significantly higher level than other countries that have lower GDPs and universal health care. A good reform would establish clinics in every community, take over private hospitals, and socialize medical research. Research and development in the medical field must be centralized in public-funded and administrative agencies that remove the pharmaceutical giants from profiting from illness. The drug companies now want to extend their profits from high-priced patented medications even further, with longer patent periods and enforceable intellectual property rights in trade agreements.

Quality Education at All Levels and Free Higher Education For All The students of Montreal, Quebec, and Santiago, Chile, had it right in demanding support for free higher education. Education at all levels is a public right, not a commodity to be privatized and made costly. Students demonstrating in Amsterdam paraded with a large banner "WE ARE NOT ASKING FOR A FREE UNIVERSITY, WE ARE ASKING FOR A FREE SOCIETY BECAUSE A FREE UNIVERSITY IN A CAPITALIST SOCIETY IS LIKE A LECTURE HALL IN PRISON." During the 1960s, university students in the United States demanded and got reasonable financing for their studies, and succeeded in making colleges and universities open to programs geared to social change, Black and Ethnic Studies programs, Women's Studies….The City Colleges of New York even instituted, for a time, open admissions and free tuition. My personal graduate education from the BA through the MA and Ph.D., coming from a background as a poor kid from the sticks, was very generously funded. Not these days; higher education is a commodity to consume, at enormous cost in student loans, and no longer a certain avenue of social mobility. Today, in the United States, working-class youth is being excluded from higher education by the exorbitant cost, middle-class students with family backing need incur huge debt to study, becoming subject to "debt sentences." Again, we need tactics that flow from the strategy of raising the level of demand. Defensive struggles against increases in tuition, the elimination of critical studies in favor of business and technical training, the increasing subservience of higher education to business interests, must eventually be raised to the level of generalized social demand for equal opportunity and free quality education. This is a key to the mobilization of youth as the fountain of social change.

Support for the struggles of teachers' unions and parents to stop the remodeling of public education into forms of indoctrination and technical training consistent with corporate ideology are indispensable. Improving the quality of education is a public investment that will help the stagnant economy and open young minds to critical thinking. The purpose of programs such as President Bush's "No Child Left Behind" and Democrat Rahm Emanuel's Chicago program is to create a climate wherein docile workers are trained to fill the niches in the low-waged service sector, while expensive private schools groom the sons of the "haves" to fill the commanding positions within the economic and political order. The Department of Education under Obama has been behind the educational "reforms" that have resulted in an expensive system of indoctrination of the student population. The idea of accountability enshrined in standardized tests; the fallacy of choice in charter schools that undermine public education; the de-professionalization of the teaching profession; the drive to undermine and destroy teachers' unions; the conversion of schools to custodial, disciplinary institutions; the elimination of curricula and programs that stimulate creativity and thought—in short, the corporate efforts to transform education into a culture of banality, conformity, and ignorance—are to be strenuously resisted until such time that education becomes a foundation for a free, open, and democratic society. This is likely to be easier with the extremes that will be forthcoming from the Trump Ministry of Miseducation.

Notes

1. Excellent recent books on the environment are Naomi Klein, *This Changes Everything. Capitalism vs. the Environment.* Simon & Schuster, 2014, and Ian Angus, *Facing the Anthropocene*, Monthly Review Press, 2016.
2. *Washington Post*, June 6, 2015.
3. "Prisons and Executions: The U.S. Model," *Monthly Review*, vol. 53, July/August 2001.
4. Bill Quigley commentary at www.readersupportnews.org, June 4, 2015. The criminalization of poverty is dealt with extensively in Karen Doland and Jodi L. Carr, *The Poor Get Prison*, Institute for Policy Studies, 2014. A new book, *Who Do You Serve, Who Do You Protect?*, was released in May 2016 by Haymarket Books. Other recent books on the criminal justice system include Dennis Childs, *Slaves of the State*, University of Minnesota Press, 2016; Elizabeth Hinton, *From the War on Poverty to the War on Crime*, Harvard University Press, 2016; Alexes Harris, *A Pound of Flesh*, Russell Sage, 2016.
5. Bernie Sanders, "Racial Injustice," www.readersupportednews.org/opionion2/277-75/31883-focus-racial-justice

CHAPTER 12

Some Tactical Considerations

The first consideration in formulating strategy for change is that ethics guides actions. To pretend that war, terror, and torture is not one's concern; to let Wall Street tycoons have economic power that translates to political power; to allow insurance and pharmaceutical companies to profit from illness and condemn the uninsured to die; to stand by while our natural environment is raped; to wonder why the biggest criminals are immune from prosecution; to submit to the inhumanity of destruction of social programs, to claim ignorance or innocence, passively to observe the powers-that-be move on doing the dirtiest of deeds, is to be complicit. It is a moral obligation for decent human beings to protest injustice in whatever form it takes.

The 2016 election in the United States confirms my earlier analysis of the sorry state of affairs. The ruling ideology has shrink wrapped the minds of millions, government is captive of corporate interests, the Republicans can fairly be described as Neanderthals now led by a zombie Fuhrer, and the Democrats barely qualify as the lesser of two evils when the candidate was a high-flying war hawk enamored of Wall Street.

Of course, Bernie Sanders was the shining light in this dark political gloom. He wants to continue a "political revolution" by reforming the Democratic Party and encouraging social movements. If the movements make enough noise, perhaps the Democrats can become more democratic. Since Bill Clinton, the Party has been obsequious to established corporate power, and the pomp, and ceremony, and money that make

© The Author(s) 2017

D.L. Johnson, *Social Inequality, Economic Decline, and Plutocracy,*
DOI 10.1007/978-3-319-49043-4_12

political office so attractive. Making the Democratic Party truly progressive would be welcome, but is an unlikely scenario. A third party is an option. Perhaps, over time, the progressive Democrats can manage to split the Party into a moderately socialist party and a center-right party. In American history, third parties have emerged at critical junctures and had an impact (see Howard Zinn, *A Peoples History of the United States*). Since the 1900s, third parties have not fared well in the entrenched two-party system. The libertarians in 2016 did not take enough conservative votes to defeat Trump. In 2012 and 2016, the Green Party had excellent platforms but got few votes. Sanders refused to join forces with the Green Party in favor of supporting the democratic status quo. The earlier formations of the Rainbow Coalition and Ralph Nader's candidacy did not have much impact. The conservative populist Ross Perot got 15% of the vote in 1992.

Bernie's revolution, welcome as it may be, does not go far enough. What is needed is a political vehicle for the total elimination of capitalism as a system. A viable third party in the United States, even if successfully founded, is trapped in a rigged two-party arrangement and an electoral college system that gives disproportionate weight to rural and less populated states where Republicans rule.

A group of movement activists have been circulating a position paper on the development of strategy for revolutionary change. "The type of strategy that is necessary to build …would: (1) imagine and formulate a vision of an alternative to capitalism; (2) analyze the current conditions both on our side (the working class, organized forces, and the left overall) as well as the opposition (the ruling class and the capitalist state); and (3) work toward that vision through devising a continually evolving program that would strengthen the forces for liberation and weaken the capitalist forces."[1]

Another group, Left Roots, envisions the eventual formation of a political party of a socialist character. While the grassroots movement of Occupy and the many others currently active seem to have definite anarchist tendencies, this formation advocates a unity based on these principles (stated only in brief):

- "Socialism is the future! Let's build it now! …"
- "End all oppression for lasting human solidarity…"
- "Victory will require both popular movement and an organized left. Liberation will only be achieved as a result of the power of

the people...reform struggles and survival projects will be two important expressions of popular struggle. It is the task of leftists to support struggles and help guide them away from reformism and towards strategic challenge and fundamental break from the existing system..."

– "Stewardship, not ownership, interdependence, not exploitation..."
– "Liberation must cross all borders..."
– "Transform society, transform ourselves....The struggle for liberation must not only aim to transform society and its institutions; it must aim to transform us as agents of change..."
– "Strategy, not dogma, must be our guide..."[2]

There are post-Sanders party formation efforts, a Peoples Summit on June 17, 2016, in Chicago and People's Revolution in Philadelphia just before the Democratic Convention. It seems that Sanders' campaign has unified some groups around a common goal of party building. There is also the Working Families Party formed by several labor unions.

The organization *The Other 98* appears to be an effective promoter of resistance and revolutionary change. Their websites are www.theother98.org and www.inequality.org There are hundreds of action groups that have informative websites, see the Appendix for a lengthy list.

The Green Party has been in the last two presidential elections with Jill Stein as the candidate and an excellent platform, but has not done well. There was some urging that Bernie Sanders, falling behind in becoming the Democrats candidate, should run on the Green Party ticket. This would have been a formidable third party movement with the potential of breaking up the two-party monopoly. Sanders was reluctant to take that step. The Green Party goes further in reforms than Sanders. Jill Stein talks about a "Green New Deal." She advocates total reform of the criminal justice system, ending all wars and drone attacks, $15 minimum wage, national health care system, free education, abolishing student debt, nationalizing the Federal Reserve, ending dependence on extractive energy and confronting global warming.

Z Communications has spearheaded the organization of an international left-wing organization, International Organization for a Participatory Society (IOPS; www.iopsociety.org). There are thousands of members; however, the organization does not seem to have done very much to date.

While in my personal exile abroad (Costa Rica) and being only a media observer not a direct participant in U.S. struggles, there seemed to me to be a creative tension in the American movement between anarchism and socialism, between community entrenchment and control, and moving toward influencing and eventual capture of state power. The anarchist thrust was evident in the anti-globalization movement of the late 1990s and in the horizontalism and militancy of the Occupy Movement. On the other hand, democratic socialism in most places in the world is viewed as the viable alternative (although its past party form is rather discredited in Europe, being superseded by new left-wing socialist parties). Even in the United States, Bernie Sanders is popularizing democratic socialism and achieving a considerable audience. The Greek party Syriza rose out of social movements against austerity and economic disaster being imposed by the European Union. But, in 2015, the party split and largely collapsed. There is always a tension between social movements and a party, very evident now in Europe. Movements identify issues that party politicians too often prefer to manage or ignore and, when formed, parties tend to compromise away on issues, or even principle, to reach out to capture more votes. Sanders seems to be doing this by supporting Clinton. He denounces inequality that has a wide appeal but says very little against the imperial vision that guides official terrorism, interventionism, and war that Clinton was part of building. My sense is that it is premature to envision a future utopia for America Inc. beyond the general aims of building a society in which people can live full and creative lives free of oppression, and establishing an economy that responds to human need, not private profit; sustainable development not degenerative development. Future forms will be defined as the movement develops. To pose this future in terms of the issues about consciousness discussed in Chap. 10, a dialectic can be posed:

Capital's hegemonic project/People's counter-hegemony
Social Darwinism/Cooperation and social harmony
Plutocracy/Decentralized substantive democracy
Inequalilty and social injustice/Equality, fraternity, and justice
Repression and war/Freedom, non-violence, and peace
Labor as commodity/Labor for the social good
Private property/Public good through public enterprise
Social privilege and division/An end to racism, sexism, privilege and all forms of social division

---

TACTIC: DEMAND THE IMPOSSISBLE

In 1968, the worldwide student revolt had a slogan: "Be Realistic, Imagine the Impossible." An imperative in furthering the movement is to "demand the impossible." In this dictatorship of money, in confronting the forceful authoritarian system of the repressive apparatus, in facing this new ugliness of fascism spouting the dogmas that mind-shrink people, there is not much space for reform. So, demand the impossible! Or, better stated, the "for now impossible." *Dismantle the State of National Insecurity that does the bidding of the moneyed plutocracy. Abolish the CIA! Take down the NSA! Do in Homeland Security! Curb the FBI. De-militarize and disarm the police! Open the doors of prisons and stop incarcerating the immiserated. Oppose any killing of Muslims and Middle-East wars! Demand non-intervention in countries seeking a more just future.*

Obstruction/Disruption as Tactical Advantage

If demanding the impossible is a strategic guideline, then militancy in expressing demands is the tactical imperative. Militant non-violence and civil disobedience are long-established and often effective tactics. With social media and cellphones, it is now easier to coordinate activities. To keep the repressive forces confused, encrypted messages can now be sent using the latest technology that does text, voice, and file-sharing of videos, music, and photos.

Just before his death a few years back in 2010, the great American writer of "history from the bottom up," Howard Zinn (*A People's History of the United States*) made a straightforward statement very pertinent to questions of movement tactics: *Go* where you are not supposed to go. *Say* what you are not supposed to say. *Stay* when they tell you to leave. His book goes into the diverse means of resistance that people in adversity and struggle have evolved throughout American history. Many of these forms of resistance have relevance to today's struggles, Zinn is a must-read, as is Frances Fox Piven.[3] Disruption of normal routines in protest championing a just cause, occupation of public space that the Occupy Movement used to such good effect, obstruction of normality in corporate and governmental activity, street blockades by thousands of marchers.... These are the main means to get attention and therefore achieve the broadcasting of just causes to a wide audience. Otherwise, protest is ignored or, if reported, trivialized. Of course the corporate controlled media will slant a negative coverage, but the word still gets out. The power of the downtrodden lies mainly in making normality unworkable, in placing bodies in places so the wheels of routine don't turn. Institutional routine is disrupted when people withhold their expected cooperation.

For sure, the forces of law and order will suppress disruption, be it the local police or National Guard. In cases of prolonged occupation of public spaces, control will pass to hands of federal law enforcement that coordinates control of untoward events. Vigilante groups may be winked the green light.

Given that our oppressed population is divided by race and ethnicity, gender, and social stratifications, it is logical that there are segmental movements of protest—against police violence, against Wall Street, against home foreclosures, against sexism, against.… It is unclear whether a thousand mutinies will eventually ignite the whole, but we are caught in specific historical circumstances that limit what can be accomplished in the short and medium runs.[4]

There are also tactics that do not require direct disruption of normality. Boycotts, divestment, and sanctions, discussed later, can be quite effective when directed against appropriate targets.

When combined with disruption of normality, the movement could confront the organizations and "think-tanks" that produce plutocratic ideology and policy. There is a large number of such organizations, super-pacs, foundations, and many other organizations that promulgate plutocratic thinking and that fund political campaigns. One such think-tank is the Council on Foreign Relations, which has guided the imperial vision for many decades. A recent good study of this is Laurence Shoup, *Wall Street's Think Tank*.[5] There are many such think-tanks, the Brookings Institution, the Rand Corporation, and many others, including university-based institutes such as Stanford's Hoover Institution, all could be subject to divestment demands or disruption of their meetings and activities.

What is tactically important is that protest not be of a nature that allows the forces of repression to come down really hard and kill a lot of people. Civil disobedience, yes. Taking up arms, suicide. (As I was doing a proof reading of this manuscript on July 8, 2016, a sniper killed and wounded police officers at a Dallas demonstration against police killings. Such killings will only escalate violence and be counter-productive). Non-violence as a strategy has made more advances historically than armed struggles (we have to grant, of course, that China, Vietnam, and Cuba could not have made revolutions by non-violent means). We see that armed Islamic retaliation against Western targets feeds the beast what it needs to escalate. It gives the forces of repression the excuse to label protest as terrorism and come down really hard. We know how protest in "terrorist" form in the Muslim world is dealt with, no reason to risk the State of National Insecurity bringing official terrorism home in escalating and deadly form. The New York Police Department now has a large special force armed with machine guns and all the lethal array of weaponry and crowd suppression technology to deal with just such events. News reports are that this special force is supported by the presumably progressive New York mayor! Chicago police even had their black site for secret rendition. Most urban police forces are now armed with an array of military equipment to deal violently with protest. America is not a Vietnam where armed insurrection against foreign occupiers and subservient local powers is the only road to freedom. Neither is America like Russia in 1917, where revolution can be gained by general uprising and force of arms. Non-violent resistance is the two steps forward to a better future, even while being pushed one step backward by the repression.

Strategically, "Demand the Impossible" raises people's consciousness to new levels that will eventually fit into a project of counter-hegemony as a result of people's changing consciousness and activity. In the interim, given substantial movement advances, some reform might be forced upon a very reluctant and resistant establishment.

Most likely, in the years to come, the movement will not embrace a coherent vision of the future, and suffer confusion and setbacks on strategies and tactics to achieve a New America. A counter-hegemony project takes time and experience to bring about. But positing alternatives to *what is* will gradually erode the hegemony of capital and move in the direction of *what ought to be*. In the realm of ideology, the idea of the war of all against all will be challenged by ideas and actions forging solidarity among the disadvantaged and oppressed. To counter the economic and social conditions of inequality, the ideas of justice and equality will emerge with demands for redistribution, progressive taxation, and the diversion of funds away from war and repression to the promotion of the common good. The policies of neo-liberalism can be effectively countered by "No" to privatization, to curtailment of public benefits, to savage capitalism, to degenerative development. Control by capital and by the plutocracy and its police forces can be answered by democratization of institutions and participation by citizens. The rule of financial oligarchs can be crimped, and eventually demolished, by the socialization of banks and an end of impunity for corporate criminality. At some point, as we learned in the case of the former USSR, authoritarian regimes can collapse. Once the forces of repression are demoralized and the violence unleashed curtailed by mass opposition, the possibility of regime collapse opens. Oppressive regimes have a life span; revolutions are living entities in the making.

Prioritizing Demands

This is a very complex question. In good measure, what the movement as a whole should take up and move with is determined by the issues of the day. In the Vietnam era and, again, in mobilizations against the Iraq invasion, it was militant protest of war. In 2011, the Occupy Movement made Wall Street and the power of the financial oligarchy, the 1% and the 99%, the issue of the period and it found great resonance in the population. The 2016 presidential campaign has renewed these issues as central concerns. In 2012–2013, there was considerable activity on the environmental front, in 2016 revived by steadfast protest against the North Dakota shale oil pipeline. In 2015, the emphasis shifted to killings of black people and the criminal justice system. Black Lives Matter became a social movement and will likely remain so. But shifting issues, defined all too often by the extent of media coverage, begs the larger question of strategies for mobilizations that will reach the broadest constituency with the most critical issues to confront.

In Chap. 11, I posed as priorities for mobilization: war and terror, the environment, the criminal justice system, the extension of social programs, and the nationalization of banking. Since capital's hegemonic project is spearheaded by the financial sector, it makes a good deal of sense to prioritize actions against Wall Street and its oligarchy of financiers. Another Occupy Wall Street would be timely, but the real possibilities remain a big question. Dissident Democrats such as Elizabeth Warren and Bernie Sanders continue to keep putting Wall Street, and combating inequality that the Street's path of degenerative development entails, in the public attention. However, legislation to regulate finance will not suffice. Campaigns for nationalization of all large banks and establishment of community controlled banking is a first step.

One should not be taken in by regulatory remedies for the financial system, if they ever get on the agenda, as regulation will not have any real meaning. It is abundantly clear that Obama was servile to financial interests and Donald Trump will likely go further than Obama in facilitating the rule of finance capital and corporations in general. Trump is appointing a top banker to the Treasury and financial oligarchs, the very rich, and warlord generals complete his cabinet and advisor councils.

Obama did some things to moderate the extremes of guarding and promoting empire. He curbed CIA torture, or at least we are told that black sites are no longer operative (except that Guantanamo still interns prisoners), although drone attacks continue. In the last year or so of his second term, Obama established diplomatic relations with Cuba, although with the apparent aim of subversion of the revolution by means other than failed embargo. A deal was finally negotiated with Iran (better said, forced upon Iran by extreme coercion) to end that nation's possibility for gaining nuclear weapons, much criticized by the Republican war establishment and the Israeli lobby. (No problem with Israel having a nuclear arsenal to unleash against Iran). However, American warships and planes continue the close patrol of the borders of the Iranian coastline. If peace with Iran is the goal, then stop threatening the country by military maneuvers. The same holds even more so with North Korea, which seems to have little choice but to develop superior weaponry to defend itself. Herr Donald trumpeted some isolationism, as well as to repair damaged relations with Russia. But his appointments to the war establishment appear much more dangerous than even Obama's and Hillary Clinton's. Trump is a loose missile armed with a nuclear warhead.

In a July 2015 speech to the NAACP, Obama made quite an insightful statement on the need for reform of the criminal justice system. Trump is all "law and order." But with respect to the power of finance, Obama, his successor, and both political parties have demonstrated time and again obsequious subservience to high finance. As documented in previous analysis, all Obama's appointments to the Treasury, the Fed, SEC, and commerce are drawn from the Wall Street crowd. The Treasury, in particular, is a revolving door between Wall Street and government and back to Wall Street after servicing finance at the Treasury. There is no reason to suppose that Trump will not continue this cozy relationship with Wall Street. Then, in his final year, Obama did the biggest favor ever in history to Wall Street and the big corporations with global ambitions—promoting and fast tracking the trade agreements with Pacific countries and Europe. This is nothing more than an obscene power grab by corporations to the detriment of the American people and the peoples of those countries whose ruling, compliant politicians agree to participate in the global strategy of capital. Trump got a considerable amount of favorable voter attention for opposition to "free trade" agreements, and promises to kill those pending and to revise those in existence, such as NAFTA with Mexico and Canada. He wants to penalize China with protectionist policies against Chinese imports. China will not put up with it and will retaliate, and American corporations manufacturing in China will not be happy.

THE LIMITS OF REFORM

In previous analysis, I stated a theoretical proposition "the state is an expression of class relations." Another generalization was that "multiclass relations are fixed in a bi-polarizing structure." The "rule of law" has, as its primary purpose, the protection of property and the "rights" of capital. At the same time, some elements of law remain embedded in constitutions, international law on human rights adopted by states, and state institutions and procedures that place limits on the repressive apparatus. The right to peaceful assembly and protest of injustice, the presumption of innocence (unless, of course, a suspect suffers rendition to a black site for torture and perpetual internment) remain to some degree in force, even in the American plutocracy administered by the State of National Insecurity. Not all the rights and benefits of being a citizen are yet eliminated. Many gains of long years of class struggles are still reflected in modern states. The question becomes how the diverse struggles of different segments of the class structure can be raised to the reflective level of state policy and activity, when these struggles are caught within the bi-polarizing structure—plutocracy versus all the subordinated classes and segmented groupings of peoples oppressed by racism, ethic prejudice, scapegoating, sexism…

Now plutocracy, aside from the moans of a few in the Republican establishment, has unleashed the fury of Trumpism, espousing the most bizarre notions and mobilizing the right-wing extremes. From mid-2015, the Republicans staged the most astounding media circuses, expounding the vilest of racism, sexism, xenophobia, and militarism as if it were the political norm of our future. They control the Congress. In this situation, the movement's cries for reform could be reduced to screams of pain in the ossified politics of rule by plutocracy as administered by Herr Kommandant Trump. Once the mechanisms of reform are closed by political impasse and Congressional intransigence, by fear-mongering and scapegoating, by closure to decency, by irrational thought, the plutocrats will have the playing field blocked to any Democratic grouping in Congress to do much of anything. So, it is up to the movement to raise hell, which seems to be in the offing. When the movement does mobilize, it is prudent to recall what Chris Hedges said about the "liberal class": "The liberal class is discovering what happens when you tolerate the intolerant. Let hate speech pollute the airways. Let corporations buy up your courts and state and federal legislative goodies. Let the Christian religion be manipulated by charlatans to demonize Muslims, gays and intellectuals, discredit science and become a source of personal enrichment. Let unions wither under corporate assault. Let social services and public education be stripped of funding. Let Wall Street loot the national treasury with impunity. Let sleazy con artists use lies and deception to carry out unethical sting operations on tottering liberal institutions and you roll out the welcome mat for fascism. The liberal class has busied itself with toothless pursuits of inclusiveness, multiculturalism, identity politics and tolerance ... and forgotten about justice."[6]

A likely scenario is that, in the coming years, the economy will continue in its degenerative phase with stagnation of the real economy and most likely another deep crisis. In that situation, which is predictable (review Chaps. 2 and 3), there may be official response to multiple reform demands to pursue a more Keynesian recovery strategy and the enactment of ameliorative programs, especially if disadvantaged sectors of capital drift away from the dominant oligarchy, people have had enough of Trump, and the Democrats regain control of the Congress in 2018. Reform from above will always be within the limits of the system, yet open avenues for the institutionalization of popular demands.

U.S. demographic trends favor the Democrats' lesser of two evils electoral choice—and also movement aspirations and social base, and a viable third party. From 1960 to 2010, the percentages of Americans identifying themselves as black, Hispanic, Asian, or other minority increased from 15% of the population to 36%. In 2013, the population was 62% white, 12% black, 17% Hispanic, and 8% other. By 2020, the white population is predicted to decrease to 59.7% and, in 2040, to 51%. Hispanics, on the other hand, will likely increase from 19.1% in 2020 and to 25% in 2040, probably even with increased immigration controls. (The Great Wall of Trump on the Mexican border and deporting millions of undocumented are, hopefully, not feasible under foreseeable circumstances.) The black and other minority populations will also increase in those years. Given that degenerative development will continue with stagnation and crisis tendencies, we can expect that there will be an expanding base for movement activity and progressive politics.

The 1%–99% discourse is statistically sound as symbolic figuration, but lacks in validity as a percentage of enemies and a percentage of friends. Throughout the book, I have been citing percentages disadvantaged by the system, settling in at around 90% when the class of the line and staff of corporations and the State of National Insecurity are added to the 1%. True enough, but this does not mean that all 90% is a constituency for a New America. Millions are taken in by the ruling ideology and, in fact, constitute a mass base for right-wing extremist mobilization, as we witnessed in the Republican 2015–2016 campaign. Donald Shrill Trumpet is joined by the other Republican candidates and pundits, anti-intellectuals, Christian fundamentalists, Fox and even CNN commentators, in propounding insulting, misogynist, racist, and ignorant rantings. They all pander to fear and nativism, and do reach an audience. In Chap. 7, the noxious effects of bigotry, ethnocentrism, hate, and perception of threatened privilege serving to divide and conquer was analyzed in some depth. In Chap. 8, fascism American-style was explored. The perception of threatened privilege especially victimizes white men, although there are many women admirers of Sarah Palin and Carly Fiorina, even Donald Trump.

In the media, Trump's victory was often ascribed to the high vote from the white working-class people suffering from deteriorating employment situations. Trump's anti-immigrant scapegoating and anti-free trade stance were said to be appealing to this sector. In fact, a better explanation is that the voter turnout was very low, 55% as compared with 61.6% in 2008 and 58.6% in 2012. That 45% of those eligible declined to vote seems to indicate indifference or discontent with both candidates and parties. Since Clinton won the popular vote by a good margin, this indicates that only about 25% of the eligible voters went for Trump. This 25% was largely the long-standing Republican base. Surveys during the primaries indicated that the medium income of Trump voters was higher than Clinton's. Trump voters were largely from the more privileged sectors, the Republican base. Clinton voters were lower- and middle-income voters, and Sanders attracted large numbers of youth.

The proportion of the white population will continue to decrease. Additionally, the population will gradually become younger as minorities have higher birth rates and men continue to die at a younger age than women—the proportion of the population over 55 (that tend to be more conservative) in 2014 was 27% of the population, but women substantially outnumber men (generally, the most intransigent) due to less male longevity. White men, it turns out, now have an increased death rate. I don't know how with any exactitude to reduce the 90% to a more realistic figure. I would say that among the approximately 10% of the population once considered middle-class now being downgraded, perhaps half will be victims of sentiments of "aggrieved privilege," and there are some white working-class people who cling to white-skinned privilege, perhaps another 5% of the population. The ethos of white privilege remains quite strong in the South, and conservatism and religious fundamentalism is rampant in mid-western rural areas. These areas hold around 30% of the U.S. population. Perhaps half those persons will side with reaction. So, we need add to the 10% of the upper echelons of class at least 30% of the objectively downgraded in the social structure and those firm believers in retrograde ideology as siding with their real enemies. We are then left with 60% of the population with the potential for mobilization for justice. In time, a mobilized majority can overcome.

So, who is on the side of righteousness and redemption from evil? The many millions of black, brown, and other oppressed minorities; most women, increasing aware of their oppression, but especially working-class and poor women; the working class with a revitalized unionism; most teachers and social workers now subordinated to act as guard labor; college students and youth in general; older folks of the 1960s generation and senior citizens that social security does not reach for living; the poor in general and sectors of the underclass, if offered hope for salvation; the good, decent folk of all classes who have managed to retain their humanity against the forces of dehumanization. Numbers are on our side. I might add here a note on *déclassé* intellectuals (in which I include myself, forced out of a university professorship years ago): educated middle-class people denied opportunity, artists without studios, actors without theaters, Ph.D.s with academic careers blocked, teachers without jobs, journalists without freedom of expression, even lawyers without clients—all articulate an increasingly anti-system stance as they are denied their place.

Boycotts, Divestment, and Sanctions

An effective tactic for the movement is boycotts, divestment, and sanctions (BDS). Boycotts of products and businesses, divestment campaigns against corporations that engage in destructive activity, and sanctions against governments and entities that violate human rights and international law have been relatively effective measures to draw public attention to issues and, in some instances, to force fundamental change.

Boycotts against colonialism have been central to independence struggles for a very long time, going back to American colonial subjects' boycott of British goods, such as the Boston Tea Party. Boycotts of British activity in the Indian colony were effective tactics for the independence movement led by Gandhi. The United Farm Workers' boycott of California grapes curtailed the anti-union activity of the agri-business. Boycotts and sanctions against the racist regime in South Africa were important in bringing an end to apartheid and enabling democratization that led to the ascension to office of Nelson Mandela and the African National Congress. In the United States, the Montgomery Bus boycott gave a jump-start to the civil rights movement. Environmental groups such as Greenpeace, Friends of the Earth, and People and Planet have initiated boycotts and divestment of Esso/ExxonMobil, and BP has been targeted over the Deepwater oil spill. Four hundred institutions have divested $2.6 trillion in coal, oil, and gas companies. The state of Arizona lost conventions because of its racial profiling practice and racist laws. Financial services customers have been asked to transfer their deposits and not to deal with big banks that are fleecing customers and engaging in foreclosure fraud. The AFL-CIO maintains a "do not buy" list of products from companies with anti-union policies. The American Federation of Teachers initiated a boycott of Coca-Cola for condoning employment of child labor in sugar cane fields in Central America and the murder of trade union leaders in Colombia. Students at Columbia University persuaded the University to divest in G4S, the international security firm operating in Israel, and in the private prison company Corrections Corporation of America (the shooter in the Orlando massacre of June 2016 was a security guard for G4S). In 2015, Santa Cruz, California, declared that the municipality will remove deposits and not use investment services or buy commercial paper with five big banks that have been involved in criminal activity. A good example for other cities, counties, and public and private entities to follow. For BDS to be most effective, alternatives need be pursued. If movements can get city and state treasurers elected, they can use the movement of public funds out of target corporations to alternative public options to effect change.

Currently, there is an international campaign of boycott, divestment, and sanctions against Israel for its policies of annexation, murderous attacks on Palestinians, and apartheid. Sponsors view Israel as a state guided by racist ideology pursuing official terrorism. The BDS has a good deal of support in Europe. Europeans demand of international corporations that they not do business in Israel, especially with those businesses operating out of occupied Palestine. The EU issued guidelines against funding Israeli projects and entities in the occupied territories. The Dutch pension fund divested in five Israeli banks because of involvement in the occupation. British cultural figures and Spanish university professors adhere to a cultural and academic boycott of Israeli institutions. European consumers are urged not to buy Israeli products. Norway has divested in several Israeli companies, as well as the German HeidelbergCement Group and the Mexican Cemex over use of Palestinian natural resources. Israel is a good target for the American movement since the United States is responsible for the political support and sophisticated armaments that allow the Israeli atrocities to continue. In the United States, the Methodist Church and the Gates Foundation divested in G4S, the security company involved in prisons where Palestinians are incarcerated. The United States and the European Union have no hesitation in applying sanctions against Russia, Iran, North Korea, or Venezuela but the people, more than established governments, support sanctions against Israel. The Association of University Teachers began a boycott of Israeli universities in 2005, because these institutions largely support official policies. This was followed by a BDS campaign by the American Studies Association. Faculty and students at American universities demand boycott and divestment by university governing boards (links in endnote).[7]

Many Jews in America and Europe support BDS, including 327 Holocaust survivors placing an advertisement in the *New York Times* against Israeli policies. These actions against Israeli policies have generated a strong reaction from right-wing Zionists, especially in the United States. Proponents are labeled anti-Semitic, and university professors and student groups have been subject to sanctions. Very wealthy Zionists are funding campaigns against BDS and attack proponents. Also, the current trade measures subjected to fast track by Obama contain measures for penalties against groups or businesses complying with BDS. The complement to TPP that may or may not move through Congress in 2016 is the Trade Facilitation and Enforcement Act (perhaps as amended by Trump). The bill requires the President to report annually to Congress on politically motivated acts of boycott against, divestment from, and sanctions against Israel. The State Department can blacklist companies, organizations, and individuals that adopt BDS. Several state governments controlled by Republicans are considering laws that penalize persons or groups sponsoring BDS. Hillary Clinton pronounced against BDS.

Given the potential, the American movement can use BDS to good effect on a multiple range of issues, from environmental degradation to corporate evil and support of labor struggles. A good resource is www.boycotts.org, and www.co-opamerica.org has information and guidelines.

* * *

If the reader has got this far, thank you for your patience with my varied style and mix of polemic with scholarship. The original version of this book that I wanted to publish had this analysis but included a great deal of poetry, satire, and spoof, with the hope that I could reach the attention of movement activists and present a more lively reading. Publishers told me they don't like to mix genres with their publics, so I went with the (more or less) scholarly discourse which will reach a more limited audience. I am trying to get out a second book, *America, Dystopia Inc.* co-authored by my ghost writers, Per Leonardo Janssen and Dalio de la Indignación Janssen (Dale L. Johnson being sequestered to a CIA black site charged with being a curmudgeon terrorist). Meanwhile, a Word copy can be obtained at troporg(a)racsa.co.cr (NSA—please note the email address to follow what might come next).

Notes

1. http://portside.org/2015-06-09/audacity-win-call-strategy-us-left
2. www.leftroots.com Martha Harnecker wrote on the strategy of the Cuban Revolution and its leaders in a tribute to Fidel Castro on his 90th birthday. http://links.org.au/harnecker-fidel-castro-tribute-political-strategy Fidel died in November 2016, leaving an admirable legacy of strength, will, and intelligence.
3. Howard Zinn, *A Peoples History of the United States*, Harper, 1980. Available at Amazon and in audio form at Audible.com; Frances Fox Piven, *The Importance of Being Unruly*, 2016.
4. On this question, the lessons of Occupy are important. See Michael Levitin, "The Triumph of Occupy Wall Street," *The Atlantic*, June 11 2015. Also read Chris Hedges, *Wages of Rebellion*, Penquin, Random House, 2015.
5. Laurence Shoup, *Wall Street's Think Tank: The Council on Foreign Relations and the Empire of Neoliberal Geopolitics, 1976–2014.* Monthly Review Press, 2015.
6. Chris Hedges, http://readersuportednew.org/off-site-opinion-section/63-63/5278
7. The call for BDS can be viewed at http://pacbi.org/etemplate. php?id=869 Updated guidelines appear at http://www.pacbi.org/etemplate.php?id=1108 See also the call at http://www.usacbi.org/mission-statement Websites useful for BDS are www.boycotts.org and www.co-opamerica.org

Epilogue: The 1960s Movement Culture

As an old guy from the 1960s, my expectations reside with today's youth. Here are some choice statements from the epoch.

The Civil Rights and Black Power Movements

Martin Luther King Jr. often repeated "We must learn to live together as brothers or perish together as fools." And also "Freedom is never voluntarily given by the oppressor; it must be demanded by the oppressed." There were many who did not have the patience of Dr. King. "Burn Baby Burn" was a response to Ghetto riots. "Off the Pigs" was often heard on the streets.

After his death in 2016, quotes from Muhammad Ali flooded the internet. "Impossible is just a big word thrown around by small men who find it easier to live in the world they've been given than to explore the power they have to change it. Impossible is not a fact. It's an opinion. Impossible is not a declaration. It's a dare. Impossible is potential. Impossible is temporary. Impossible is nothing." In the 1960s, he received considerable official notoriety and was convicted of draft dodging. At the time, he said: "I ain't draft dodging. I ain't burning no flag. I ain't running to Canada. I'm staying right here. You want to send me to jail? Fine, you go right ahead. I've been in jail for 400 years. I could be there for 4 or 5 more, but I ain't going no 10,000 miles to help murder and kill other poor people. If I want to die, I'll die right here, right now, fightin' you, if I want to

© The Author(s) 2017

D.L. Johnson, *Social Inequality, Economic Decline, and Plutocracy,*

DOI 10.1007/978-3-319-49043-4

die. You my enemy, not no Chinese, no Vietcong, no Japanese. You my opposer when I want freedom. You my opposer when I want justice. You my opposer when I want equality. Want me to go somewhere and fight for you? You won't even stand up for me right here in America, for my rights and my religious beliefs. You won't even stand up for my right here at home."

The Anti-Vietnam War Movement

"Hey, hey, LBJ, how many kids did you kill today?"—Anti-war chant. (Today's equivalent, "Hey, hey, Obama, how many wedding parties did you drone today?")

"How many deaths will it take 'til he knows, that too many people have died?"—Bob Dylan ("Blowin' in the Wind" lyric)

"All we are saying is give peace a chance"—John Lennon ("Give Peace a Chance" lyric)

"The draft is white people sending black people to fight yellow people to protect the country they stole from the red people" The musical *Hair*.

"Hell no, we won't go!" "Shut Down DC"—2001 massive Washington demonstration.

Flowerjock speak: "War is not a team sport—everyone loses."

The New Left

"You don't need a weatherman to know which way the wind blows"—Bob Dylan ("Subterranean Homesick Blues" lyric). The Weathermen later became an underground movement. Bob Dylan sang "The battle outside ragin' will soon shake your windows and rattle your walls" ("The Times They Are A-changin'" lyric).

"If it takes a bloodbath, let's get it over with."—Ronald Reagan, then Governor of California, on how to deal with student unrest.

"The purpose of this program is to expose, disrupt, and otherwise neutralize the activities of the various new left organizations, their leadership, and their adherents..."—FBI Director J. Edgar Hoover in *Disruption of the New Left*, counter-intelligence memo dated May 14, 1968.

"I wrestled with an alligator, I tussled with a whale, I handcuffed lightning, thrown thunder in jail, I'm bad man... Last week I murdered a rock, injured a stone, hospitalized a brick. I'm so mean I make medicine sick,"—Muhammad Ali.

"I like ideas about the breaking away or overthrowing of established order. I am interested in anything about revolt, disorder, chaos... It seems to me to be the road towards freedom—external freedom is a way to bring about internal freedom."—Jim Morrison.

"I've been smiling lately, dreaming about the world as one. And I believe it could be, someday it's going to come."—Cat Stevens ("Peace Train" lyric).

Che portraits were everywhere—"Aqui se queda la clara, la entrañable transparencia de tu querida presence, Comandante Che Guevara" ("Here is the clear, endearing transparency of your beloved presence, Commandante Che Guevara"). "Y el canto de todos que es mi propio canto. Gracias a la vida." ("And the singing of all that is my own song. Thanks to Life.")—movement folklorist Victor Jara, murdered by the Chilean military on September 11, 1973.

"It riles them to believe that you perceive the web they weave...so keep on thinking free!" The Moody Blues ("On the Threshold of a Dream" lyric).

Along with Victor Jara, Leonard Cohen expressed universalism of love and struggle: "Now Suzanne takes your hand and she leads you to the river She is wearing rags and feathers from salvation army counters And the sun pours down like honey on our lady of the harbor and she shows you were to look among the garbage and the flowers There are heroes in the seaweed There are children in the morning they are leaning out for love and they will lean that way forever While Suzanne holds the mirror and you want to travel with her and you want to travel blind and you know that you can trust her for she's touched your perfect body with her mind." ("Suzanne" lyric)

"It riles them to believe that you perceive the web they weave...so keep on thinking free!" The Moody Blues ("On the Threshold of a Dream" lyric).

In my personal political formation, I benefited from the culture of the 1920s and the 1930s. Woodie Guthrie, Pete Seeger.... The first song I learned was a Joe Hill Classic "Pie in the Sky-" "Long-haired preachers come out every night, try to tell you what's wrong and what's right, But when asked how 'bout something to eat' They will answer with voice so sweet: You will eat, bye and bye, in that glorious land above the sky: Work and pray, live on hay, You'll get pie in the sky when you die." The labor song "I dreamed I saw Joe Hill Last Night" was a movement classic, favorite of Woody Guthrie, Pete Seeger, and Phil Ochs and made famous by Joan Baez's performance at Woodstock in 1969 and in the film "Woodstock." "The copper bosses killed you Joe. Takes more than guns to kill a man what they forgot to kill went on to organize." Joe Hill wrote "Casey Jones" given new versions by the Grateful Dead and Johnny Cash.

The Hippies

Hippie culture was widely shared among millions of young men and women in the 1960s. "Make Love, Not War" "If it feels good, do it!" was current street talk. "All you need is Love"—The Beatles. There was a chemical ethos in America, Dow Chemical's advertisement was "Better living through Chemistry." There was a drug culture among the hippies, but it has been somewhat exaggerated, or not comparable to what came later. Jimi Hendrix, in his song "Purple Haze," expressed the hard side: "Purple Haze all in my brain, lately things don't seem the same. Actin´ funny but I don't know why. ´Scuse me while I kiss the sky." But the most famous hippie of all, Abbie Hoffman, said "Avoid all needle drugs. The only dope worth shooting is Richard Nixon." Hippies boosted the ecology movement. They took on racism and practiced sexual liberation from convention. They questioned materialism. They fought against the Vietnam War. Sometimes they gathered in great numbers as at Woodstock, New York, in 1969. Arlo Guthrie, about to perform, said "Look at all the freaks!"

Appendix: *Movement Websites*
(Be informed! For private encrypted
communication get Whatsapp—neither
local police nor the NSA can, at least
not yet, read you.)

News and Critical Analysis (by subscription
at website, delivered to your email)

Truth-out.org	Truthdig.com	rsn.com	Upsidedownworld.org
Occupy.com	credo.com dailykos.com	Portside.org	Nation.com
inthesetimes.com	lemondediplomatique.com	theguardian.com	huffingtonpost.com

Labor News

Portsidelabor.org	AFL-CIO/CWA (Communication Workers)	aflcio.org/home.htm	ueunion.org
Stateofworkingamerica.org	Labormovementnews.org	USLaborAgainstthe War	workinginthesetimes.com

© The Author(s) 2017
D.L. Johnson, *Social Inequality, Economic Decline, and Plutocracy,*
DOI 10.1007/978-3-319-49043-4

Periodicals with Critical Viewpoints

monthlyreview.com	Inthesetimes.com	Huffingtonpost.com	rollingstone.com
nacla.com	tomdispatchacla.org	frontline.com (India)	indymag.org
znet.com	dollarsandsense.com	Science and Society	nation.com
Latin American Perspectives	commondreams.com	alternet.com	Sojourners.com
Yes! Magazine.com	counterpunch.com	the independent.com	Populareconomics.org
criticalsociology.org	Adbuster.com	Counterpunch.com	Freedomlake.com
The Independent	Nation of Change	OWNI	Links.org.au
Populareconomics.org	Jocobinmag.com	ROAR	graffiti.net
newpolitics.com	wagingnonviolence.org	theintercept.com	alternet.com
urpe.com	sojourners	nationofchange.com	counterpunch.com
solidarityweb.com	handsoffsyria.org	bitchmagazine.com	raceandclass.com

Movement Sites

blacklivesmatter.org	moveon.org	upsidedownworld.org	rollingrebellion.org
worldbeyondwar.org	demandprogress.org	sierraclub.org	flushtheTPP.org
Mayfirst.org	350action.org	someofus.org	gregpalast.com
veteransforpeace.org	ourfuture.org	nationalpeoplesaction.org	lawg.org
workinginthesetimes.com	justforeignpolicy.org	aclu.org	change.org
allianceforajustsociety.org	SAaction.org	democracyforamerica.com	fwwatch.org
salsalabs.net	bitchmedia.org	afsc.org	peoplefortheamericanway.org
jubileeusa.org	unitedwedream.org	occupy.com	onebillionrising.org
blackagenda.com	colorofchange.org	leftforum.org	rootsaction.org
nationalpeoplesaction.org	ontheissues.org	greenparty.org	usaaction.org
socialistproject.ca	Socialistworker.org	wagingnonviolence.com	ourfuture.org
citizenstradecampaign.org	sipaz.org	standupfortruth.org	allianceforglobaljustice.org
globalclimateconvergence.org	Poorpeopleseconomicand humanrig htscampaign.org		
organicconsumersassociation.org		Popularresistance.org	risingtideNA.org
beyondextremeenergy.org	credomobilize.com	credoaction.com	
billofrightsdefensecommittee	blueamerica.com	demandprogress.org	Sum of Us.org
orgenvironmental-action.org	fightforthefuture.org	justforeignpolicy.com	
RHrealtycheck.com	winwithoutwar.org	theother99%.org	zcommunications.com
ciponline.org	witnessforpeace.org	350.org	movementgeneration.org
epic.org	indymedia.org	utnereader.com	yellowtimes.org
gasandoil.com	commondreams.org	globalpolicy.org	bdsmovement.net
fightforreform.org	grrn.org	noburn.org	zerowasteamerica.org
Energyjustice.net	NewUrbanism.org	occupystudentdebt.org	projectcensored.org
strategic-culture.org	theglobalpowerproject.org	participatorybudgetingproject.org	

(continued)

(Continued)

centerforpopulardemocracy.org	Antiwar.com	billofrightsdefensecommittee.org	
codepink	vetransforpeace.org	Cursor.org	nuclearresister.org
allianceforglobaljustice.org	Poorpeopleseconomichumanrightscampaign.org		answer.org
popularresistance.org	workersworld	freedomroadsocialistorganization.org	
Partyofsocialismandliberation.org		panleftvideocollective.org	
globalclimateconversion.org	campaignforlaborrights.org	women'sfightbacknetwork.org	
arizonapeacecouncil.org	Jewishvoiceforpeace.org	anti-warcommitteechicago.org	fightback!news.com
#NoDAPL	fightfor15.net	nakedcapitlism.org	
Nationalcampaignfornonviolentresistance.org		unitedforpeaceand justice.org	warresistersleague
wilpf.org	PeaceNoWar.net	activistVideo.org	iacenter.org
tidalmag.org	ourfuture.org	change.org	consortiumnews.com
uprising.org	nodo50.org	act.demandprogress.org	therealnews.com
americasvoice.com	environ.org	USUncut.org	worldwithoutwar
Justice-integrity.org	gofossilfree.org	OWNI.org	foe.org
worldsocialforum.org (see for list of member organizations worldwide)			AFGI.org
greenpeace.ocr	citizen.org	socialwatch.org	tni.org
strategic-culture.org	iopsociety.org	zcommuncations.org	theopedpojection.org
demandprogress.org	leftroots.net	alternet.net	Sojourners
Alliance For Global Justice afgj.org		couragecampaign.org	EconomyInCrisis.org
platformcooperativism.org	counterpunch.org	jubileeusa.org	theintercept.com
wagingnonviolence.org	UsAgainstGreed.org	PayUpNow.org	RappingHistory.org
USUncutChicago.org	codepink.org	usaction.org	trade4people.org
Friends of the Earth	People and Planet	USlaw.org	couragecampaign.org
colorofchange.org	greenpeace.org	inequality.org	democracy at work.info
Lcvo.org (league of conservation voters)		justforeignpolicy.org	other98.com
inequality.org	cdpaction.org	fightforfreedom.org	creativeresistance.org
battleforthenet.com	flushtheTPP.org	rollingrebellion.org	itsoureconomy.us
	cleanupthemines.org	wearecovepoint.org	

Blog Sites

wordpress.com	zcommunications/zspace	desmogblog.com	touchstone.com
posterous.com	actionforum.com	ezinearticles.com	topica.com
LAPerspectivesblogspot.com	triplecrisis.com	NewleftBlogosphere.com	touchstone.com
DSmogBlog.com	fictionblog.com	openmicvoices.org	
activistpost.com/forum word.		socialistworkers.org	wisebread.com
world-citizenship.org			
commondreams.org	indignados.org	thepublicintellectual.org	
wagingnonviolence.org	worldcitizenship.com	socialistworkers.org	wisebread.com
wiki.occupy.net	triplecrisis.com	commondreams.org	
newleftblogosphere	openmicvoices.org	activistpost.com/forum	
		tomdispatch.com	
orchestratedpulse.org	forumsocialmundial.org		
	(see for hundreds of worldwide		
	organization participating in the		
	World Social Forum)		

Publishers

Monthly Review Press	PM Press	Beacon Press	Haymarket Books
Verso Books	Nation Books	City Lights Press	Zuccotti Park Press
Pluto Press	Tom Dispatch	Red Pepper	AK Press
Alternative Press Index	Burning Books	Metropolitan Books	International Publishers
Revolution Books	Zero Books	New Press	Seven Stories
Loud Mouth Press	New Village Press	Consortium/Perseus	Flashpoint Press
Trade Root	Switchblade	Big Noise	Busboys and Poets
Common Notions	Green Arcade	Outspoken Authors	Metropolitan Press

Economic, Social, and Political Research, and Analysis and Legal Defense

Center for Economic and Policy Research, cepr.net		Political Economy Research Institute, peri.umas.edu
Institute for Policy Studies, ips.DC.org		bakerinstitute.org
Center for Economic and Policy Research, cepr.net		Economic Policy Institute, epi.org
Union of Radical Political Economists, urpe.org		Southern Poverty Law Center
National Council of La Raza nclr.org		aclu.org
National Hispanic Media Coalition nhmc.org		theantimedia.org
Mexican-American Legal Defense and Educational Fund maldef.org		Center for Popular Economics, populareconomics.org
	Planned Parenthood	SisterSongWomenofColor
Reproductive Justice Collective	Immigrant Youth Justice League	Mexican American Legal Defense and Educational Fund
Council on America-Islamic Relations		Trevor Project
Natural Resources Defense Council	Rethinking Schools	Sacred Stone Legal Defense Fund
NAACP Legal Defense Fund		National Lawyers Guild

GLOBAL RESISTANCE. EN ESPAÑOL, AMERICA LATINA Y ESPAÑA. EUROPEAN, AFRICAN, AND ENGLISH LANGUAGE SOLIDARITY SITES

Resumenlatinoamercano.org	CubaNews@groups.yahoo.com/CubaNews		Cispes.org	presente.org
telesur.net (Venezuela)	resumenrebel.org	colombiasupport.net	igc/isla.co	haitisolidarity.net
mayfirst.org	wola.org	lanic.utexas.edu	globalexchange.org	amnesty.org
rebelion.org	puestaenlinea.nacion.com	worldlearning.org/star	unitedwedream.org	nuso.org
salsa.wiredforchange.com	cipamericas.org	immigrantsolidarity.org	ActionLA.org	viacampesina.org
Lawag.org	twnafrica.org	forumsocialmundial.org.br/ see for long list of worldwide participants		
Cuba news in English en.granma.cu		en español granma.cu	noticiasclacso.edu.ar	salsalabs.com
derechoshumansocoalition	nationalnetworkoncuba.org	ChicagosolidaritywithALBA		

There are excellent resources on Latin America in English including: http://www.cipamericas.org/, http://nacla.org, http://venezuelanalysis.com *and* http://upsidedownworld.org/main, *as well as activist solidarity groups such as* http://www.cispes.org, http://nisgua.org, http://www.hondurassolidarity.org, http://www.nicanet.org, *and* http://colombia-support.net

España:	claroquepodemos.es	ahoramadrid.es	programa.ahoramadrid.org
	Barcelona en comú.es	Zaragoza en comú.es	lamariaatlantica.es
	movimientossociales.es	Monthlyreview.es	
Australia:	greenleft.org.au	links.org.au	Council of Trade Unions actu.asn.au
France:	gauchefrancaise.fr	fph.fr	alliance21.org attc.org.fr Parti de gauche.fr
Sweden:			vansterpartiet.sv
Germany:	en.die-linke.de (English. Deutsch: die-linke.de)	berlin-gegan-belin-kreig.de	opendemocracy.net/…/antirepresentative
Italy:	5stelleeuropa.it	beppegrillo.it/movimento	
Israel:	+972mag.com		
Europe:	European United Left-Nordic Green left, guengl.eu cedetim.org etuc.org	European-left.org unimondo.org	euobserver. com oxfam.org

Brazil:		cartamaior.com.br	abongdiretoria abong.org.br
Portugal:		bloc.org	
Canada:		globalresearch.ca	
Asia:	asianexchange.org	kctu.org (Korea unions)	wsfindia.net
Africa:		Africa Trade Network twnafrica.org	Development Center aidc.org.za
Mexico:		Subversiones.org	
Venezuela:		Humandidadred.orgve	

Index

Note: Page numbers followed by "n" refer to notes.

D.L. Johnson, *Social Inequality, Economic Decline, and Plutocracy*,
DOI 10.1007/978-3-319-49043-4

GPSR Compliance
The European Union's (EU) General Product Safety Regulation (GPSR) is a set
of rules that requires consumer products to be safe and our obligations to
ensure this.

If you have any concerns about our products, you can contact us on

ProductSafety@springernature.com

In case Publisher is established outside the EU, the EU authorized
representative is:

Springer Nature Customer Service Center GmbH
Europaplatz 3
69115 Heidelberg, Germany